Winning CFOs

Winning CFOs

Implementing and Applying Better Practices

DAVID PARMENTER

WILEY
John Wiley & Sons, Inc.

Published by John Wiley & Sons, Inc., Hoboken, New Jersey.

Published simultaneously in Canada.

Note: This is the new edition to *Pareto's 80/20 Rule for Corporate Accountants,* © 2007, Published by John Wiley & Sons, Inc.

For general information on our other products and services or for technical support, please contact our Customer Care Department within the United States at (800) 762-2974, outside the United States at (317) 572-3993 or fax (317) 572-4002.

Wiley also publishes its books in a variety of electronic formats. Some content that appears in print may not be available in electronic books. For more information about Wiley products, visit our web site at www.wiley.com.

Library of Congress Cataloging-in-Publication Data:
Library of Congress Cataloging-in-Publication Data
Parmenter, David.
    Winning CFOs : implementing and applying better practices / David Parmenter.
        p. cm.
    Includes index.
        ISBN 978-0-470-76750-4(book); ISBN 9781118025789(ebk); ISBN 9781118025796(ebk); ISBN 9781118025802(ebk)
        1. Chief financial officers.   2. Organizational change.   3. Leadership.   I. Title.
    HG4027.35.P35 2011
    658.15--dc22

                                                                        2010045646

Printed in the United States of America

10   9   8   7   6   5   4   3   2

Contents

Acknowledgments

I would like to acknowledge the commitment and dedication of Waymark Solutions staff members over the years it took to complete this project (Dean, Roydon, Matt, Louis and Jennifer) I thank my partner, Jennifer Gilchrist, and my children, Alexandra and Claudine who are so understanding during my absences which are so much a part being a writer and speaker.

I am grateful to Harry Mills, Matt Clayton, and Jeremy Hope for their "sage" advice over the years and to Sheck Cho for encouraging me to do this follow on edition from *Paretos 80/20 Rule for Corporate Accountants*.

My gratitude goes to Ian Niven, Wayne Morgan, Ken Lever, and Eon Black (all leading CFOs), Bill Cotton and, last but not least, all those accountants who have shared their better practices with me during workshops I have delivered around the world.

A special thanks goes to my parents, who encouraged all their four children to be independent and confident in their own endeavours. To all of the above mentioned people and all the other people who have been an influence in my life, I say *thank you* for providing me the launching pad for the journey I am now on.

Introduction

All CFOs need to leave a legacy before they move on. In other words, they need to have made a permanent improvement to the organization. Yet many CFOs, and the accountants who report to them, are not producing enough added value to their organization—they are failing to make a difference. I know this from observation and my own personal experience. How many CFOs, financial controllers, management accountants, on leaving, receive an outpouring of loss from the senior management team and budget holders?

Many finance teams are merely a processing machines moving from one deadline to the next having too little time to invest in being a business partner to budget holders and senior management.

This book is a follow on edition from *Paretos 80/20 Rule for Corporate Accountants*. The Book has been extended to incorporate issues that directly relate to the CFO being a better leader and a more effective business partner with the senior management team. It has drawn from my recent book *The leading-edge manager's guide to success*. The better practices in this book are ignored at your peril, as they are based on the wisdom and better practices of over 4,000 accountants whom I have met through delivering my workshops around the world.

I would like to add that few, if any, of these practices were used by me when I was a corporate accountant; thus senior management did not shed a tear when I left the organization. It is my mission to ensure CFOs, financial controllers and management accountants leave a legacy that stays around a long time after they have left the organization.

David Parmenter
Writer, Speaker, Facilitator
Helping organizations measure, report and improve performance
PO Box 10686, Wellington, New Zealand
(+ 64 4) 499 0007 parmenter@waymark.co.nz www.davidparmenter.com
15 January 2011

Dear CFO:

Invitation to leave a profound legacy in your organization

In this book I would like to introduce you to better practices that will have a profound impact on the way your finance team functions and help you make a difference as a **leader** and **business partner**.

If you find yourself and your team locked up in the past as historians, still trapped by the archaic annual planning process, constantly fighting fires, and unappreciated by the organization at large, then maybe some of the panacea for you is here.

I have written this book from the standpoint of an accountant and observer. It is a book that you need to read before you pass it down to your direct reports. I say this because far too many CFOs have delegated continuing learning to their younger accounting staff. While the detail is the domain of the younger corporate accountants, continuing learning is a duty that all of us need to shoulder.

This book is designed to transform your contribution, increase your job satisfaction and profile in the organization, and help you leave a legacy in every organization you work for. To back this claim I ask that you at least read the following chapters:

- Introduction
- Chapter 6, covers managing and leading the accounting Team.
- Chapters 14 and 15 will help you implement quarterly rolling forecasting and planning.
- Chapters 18 and 19 will help you find your organization's critical success factors and winning KPIs.
- Chapter 24 on the foundation stones of performance bonus schemes that work.

I also ask that you spare 45 minutes of your time and make use of the support materials (webcasts, electronic templates) on www.davidparmenter.com.

I am hopeful that someday in the future we will meet, whether it is at a course or over a coffee. It is my fervent wish that you will be able to say "I used this book to make a difference." It will mean that both you and I will have left a legacy.

Kind regards,

David Parmenter

How to Use the Book

This book is divided into four sections. The table below explains the purpose of each section.

	Section	Significance
Introduction	Covers the foundation stones that will facilitate change. All accountants need to improve their work balance, the way they sell change and sort out the personal baggage they carry (we all carry some).	Failure to understand and implement these suggestions will limit how effective the rest of the book can be.
Part One	Focuses on the areas where the finance team can score the easy goals in the next six months.	The better practices in Part One, if implemented, will free up time so Part Two initiatives can be attempted successfully.
Part Two	Focuses on more wide-ranging changes, such as the introducing winning key performance indicators and quarterly rolling planning, which will require a heavy investment of time from the finance team.	These initiatives will have a profound impact on your organization.
Part Three	Focuses on areas where the CFO can and should save the organization from making costly mistakes, such as performance bonus schemes, takeovers, reorganizations, downsizing, and so forth.	The CFO can save the organization from making costly mistakes.
Appendices	The templates and diagrams in the book will take some time to absorb. Discuss these with the corporate accountants in the finance team and with your mentor.	Once understood, these templates and diagrams will have a significant impact.

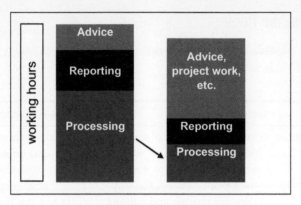

EXHIBIT I.1 Getting the Balance of Work Right

Getting the Right Work Balance

The impact of the efficient and effective practices listed in the book will, if implemented, make a major change to the nature of work performed by the accounting team. There will be a migration away from low-value processing activities into the more value-added areas such as advisory, being a business partner with budget holders, and implementing new systems. As Exhibit I.1 shows, the change in focus should mean we are working smarter, not harder. This change in workload will, over time, lead to the formation of a smaller but more experienced accounting team and a better work–life balance.

Exhibit I.2 shows the impact of this shift away from processing into more service delivery work. The key change is to radically reduce the time the accounting team spends in month-end reporting, the annual accounts, and the annual planning process. I call these three activities the trifecta of lost opportunities for the accounting team. When were you last thanked for any of these tasks?

The better practices in this book will approximately double the amount of "added value time" you and your team have.

Selling a New Process through the Emotional Drivers

The contents of this book will encourage you to change the way you do things so it is appropriate to talk about selling change.

Remember, nothing was ever sold by logic. You sell through emotional drivers. Remember your last car purchase. Many initiatives driven from the

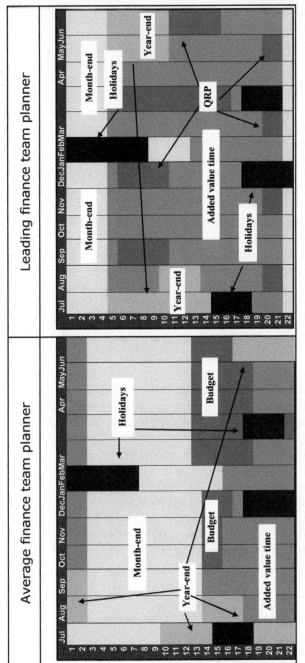

EXHIBIT I.2 How the Year's Workload Will Change (Based on a June Year-End, and a Southern Hemispher–Based Organization)

finance team fail at this hurdle because we attempt to change the culture through selling logic, writing reports, issuing commands via email. It does not work.

All major projects need a public relations (PR) machine behind them. No presentation, email, memo, or paper related to a major change should go out unless it has been vetted by your PR expert. All your presentations should be road-tested in front of the PR expert. Your PR strategy should include selling to staff, budget holders, the senior management team (SMT), and the board.

We need to radically alter the way we pitch a sale to the SMT and the board. We first have to make sure we have a good proposal with a sound focus on the emotional drivers that matter to them. We then need to focus on selling to the thought leader on the SMT and board before we present the proposal. This may take months of informal meetings, sending copies of appropriate articles, telling better practice stories, and so on, to awaken interest.

It is worth noting that the thought leader of the SMT and board may not be the CEO or chairperson respectively. Having presold the change to the thought leader, watch, after delivering your presentation, how the meeting turns to listen to the thought leader's speech of support. Your proposal now has the best possible chance of a positive vote.

Following are some of the emotional drivers regarding the annual planning process that you would use if selling the need to streamline the process and eventually migrate to quarterly rolling planning:

- Meaningless month-end reports (e.g., "it is a timing difference").
- Lost evenings/weekends producing meaningless variances comments.
- Lost months and the lost weekends with the family producing the annual plan.
- Huge cost associated with the annual plan—estimate on the high side (costs motivate boards).
- Time spent by the board and SMT second-guessing the next year—it is more efficient on a rolling quarterly basis.
- It is better practice to implement quarterly rolling forecasting and planning (e.g., 80 percent of major U.S. companies expect to be doing quarterly rolling forecasts, etc.).

Sorting Out Your Personal Baggage

This section is in the front for good reason. We will always be running with a few cylinders misfiring unless we fully understand our behavior patterns and the patterns of those around us. Skip this section and I promise that you will never reach your full potential. You will never be able to successfully implement large change, as doing so requires advanced interpersonal skills.

We inherit *baggage* from our ancestors, along with many great things. This baggage is added to by some of the negative aspects of the environment we grew up in and by the parenting we received (with either too much smothering, too little attention, too much criticism, too little quality time). One course I attended called "Turning Point" stated that we all have baggage, and our role in life is to lighten the load so that it is not crippling when we decide to start "management summiting."

There are plenty of CFOs causing havoc with every organization that they work for. Yet there are those iconic CFOs who are a pleasure to work for and who ably demonstrate the benefits of minimizing one's own personal baggage.

My point is you owe it to your work colleagues, staff, suppliers, contractors, family, partner, and offspring to do something about it. The key to making progress is the awareness of one's weaknesses and to attend some or all of these courses:

- Understand yourself by attending workshops on the Myers-Briggs, the Enneagram, and Hermann thinking style preferences. These are a must for a better understanding of oneself. (Useful places to search are www.myersbriggs.org, www.enneagraminstitute.com, and www.hbdi .com.)
- Understand the impact of using Neuro-Linguistic Programming. Go on the web and search "NLP" + "course" + (your location) to find a local course.
- Develop a decent toolkit so you learn to handle disappointment, anger, and loss; if you do not, there will be plenty of opportunities for these events to screw up your life. I benefited greatly from attending an anger management course.
- Invest in some personal development courses; the ones that are of a longer duration have the most chance of changing behaviors. The experts in behavioral change say it takes up to 8 to 12 weeks of weekly commitment to change a behavior.

We have a choice: to grow and challenge those behavior traits that will create havoc in the workplace, or to ignore them and seek new jobs like we do new partners, hooked on the romance period and leaving when the going gets tough. To make a major contribution, you will need to achieve through the contributions of others. This means acquiring a suite of behavioral skills. Periodically rate yourself against the checklist in Exhibit 1.3.

EXHIBIT I.3 Personal Baggage Checklist

Focus

Do you allocate the major chunks of your time to the major goals in your life? (as per your treasure map) ☐ Yes ☐ No

Have you determined what your goals are for the next two to three years? ☐ Yes ☐ No

Do you treat emails as you would mail, and read it at an appropriate time? (You can set up email filters to help manage the emails and better channel your time.) ☐ Yes ☐ No

Do you avoid being sucked into nonurgent, not important issues? ☐ Yes ☐ No

Do you inoculate yourself from the diversion disease? ☐ Yes ☐ No

Do you have a clear understanding of all the loose ends that are outstanding? ☐ Yes ☐ No

Do you carefully check the purpose and intent of a meeting before you agree to attend? ☐ Yes ☐ No

Ability to Finish

Do you have specific times for finishing (e.g., a finishing week each month)? ☐ Yes ☐ No

Do you minimize your involvement in new projects until your previous ones are finished? ☐ Yes ☐ No

Interpersonal Skills

Are you able to make sufficient eye contact (at least 50 percent of the time the conversation is taking place)? ☐ Yes ☐ No

Are you able to demonstrate humility when you consider yourself an expert in the subject matter? (showing that you are open to others' suggestions and opinions) ☐ Yes ☐ No

Can you remain open to ideas that initially you would like to reject out of hand? ☐ Yes ☐ No

Do you listen to tone and context of the spoken words so as to ascertain what the person is really meaning? (The poor choice of words commonly leads to misunderstandings.) ☐ Yes ☐ No

Do you allow others to complete their conversations? ☐ Yes ☐ No

Are you using your mind to create more linkages from the conversation? ☐ Yes ☐ No

Do you show interest and give back verbal and nonverbal signals that you are listening? ☐ Yes ☐ No

Are you aware of all the nonverbal cues you are giving from your body language? ☐ Yes ☐ No

EXHIBIT I.3 *(Continued)*

Can you be courteous with people and ruthless with time?	☐ Yes	☐ No
Can you be as least as patient with other people as you would wish them to be with you?	☐ Yes	☐ No

Calm in Adversity

Can you avoid taking adversity personally?	☐ Yes	☐ No
Can you look at the funny side when adversity strikes?	☐ Yes	☐ No
Can you realize that adversity is part of life and deal with it?	☐ Yes	☐ No
Can you still be courteous to people when you are on a tight deadline?	☐ Yes	☐ No

Addiction Management

Do you limit stimulants that adversely affect your behavior? (e.g., caffeine can make a substantial impact on how argumentative you become, especially if you have more than 2 strong coffees during the working day)	☐ Yes	☐ No
Are you addicted to the adrenaline rush of completion in the eleventh hour?	☐ Yes	☐ No
Have you controlled the need to work harder (or longer) than anyone else in your team?	☐ Yes	☐ No

Anger Management

Do you see anger as a negative trait rather than a good release valve	☐ Yes	☐ No
Do you handle the feelings for anger in a safe way?	☐ Yes	☐ No
Are you aware that you have a choice and alternatives? (There are many good behavioral change programs.)	☐ Yes	☐ No
Are you aware that frustration with oneself is one of the great initiators of anger?	☐ Yes	☐ No
Do you use the "time-out" technique to avoid expressing anger to your colleagues, staff, and family?	☐ Yes	☐ No
Do you view events as challenges to be overcome rather than roadblocks to your progress?	☐ Yes	☐ No

Personal Learning and Growth

Have you attended any personal development courses to overcome the defense mechanisms that you have put in place from childhood onward which may be limiting your effectiveness?	☐ Yes	☐ No
Have you attended any personal development courses to challenge your negative behavior traits? (We all have them.)	☐ Yes	☐ No

(Continued)

EXHIBIT I.3 (*Continued*)

Do you know where you lie on the Enneagram (a worldwide program to help individuals understand their behavioral weaknesses)?	☐ Yes	☐ No
Do you know your Myers-Briggs personality type (a worldwide program to help individuals understand their personality type)?	☐ Yes	☐ No
Have you attended a "Transactional Analysis" course?	☐ Yes	☐ No

Creating Win-Win Situations

Do you analyze the situation from the other side?	☐ Yes	☐ No
Can you honestly say you are focused on a mutual win-win?	☐ Yes	☐ No
If your trade suppliers, customers, and so on were contacted, do you think they would say you are fair and reasonable?	☐ Yes	☐ No

Functioning Team Member

Are you able to curb your own desires in order to function fully as a team member?	☐ Yes	☐ No
Are you able to put other team members' needs alongside yours?	☐ Yes	☐ No
Does the administrative staff willingly help you (because you have linked well with them)?	☐ Yes	☐ No
Do you share praise from others with the team rather than bag it for yourself?	☐ Yes	☐ No

Your Score   ____   ____

Your Staff Scoring You   ____   ____

Ticks	
less than 20	Treat it as an urgent priority to attend some personal development courses
20–25	Time to get serious with personal development
25–30	Still more could be done
over 30	Congratulations, you have made good progress minimizing your personal baggage. (Try having a number of other staff members score you—the results may be different.)

Note: The author has provided some complementary material on his Web site, which will be helpful to readers. This material can be accessed through www.wiley.com/go/winningcfo or www.davidparmenter.com.

PART I

Areas to Focus on in the Next Six Months

There are some steps that you can take to get started very quickly in changing the way you handle the processes within your company. They are:

Goal	Reason
1. Invest in accounts payable technology.	The accounts payable team is the center of the accounting team. Investing in accounts payable technology pays high dividends for the finance team, the budget holders, and their administrators. This will take around a six-month time frame and thus you need to start now.
2. Get month-end reporting to the senior management team (SMT) down to three working days post month-end.	If you are not this quick, too much time is being absorbed by this low-value task. We need to free up time to provide decision-based reports during the month, which are much more valuable.
3. Draft a dashboard with your key result indicators (KRIs) for your board of directors.	This will revolutionize the board's finance report and can be set up very quickly (e.g., one person did it over one evening).

(Continued)

Goal	Reason
4. Start work on your annual reporting cycle so that it can be completed and signed off by the auditors in 15 working days post year-end.	You never get thanked for this activity so streamlining annual reporting is a must.
5. If your annual planning cycle is to be completed within the next six months, plan now to complete it within a 10-working-day time frame.	Your annual plan takes too long, undermines reporting, creates dysfunctional budget holders, and smart organizations do not do it anymore. You need to adopt some of the practices suggested, which will speed up the process and prepare the way for quarterly rolling planning—outlined in Part Two.
6. The CFO and the CFO direct reports should all have their own mentor.	A mentor not only will advance your career but will save your career time and time again.
7. Start marketing the accounting team as of tomorrow.	I expect this will be a challenge but it is one you cannot delay—you have years to catch up.
8. Place more emphasis on daily and weekly reporting.	Reporting as soon as the barn door is left open will, over time, help management to learn to shut it immediately.
9. Plan for some team-building events in the next three months.	Your team deserves this: It is a better practice, productivity will improve, and you will feel good about creating an improved work environment.

A checklist has been developed covering the major steps. This is set out in Appendix A.

CHAPTER 1

Accounts Payable in the 21st Century

Many large organizations have made massive inroads into accounts payable and quite frankly will find this chapter rather basic. To those I say simply move to Chapter 2. However, many finance teams are wedded to Charles Dickens's processes and procedures.

This chapter is an extract from a white paper[1] I deliver around the world that has revolutionized many accounts payable teams.

Removal of Charles Dickens's Processes

I believe the accounts payable team is the center of an accounting function, for without its smooth operation:

- Monthly accounts cannot be prepared promptly.
- The company does not, at any point in time, know its total liabilities.
- Budget holders spend too much of their valuable time processing orders and approving invoices for payment.
- There is a low level of accuracy in the monthly accounts due to missed liabilities and posting errors.
- The processing procedures are more akin to the Charles Dickens era than to those of the 21st century. (after all, Charles Dickens had a checkbook and received paper-based invoices.)
- Suppliers are forever on the phone querying payments.
- Expense claims are a nightmare for claimants and the accounts payable team.

Let us look at some areas to attack.

Move to a Paperless Accounts Payable Function

As already mentioned, many accounts payable (AP) processing procedures are more akin to those from the Charles Dickens era than to those of the 21st century. Why do we go from an electronic transaction in the supplier's accounting system to a paper-based invoice? Surely we should be able to change this easily with our major suppliers.

Many U.S. multinationals have achieved this already. Doing so requires an investment, skilled AP staff, and retraining of the budget holders. The rewards are immense. To appreciate the benefits, I suggest the AP team regularly visit the website of the Accounts Payable Network (www.TAPN.com).

The various ways to make this move into the 21st-century AP paperless procedures include:

- Invest in an electronic ordering system (procurement system) so control is at the order stage, receipting is electronic, and supplier invoices can be automatically matched to orders and paid (see the next section).
- Introduce the purchase card to all staff with delegated authority so all small-value items can be purchased through it, thereby saving thousands of hours of processing time by both budget holders and the accounts payable teams (see "Introduce a Purchase Card.").
- Require all major suppliers to provide electronic feeds of the invoices, which will include the general ledger account codes. This requires liaison between your information technology (IT) team and the supplier's IT team.
- Process electronic expense claims through a web-based system so employees, wherever they are, can process their claims. (Purchase cards have an accompanying online system supplied by the relevant bank provider that can also accommodate cash expense items).
- Eliminate all check payments, framing the last check on the CEO's office wall; see "Mount the Last Signed Check on the CEO's Wall" later in the chapter.
- Introduce scanning technology for all paper-based invoices from your minor suppliers (all major suppliers will become electronic feeds over time). The electronic image can then be sent to the budget holder for approval if there is no purchase invoice.
- Post remittances electronically onto your website in a secure area so that suppliers with passwords can download them. This removes the need to send remittances by email or post.

Invest in an Electronic Ordering System (Procurement System)

Most accounting systems come with an integrated purchase order system. Some systems even enable the order to be priced using the supplier's online price list and then emailed automatically to the preferred supplier, providing the order is within the budget holder's delegated authority.

These systems should be purchased and implemented before the accounting team ever considers upgrading the general ledger (G/L). Increasingly today the G/L is only the holder of actuals, with the targets, reporting, and drill down being provided in auxiliary systems.

This is a major exercise and one that should be researched immediately. There should be an organization near your locality that uses the same accounting system and where the purchase order system is working well. Visit that organization and learn how to implement the system.

Introduce a Purchase Card

A purchase card is a free AP system, run by your card provider, financed by your suppliers. It is a no-brainer. Get a purchase card system implemented as soon as possible.

It has been estimated that the average cost of the whole purchase cycle is between $65 and $85 per transaction. Pretty horrific when you realize that a high portion of your transactions are for minor amounts. Exhibit 1.1 shows a typical profile of AP invoices. The bulk of invoices may be for low-value amounts, especially if consolidation invoices have not yet been organized. Remember that it costs the same to process a $10 transaction as it does a $100,000 transaction. In addition, is it appropriate to request budget holders to raise an order in your purchase order system for a $20 transaction? Surely the AP system is designed around 100 percent compliance of major invoices (say over $2,000).

Purchase cards are different from credit cards and are here to stay. There are three liability options: limited to genuine business, company has sole liability, and individual has sole liability. They work particularly well with high-value, low-volume items where you are purchasing through the same suppliers, as they will be able to insert G/L code information on the transaction (e.g., an organization has told its national stationery supplier the G/L code for stationery and has given it the department codes associated with each purchase card).

The purchase card is certainly a way for you to take control of processing these minor-value/high-volume transactions, that cannot be organized through an electronic consolidated invoice.

For more information, search the web for "purchase card" + "name of your bank."

My financial controller lobbied hard for a purchase card for all staff with all expenditure under $2,000 being processed via the card. The staff entered coding for purchases that were not already recoded by the

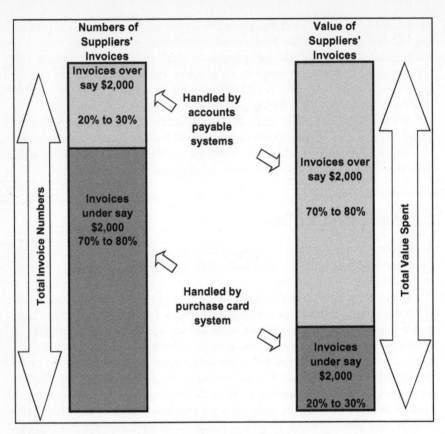

EXHIBIT 1.1 AP Invoices that a Purchase Card Is Targeting

supplier, and the approval process was online. Thousands of transactions were replaced by one electronic feed and one direct debit.
                                    CFO with blue chip international experience

The purchase card statements are sent electronically with additional vendor spend analysis and can be loaded directly into the G/L.

These systems have been working well in many companies. All you need to do is contact your bank, which will have many better practice examples.

Cut Off Accounts Payable on the Last Working Day

If AP is held open, you will find it difficult to complete prompt month-end reporting. What benefit does holding open AP for one or two days have?

EXHIBIT 1.2 Month-End Time Key

Day −2	Day −1	Day +1	Day +2
2nd to last working day	Last working day	First working day	2nd working day of new month

Better practice is to cut off AP at noon on the last working day. In my workshops I come across organizations that cut off AP even earlier, on day −2 and day −3 (see Exhibit 1.2). They manage this by relying more on recurring reversing accruals supplemented by budget holders' accruals for the larger one-off amounts. They place timeliness above preciseness. This requires good communication to budget holders and suppliers with the latter sending their invoices earlier by changing the timing of billing.

> *Your month-end result doesn't become more accurate the longer you leave it. It just becomes more expensive to produce.*
> *CFO with blue chip international experience*

Close Accruals a Day before the Accounts Payable Ledger

One smart accountant I have come across worked out that budget holders know little more about month-end purchase invoices at day +2 than at day −2. So, the accountant introduced accrual cutoff on day −2, the day before month-end. Budget holders were required to send their last invoices for processing to meet the month-end AP cutoff by noon on day −2, which gave AP 24 hours to process them before the day −1 AP cutoff. He also told them to prepare their accruals in the afternoon of day −2, directly into the G/L. Cutting off accruals early recognizes that month-end invoices will not arrive miraculously by day +1 or day +2, so staff will need to phone some key suppliers to get accrual information regardless of when the cutoff is. Another point to note is that the accrual cutoff does not need to be after the AP cutoff!. All that is required is a guarantee that all invoices approved for payment by budget holders within the deadline will in fact be processed prior to the AP cutoff or accrued directly by the AP team.

Limit the Accruals

It is important to set materiality levels for the accruals based on what is material for the whole organization. You may say to all budget holders that a department can raise accruals only if the total comes to over $5,000, $10,000, and so forth, and each individual debit is greater than $1,000 or $2,000.

For many smaller departments, their accruals will never reach these levels. They can be told, "You are too small to do accruals."

Mount the Last Signed Check on the CEO's Wall

For some time, many companies have tried to change their suppliers' preferences for checks. The benefits from using electronic funds transfers as a payment method include lower costs, predictable cash flows, and fewer supplier phone calls over late payment. The question is, how do you get the reluctant suppliers to give you their bank details?

Some progressive companies have given up mailing request letters to suppliers and have hired temporary staff to call suppliers. One company with 99 percent of accounts paying by direct debit (and they are still not happy) calls suppliers and says, "We would like to pay you but we cannot . . . pause . . . we are a modern company and pay all our accounts electronically. We have thrown away the checkbook and are at a loss as to how we can pay you as you have ignored our requests for your bank account details!" One company cancelled its check payment run and was able to obtain 120 suppliers' bank details within four hours of phoning them to say "We cannot pay you!"

I recommend that the last check be written payable to "A.N. Other" for 99 cents. This check is then ceremoniously mounted in a golden frame with a plaque saying "This is the last check and is a symbol of our drive to end all Charles Dickens processes." The framed check is then mounted in the CEO's office. The CEO will get much pleasure in answering visitors when they ask, "What is a check doing in a frame?"

Perform Frequent Direct Credit Payment Runs

It is a better practice to perform frequent direct credit payment runs, in fact treating this as a normal day-to-day activity. In organizations doing frequent runs, an invoice is received directly by AP from the supplier, and the details are matched to the order and the electronic receipting flag that says "goods/services have been received in full." Once order, invoice, and receipting match one another, a payment is processed on the agreed future payment date.

Improve Budget Holders' Cooperation

There are many ways to improve budget holders' cooperation, including:

- Increasing budget holder turnaround on purchase invoice approval by linking performance to their bonus element.
- Establishing account management within the finance team (e.g., Sarah looks after budget holders A, B, and C; Ted looks after budget holders D, E, and F).
- Sending a "welcome letter" to new budget holders to train them from the beginning and eliminate potential bad habits before they have a chance to set in.
- Holding workshops outlining how budget holders, and their relevant staff, should work with the finance systems (AP, reporting system, G/L, completion of expense claims, use of purchase card, etc.).
- Rewarding and recognizing good budget holder behavior.
- Making budget holders aware of all their errors.

Speed Up Budget Holders' Correction of Omissions

One company reports that it now has a 24-hour turnaround for all branches to approve all invoices that cannot be matched to orders and have not been electronically receipted. If a branch manager does not achieve this on one single day in the month, he or she loses one month's performance bonus. The CEO was approached and got behind this initiative. This takes clever marketing, and is well worth the effort.

This change, along with streamlining of supplier invoice timings, will have a profound impact on processing volumes, helping to smooth out the workload, as shown in Exhibit 1.3.

A Welcome Letter to All New Budget Holders

Imagine the goodwill created when a new employee receives a welcome letter from the AP department asking for a slot to deliver a 20-minute training session for the individual within the next few weeks.

Why wait till new employees are educated by the uneducated (budget holders who do not know or do not comply with the AP procedures)? Get in there first. Deliver a brief training presentation, including:

- The procedures
- The forms

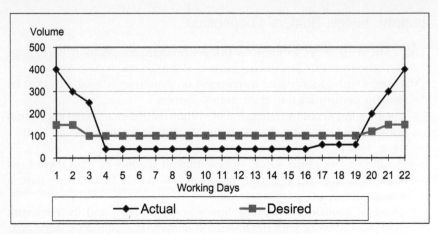

EXHIBIT 1.3 AP Invoice Processing Volumes during Month

- The problems we have and why they create a lot of wasted time
- How budget holders and the AP team can work most effectively together
- The presence of "shame and name" lists, which you point out, "but this of course will not affect you!"

This presentation is best delivered in a casual format, on a laptop supplied by the IT department, sitting on the new budget holder's desk. See Appendix J for a draft welcome letter.

Introduce "Shame and Name" Lists

If you want to change human behavior, you need to work on it for a duration of 12 weeks, and during this time the penny will drop. If you create a number of shame and name lists and publish these on the intranet and in hardcopy for the senior management team (SMT), you will, over 12 weeks, create change. I would recommend preparing a laminated card with all the league tables (i.e., lists of the culprits with the highest number of errors, exceptions, etc.), cut to fit the inside pocket of SMT members' jackets. All the SMT need to do is discuss the matter with the budget holders when they bump into them, or, when they have time, make a few career-limiting phone calls to these noncompliant staff.

The suggested lists are:

- Budget holders with the most purchase invoices without a corresponding order.

- Employees with late expense claims.
- Budget holders with purchase invoices awaiting approval that are already outside the set approval turnaround time.
- Budget holders who have missed deadlines.

Remember, you will never want to invite all the budget holders to your Sunday afternoon barbeque, so do not worry about being unpopular with a noncompliant budget holder. You need to make one thing clear: Not complying with the accounting system requirements is going to be career limiting. In other words, there are three options open to these nonconforming budget holders: You leave the organization, they leave the organization, or they change. You might, as one attendee pointed out, want to call these lists "budget holders requiring further training."

Reward Good Budget Holder Behavior

One accounting team gives a bottle of wine a month to the budget holder who provides the first complete month-end submission. This simple acknowledgment has provided the appropriate environment for timely submissions from budget holders. It is also important to record the "winner" on your intranet page so the relevant budget holder gets the recognition, which is the main reward.

Have a Closer Relationship with Your Main Suppliers

There are a number of ways a closer relationship with suppliers can improve processing. The more your key suppliers' systems are linked to yours, the better. It is simply an issue of getting the two IT departments together around the same table.

Better practices include:

- Having all major suppliers link their systems with yours and having the supplier provide electronic invoices that are already G/L coded. Set a target of getting your top five suppliers all electronic within the next three months. You will need to get on the phone today to talk to your counterpart in the supplier organization (the CFO or management accountant). Do not leave this to the IT department to organize, as they find this type of exercise personally challenging. Where have you seen an IT department full of extroverts and great communicators?

- Introducing consignment stock where the supplier is responsible for constant replenishment (e.g., core stock items [which requires online access to relevant stock records], stationery, etc.).
- Asking for consolidated invoices from suppliers, especially utilities, and stationery.
- Changing invoicing cycles on all monthly accounts such as utilities, credit cards, and so on (e.g., invoice cycle including transactions from May 28 to June 27 and being received by June 28). The accruals for these suppliers can then be a standard one, two, or three business days, depending how the working days fall.
- Asking major suppliers to request an order from your budget holders; support this by not paying supplier invoices unless there is a purchase order. Simply return the invoices to suppliers and ask them to attach the purchase order (they will not want to repeat this activity more than once!).
- Ask large-volume, small-dollar suppliers to accept your purchase card.

Use Self-Generated Invoices (Buyer-Created Invoices)

Where a supplier invoice will be received too late, where some product may be missing (raw material blown out of the truck), or where your systems are so sophisticated that you have no need for a supplier's paperwork, a "buyer-created invoice" will aid efficiency.

The supplier's shipping document is used to determine the quantity of goods supplied or, in the case of a weigh-bridge process, the actual weight, measured by the weigh bridge. The agreed weight is then multiplied by the agreed purchase contract price to calculate the amount owed. The customer then direct credits the supplier, who also is sent an electronic invoice. The invoice contains all required details, such as quantity, date of service, taxes, value, total payable, and a unique invoice number using, say, the first three letters of your company, two letters of theirs, and four numbers (e.g., invoice #dsbbd1234).

Note

1. David Parmenter, "50+ Ways to Improve Your Accounts Payable Function," www.davidparmenter.com, 2010.

CHAPTER 2

Timely Month-End Reporting: By Working Day 3 or Less

M any large organizations have made massive inroads into fast and accurate month-end reporting. I say to them "Celebrate your achievement" and simply move to Chapter 3. However, the vast majority of finance teams around the world have month-end processes that are career limiting, to say the least. This chapter is an extract from a white paper[1] I deliver around the world that has revolutionized many finance teams.

When I was a corporate accountant, each period-end was a disaster waiting to happen. Each month-end had a life of its own. You never knew when and where the next problem was going to come from. Two or three days away, we always appeared to have it under control, and yet each month we were faxing (email was not on the scene then) the result five minutes before the deadline. Our fingers were crossed as a series of late adjustments had meant that the quality assurance work we had done was invalid and we did not have the luxury of doing it again. Does this sound familiar?

CEOs need to demand a complete and radical change if they are to free management and accountants from the shackles of a zero-sum process—reporting last month's results halfway through the following month. Here are the *facts*:

- U.S. companies are now providing commentary and numbers by the first working day.
- Companies are migrating to closing the month on the same day each month (i.e., months are either five or four weeks).
- In leading companies, the senior management team (SMT) is letting go of report writing—SMT members are no longer rewriting reports. They have informed the board that they concur with the writer's findings but it is a delegated report.

See Appendix B for a checklist of implementation steps to reduce month-end reporting time frames. See Appendix C for the common bottlenecks in month-end reporting and techniques to get around them.

Rating Scale for Month-End Reporting

The following rating scale shows the time frames of month-end reporting across the 4,000 corporate accountants I have presented to in the past 10 years.

Exceptional	Outstanding	Above Average	Average
One working day	Two to three working days	Four working days	Five working days

Benefits of Quick Month-End Reporting

As a CFO of a tertiary institution said, "Every day spent producing reports is a day less spent on analysis and projects." There are a larger number of benefits to management and the finance team of quick reporting, and these include:

Benefits to Management	Benefits to the Finance Team
Reporting plays a bigger part in the decision-making process.	Staff are more productive as efficiencies are locked in and bottlenecks are tackled.
Reduction in detail and length of reports.	Many month-end traditional processes are out of date and inefficient, and these are removed.
Reduced cost to organization of month-end reporting.	Happier staff with higher morale and increased job satisfaction.
More time spent analyzing trends.	Finance staff focus is now on being a business partner to the budget holder, helping them to shape the future.
More time spent on achieving results.	The team has time to be involved in more rewarding activities, such as quarterly rolling forecasts, project work, and so forth.

Benefits to Management	Benefits to the Finance Team
Greater budget holder ownership (accruals, variance analysis, coding, corrections during month, better understanding, etc.).	More professionally qualified finance staff.
Less senior management time invested in month-end.	Likewise and also leads to a very quick year-end.

Impact of a Quick Month-End on the Finance Team Workload

The significance of month-end reporting can be seen from this comparison of three companies reporting in different time frames. Waymark Solutions analysis of over 500 finance teams shows that the quick reporting accounting teams are far more advanced in many other areas. They should be, as they have much more time on their hands, as shown in Exhibit 2.1.

It is important to cost out to management and the board the month-end reporting process. When doing this exercise, remember that senior management barely has 32 weeks of productive time when you remove holidays, sick leave, travel time, and routine management meetings. Thus a cost of $1,000 per day is not unrealistic.

Such an analysis can be easily performed by your accounting team in 30 minutes, and will be valuable in the sale process of changing month-end reporting time frames. Exhibit 2.2 shows the time invested in an organization with five business units with around 500 to 700 staff.

EXHIBIT 2.1 Impact of Quick Month-Ends Based on a 22-Working-Day Month

Tasks	Day 1	Quick Month-End	Slow Month-End
	No. of working days a month		
Month-end reporting completed	1	4	9
Remaining days	21	18	13
Percentage of extra time for project work and daily routines	60% more time	40% more time	
Based on a 22 working day month			

	Days
Drafting papers	2–4
Review and redrafting	1–2
Total days of effort by each unit	3–6
5 business units	15–30
Support function reports	10–15
Review by CEO, etc., and redrafting	1–2
Total senior management effort each month	26–47

EXHIBIT 2.2 Senior Management Time Invested in Month-Ends

Major Steps You Can Do before Your Next Month-End

Set out next are the major steps you can achieve within the month you are currently in.

Establish Reporting Rules within the Finance Team

Members of the finance team have to realize that they are artists, not scientists. There needs to be recognition that the monthly accounts are not precise documents. Assessments need to be made, and the monthly accounts will never be right; they can only be a true and fair view. We could hold the accounts payable open for six months after month-end and still not have the plumber's invoice that arrives when the plumber's company is doing its year-end and realize that it has forgotten to invoice for work done. We therefore need some rules about the month-end reports. The month-end financial report should:

- Not be delayed for detail.
- Be consistent—between months, judgment calls, and format.
- Be a true and fair view and error free.
- Be concise—less than ten pages (include the major business units' one-page reports).
- Be a merging of numbers, graphs, and comments on one page.

Ban Spring Cleaning at Month-End

Month-end reporting is not the time for spring cleaning, no matter how tempting it can be. This fact requires a reeducation of the finance team and of budget holders.

All miscoding, unless resulting in a material misstatement of the profit and loss statement (P&L), is processed during the following month. Budget holders are educated to review their cost center numbers via online access to the general ledger (G/L) during the month and are requested to highlight any discrepancies immediately with the finance team.

Only month-end adjustments that are for material P&L corrections are processed.

Avoid Intercompany Adjustments

Clever organizations ban all intercompany adjustments at month-end except for major internal profit adjustments. They have automatic interfaces with intergroup transactions where one party does transactions for both G/Ls.

When there is a difference, instigate a rule that the accounts payable or accounts receivable ledger is always right, and adjust accordingly, leaving the intercompany parties to sort the issues out in the following month.

This change requires a memo from the CEO. See Appendix J for a suggested memorandum from the CEO.

Avoid High Processing at Month-End

It is important to push processing back from month-end by avoiding a payment run at month-end. It is a better practice to have weekly or daily direct credit payment runs with none happening within the last and first two days of month-end. The last thing you need is to receive a large pile of invoices on the last day of cutoff, as shown in Exhibit 2.3.

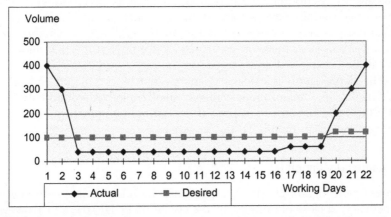

EXHIBIT 2.3 Accounts Payable Invoice Processing Volumes during Month

Change invoicing cycles on all monthly accounts, such as utilities, credit cards, and so forth, as discussed in Chapter 1 (e.g., invoice cycle including transactions from May 28 to June 27 and are received electronically by June 28).

Early Closing of the Accounts Payable Ledger

I have not come across a company that can justify closing off accounts payable after the last day of the month. Whatever date you pick to close accounts payable, you will never capture all the invoices. Remember, we are after a true and fair view and we are sculptors rather than scientists (see Chapter 1).

Early Accruals Close-off

Cutting off accruals before accounts payable, say day −2, is both possible and desirable (see Chapter 1).

Early Close-off of Accounts Receivable

Close off accounts receivable immediately on the last working day, or better still, at noon on the last working day, with transactions in the afternoon being carried forward to the first day of the new month.

Remember that training will be required in dispatch and accounts receivable to ensure cut-off is clean each month-end.

Early Capital Expenditure Cut-off

Why are we performing depreciation calculations at month-end when clever organizations have already done this much earlier? They close off capital projects at least one week before month-end. Any equipment arriving in the last week therefore is treated as if it arrived the next month. It still can be unwrapped and plugged in.

The depreciation is calculated and posted before month-end, at the latest by day −3. Organizations with very small capital expenditure are even using the depreciation calculations done during the annual plan and correcting to actual in month 11 and month 12.

Early Inventory Cut-off

Sophisticated organizations can get their month-end inventory cut-off immediately at close of business on the last working day (day −1). However, many manufacturing organizations take a few days into the next month to manage this process. This creates an unnecessary delay in month-end accounts.

If your systems are not state of the art, make the inventory cutoff at close of business on day −2, with all production on the last day being carried forward to the next month. This gives one day to check the valuation and records.

Always avoid a month-end stock count; these should be done on a rolling basis and be held no nearer to month-end than the third week of the month (e.g., one jewelry chain counts watches one month, gold chains the next month, etc.). The close-off transfer of work in progress to finished goods also is done on day −2, with day −1 production treated as the next month's.

These early cutoffs will require cooperation between accounts payable and inventory staff to ensure raw materials arriving on the last day and the matching liability are treated as the next month's transaction or accrued.

From 5 P.M. Last Day to 5 P.M. First Working Day

What happens in the next 24 hours is critical to the success of month-end reporting.

At 5 P.M. on the last working day, all the cutoffs should be done. We can print off the first cut of the numbers. All the management accountants should take a copy home and look for areas where they think the numbers could be wrong. In addition budget holders should be sent their accounts and they should be given until noon Day +1 to complete their commentary on major variances. The variance must be over $•• (based on materiality level for whole organization) and >10% of budget before a comment is required.

At 9 A.M. the following day, all the accountants meet to discuss the areas where further work is needed to be sure that the numbers are "true and fair." At the meeting, "who is reviewing what" is decided and a time is set to meet again before the flash report numbers are finalized that day.

One of the most important better practices is to catch all material adjustments the accountants find and see the net result before you decide to adjust. Two "overs and unders" spreadsheets can be set up (see Exhibit 2.4), one to trap major adjustments, say, over $5,000, $20,000, or $50,000 depending on the size of the company, and one for smaller items that can be tidied up in the quiet times in the following midmonth. The accountants, if they find adjustments, will enter the adjustments on the appropriate spreadsheets, which reside on a shared drive on the local area network.

At between 3 and 4 P.M. on the first day, you call all the accountants back and ask, "What did you find?" "Are there any adjustments highlighted. by the budget holders' comments?" More often than not you will note that adjustments have a tendency to net each other off. Book only the

EXHIBIT 2.4 Maintaining an "Overs and Unders" Schedule

Source	Raised by	JV #	Adjustment		P/L Impact		B/S Impact	
					Dr	Cr	Dr	Cr
xxxxx	Pat	1	Dr	xxxxxxxxx xxxxx xxxx	45			
			Cr	xxxx xxxxx xxxxx		45		
xxxxx	John	2	Dr	xxxx xxxx	10			
			Cr	xx x x xxxxxxxxx		10		
xxxxx	Jean	3	Dr	xxxx xxxx	25			
			Cr	xx x x xxxxxxxxx				25
xxxxx	Dave	4	Dr	xxxx xxxx		15		
			Cr	xx x x xxxxxxxxx			15	
		etc.						
					80	70		
					−70			
				Net impact on P/L	10			

adjustments required to restate the numbers as "true and fair." You are now in a position to prepare the one-page flash report for the CEO.

Deliver a Flash Report at the End of Day 1

Issuing a flash report on the (P&L) bottom line to the CEO stating a level of accuracy of, say, +/–5% or +/–10 by the close of business on the first day is a very important practice. There is not a CEO on this planet who would not welcome a heads-up number on such a timely basis. See Exhibit 2.5 for an example of a flash report.

It is important not to provide too many lines because you may find yourself with another variance report on your hands if you have a CEO who fails to look at the big picture. Remember to state your degree of accuracy (e.g., +/–5%, +/–10%). Never attempt a flash report until the accounts payable, accounts receivable, and accrual cutoffs have been successfully moved back to the last working day of the month. Otherwise you will be using the accruals to change final numbers so they can closely match your flash numbers, a practice I would not recommend.

Major Quality Assurance Tasks after Day 1

When the flash report is done and has been discussed with the CEO, we need to focus on the reporting pack. The important issue to remember

Flash Report for the Month Ending 31 December 20XX

	Actual	Target	Variance	>$100K
	This Month $000s			
Revenue				
Revenue 1	5,550	5,650	(100)	⇔
Revenue 2	3,550	3,450	100	⇔
Revenue 3	2,450	2,200	250	✓
Other revenue	2,250	2,350	(100)	⇔
Total Revenue	13,800	13,650	150	⇔
Less: Cost of sales	(11,500)	(11,280)	(220)	⇔
Gross Profit	2,300	2,370	(70)	
Expenses				
Expense 1	1,280	1,260	(20)	
Expense 2	340	320	(20)	
Expense 3	220	200	(20)	
Expense 4	180	160	(20)	
Other expenses	170	110	(60)	
Total Expenses	2,190	2,050	(140)	⇔
Surplus/(Deficit)	110	320	(210)	✗

Areas to Note
1. xxxxxxxxx xxxxxxx xxx Xxxxxxxxx xxxxx xxxxx xxxxxxxxx xxxxxxxxxxxxx
xxxxxxxxxxxxxxxxxxxxxxxxxxxxxxxxxxxxxxxxxxxxxxxxxxxxxxxxxxxxxxxxxx
xxxxxxxxxxxxxxxx xxxxxxxxx xxxxxxx xxxxxxxxxxxx xxxxxxxxxxxxxxxxxxxxxxxxxxxxxxxxxx
2. Xxxxxxxxxxxxxxxxxxxxxxxxxxxxxxxxxxxxxxxxxx
xxxxxxxxxxxxxxxxxxxxxxxxxxxxxxxxxxxxxxxxxxxxxxxxxxxxxxxxxxxxxxxxxx
xxxxxxxxxxxxxxxx xxxxxxxxx xxxxxxx xxxxxxxxxxxx xxxxxxxxxxxxxxxxxxxxxxxxxxxxxxxxxx
3. Xxxxxxxxxxxxxxxxxxxxxxxxxxxxxxxxxxxxxxxxxx
xxxxxxxxxxxxxxxxxxxxxxxxxxxxxxxxxxxxxxxxxxxxxxxxxxxxxxxxxxxxxxxxxx
xxxxxxxxxxxxxxxx xxxxxxxxx xxxxxxx xxxxxxxxxxxx xxxxxxxxxxxxxxxxxxxxxxxxxxxxxxxxxx
4. Xxxxxxxxxxxxxxxxxxxxxxxxxxxxxxxxxxxxxxxxxx
xxxxxxxxxxxxxxxxxxxxxxxxxxxxxxxxxxxxxxxxxxxxxxxxxxxxxxxxxxxxxxxxxx
xxxxxxxxxxxxxxxx xxxxxxxxx xxxxxxx xxxxxxxxxxxx xxxxxxxxxxxxxxxxxxxxxxxxxxxxxxxxxx

EXHIBIT 2.5 Flash Report to CEO at End of Day 1

here is that the month-end can never be right, it can only be a true and fair view.

TRUE AND FAIR VIEW AND ERROR FREE I always point out to workshop attendees that if we took one organization's month-end financial information and gave it to all the finance teams present at the workshop to work on, no one team would get the same month-end result. All the "net results" presented by those teams would all be different, as the accountants would have made different calls on materiality, depreciation, and accounting policies. Yet over 60 months—five years—the consolidated results would be very similar. I say to the attendees that we are all artists, not scientists; we sculpt the numbers. Thus once we have reached what we consider a true and fair view, we should cease to review or adjust the numbers any further.

BAN ALL LATE CHANGES TO THE REPORTS Once the flash report has been issued, at the close of business on the first working day, teams should continue with recording any adjustment found in the relevant "overs and unders" spreadsheet.

No changes are permitted to the numbers reported in the flash report until the entire review has been completed. The accounting team can then assess which adjustments are worthy of processing. As many have no P&L impact, they would be held back for adjustment in the following month.

Once the reporting pack is prepared, no adjustments are allowed unless they are very material. There is nothing worse for the finance team than to submit a finance report to the CEO that is inconsistent. This is frequently caused by a late change not being processed properly through the report. As night follows day, the CEO will be sure to find it. I am sure many readers have been guilty of this one.

It is far better to hold back the adjustments. If the CEO says to you, "I thought the sales were higher," you can say, "Pat, it is a pleasure working for such an astute CEO. You are right, the sales are understated by $13,000; however, there are adjustments totaling $7,000 going the opposite way, so I have not booked the adjustments as the net difference is immaterial. I am booking these through this month. However, if you like I will adjust this month's report." Most CEOs will feel pleased with themselves for spotting the shortfall and then move on to another issue.

THE CEO WILL BE LESS INTERESTED IN THE FINAL MONTH-END REPORT The flash report has been a great appetizer, and the CEO's appetite for month-end information has been largely satisfied. This then creates a great opportunity to reduce the volume of reports we give the CEO, further making the month-end process more efficient.

QUALITY ASSURANCE CHECKS REDUCE WITH MORE CONFIDENCE Most of the work from day 2 onward is report preparation and quality assurance work. Once everybody has become used to the new regime, you will note that the error rate starts reducing. The accountants can then have more faith in the numbers and spend less time checking them.

Major Steps You Can Do within the Next Six Months

Note that accounts payable improvements that were discussed in Chapter 1 have been excluded.

Avoid Late Time Sheets

Get staff to complete non-revenue-generating time sheets by day −3 and to include their best guess for the remaining two days. You could even get them to project forward for the full week. Even if the estimates were 100 percent wrong, there would not be a material misstatement. You work it out!

Get all relevant staff to complete revenue-generating time sheets by noon on the last working day, with a best guess for the afternoon and corrections processed on the next week's time sheet. If by lunchtime staff members do not know what they are doing that afternoon, maybe they should be working for your competition.

Minimize Budget Holders' Month-End Reporting

Budget holders' reports should be limited to half an hour of preparation. A one-page report should suffice, or two pages if you are using performance indicators.

I once saw a pile of reports on a finance manager's desk. When I asked what they were, he said they were the budget holders' month-end reports. "What do you use them for?" I asked. "I do not use them; I call the budget holders if I need an explanation of a major variance," he replied. Hundreds of hours of budget holder time were wasted each month that could have been better spent getting home at a reasonable hour.

A good starting point is to cost out the monthly report preparation, as described earlier.

Avoid the Rewriting of Reports

Some organizations have made a major cultural change to report writing, committing the board, CEO, and the SMT to avoid rewrites at all costs, saving thousands of dollars a month of management time. The board no longer considers the quality of the board papers as a reflection of the CEO's performance. The organizations have learned to delegate and empower their staff so that the SMT and board papers are being written with limited input from senior managers and are being tabled with few amendments, provided that the SMT agrees with the recommendations. The CEO can choose to put a caveat on each report: "While I concur with the recommendations, the report was written by XXXXX."

The board understands that the report is not written in SMT-speak. Board members are encouraged to comment directly to the writer about strengths and areas for improvement in report writing. The writers are also the presenters, where necessary. The organization thus has a much more relaxed week leading up to the board meeting, having largely delegated the report writing and the associated stress. The rewards include motivated and more competent staff and general managers being free to spend more time contributing to the bottom line.

Replace the Monthly Forecast with a Quarterly Forecast

The last exercise that delays the monthly report is the reforecast for year-end. We, as corporate accountants, seem to believe that if the last month is a good month, this benefit will remain at year-end. Our year-end forecast yo-yos every month. The only thing consistent is that all the forecasts turn out to be wrong. In fact, we should put a note by the forecast: "This forecast: is wrong, will be changed next month." It is far better to hold the forecast and redo it properly, bottom-up, once a quarter as part of a quarterly rolling forecast process, see Chapter 15 and www.davidparmenter.com for a web seminar and article on the quarterly rolling forecasting and planning.

By removing the forecasting exercise from the month-end reporting cycle, you will have saved at least half a day without any loss in the report's quality.

Close on the Same Day Each Month

Julius Caesar gave us the calendar we use today. It is not a good business tool because it creates 12 dramas a year for the finance team and budget holders, with each month being slightly different.

Between three and five months every year will end on a weekend, and finance teams often find that the month-end processes are smoother for these months. Why not close off on the nearest Friday/Saturday/Sunday to month end as many U.S. companies do? The benefits of this include precise four- or five-week months, which make comparisons more meaningful, and there is less impact on the workweek as the systems are rolled over at the weekend.

Otherwise, every month is a drama because we close on a different calendar day. Every month we have to issue detailed instructions that effectively say "What you did on Wednesday last month please do on Thursday, what you did on Thursday . . ."

Closing off at the weekend can be done for all sectors; some will require more liaison than others. It also would make a big difference in the public and not-for-profit sectors. You simply present to the board June's results and balance sheet. You do not need to highlight the July 2 close. At year-end, the missing two or extra two days of income and balance sheet movement will be taken up in the auditor's "overs and unders" schedule.

You need to choose whether it is to be the last Saturday or the nearest Saturday, last Sunday or nearest Sunday to month-end, and so on. The last Saturday can have you closing six days before month-end, whereas the preferred option of the nearest Saturday will be a maximum of only two working days out.

By making this change you are beginning to create 12 nonevents a year, the El Dorado of all corporate accountants.

Introduce a Friendly Front End to the General Ledger

It is important that budget holders take ownership of their part of the G/L. To this end we need to offer them a user-friendly interface to their part of the G/L. There are a number of reporting tools (e.g., Crystal, PowerPlay) that can make any G/L look good. Companies are reporting that they have had great success by downloading transactions (daily or weekly) from the G/L into these drill-down tools, allowing read-only access to budget holders.

With a drill-down tool, budget holders never look at the G/L. Management accountants and budget holders also will use this reporting tool when analyzing costs because it contains prior months' figures in a continuous stream, enabling them to do cross-year financial comparisons seamlessly.

A by-product of these reporting tools is that CFOs are now questioning why they need to invest in the first-tier accounting systems. In Australia, one CFO is running the G/L of an organization with 400 full-time employees on the mind-your-own-business (MYOB) accounting G/L. As he said, "Why invest more than $300 when all the G/L does is to hold the historic numbers and is only accessed by a couple of accountants? In our company all the reporting against budget and drill-down access used by budget holders is performed in auxiliary systems."

No Need to Change Your Accounting System

Companies should be able to achieve day 3 reporting no matter how antiquated their accounting system is. Much can be achieved with an old system. An old G/L is not an excuse for not reaching day 3 reporting!! If you still believe the G/L is the problem, you need a paradigm shift in your thinking.

Far too much money is reinvested in upgrading G/Ls. In a modern company, the G/L only does the basic task of holding the financial numbers for the year. Monthly reporting, latest forecast numbers, budget numbers, and even the drill-down facility available to budget holders often reside outside the G/L package, so why reinvest?

Worse still, many CFOs are party to huge investment in large G/Ls that serve to lock in analysis at the micro level. Jeremy Hope, of *Beyond Budgeting* fame, points out in his recent book[2] that many such systems are dubious. I concur, for these systems often are designed by the people who always wanted to be NASA scientists and who have never run a finance team in their life.

> *Business upgrades to G/L and other core systems often simply replicate existing processes and do not take the opportunity to redesign those processes into new systems. There are many tools in modern systems that are never used!*
>
> *CFO with blue chip international experience*

Most accounting systems come with an integrated purchase order system. Some systems even enable the order to be priced using the supplier's online price list and then emailed automatically to the preferred supplier, provided the order is within the budget holder's delegated authority. These systems should be purchased and implemented before the accounting team ever considers upgrading the G/L.

Removing Excel from the Month-End Routines

Excel has no place as a reporting or consolidation tool as it is too prone to disaster. There is no problem when a system automatically downloads to Excel, with all the programming logic being resident in the system and thus bomb-proof. The problem arises when the system has been built in-house, often by someone who has now left the company, with the accuracy of reports relying on Excel formulas reading the imported G/L download. This is, as you will have personally experienced, this is a disaster waiting to happen.

History of Quick Month-End Reporting

Quick month-end reporting has been around since the early 1990s, when farsighted CFOs starting looking at the concept of day 1 reporting (DOR).

However, this has been superseded by those who have developed systems capable of giving the CFO a full accrual net result at any time during the month. The virtual close, as it is called, is performed by CISCO, Motorola, Oracle, Dell, Wells Fargo, Citigroup, JP Morgan Chase, and Alcoa.

What Is Day 1 Reporting?

DOR is the condensing of the monthly reporting process down, so that the month-end processes are completed and management reports are issued all within day 1, the first day after the previous month-end. Organizations that are achieving DOR complete all of the next tasks by 5 P.M. on day 1:

- Transaction information processed
- Accruals raised
- Consolidations complete
- Reports prepared
- Commentary/analysis added
- Reports issued to CEO

The introduction of DOR has created a precedent that means that reporting five, six, seven, or eight working days after month-end will soon be a perilous activity for the CFO. How will you explain this time wasting to a CEO who was used to day 1 reporting in his or her previous employment?

In other words, soon it will not be acceptable for organizations and will be career limiting for CFOs to be responsible for time-consuming and costly month-end processes.

Case Study: Johnson & Johnson Vision Products USA

Around 1980, the first articles about DOR started to appear, and one of the first companies to do it was Johnson & Johnson Vision Products USA, the makers of Acuvue soft contact lenses. The company had not realized there was a real problem until it benchmarked against other companies. It found to its horror that its two weeks to close was resulting in the company "paying more to have monthly reports later." In other words, the quicker companies had less accounting resources. Then J&J started the move to day 1 reporting (see Exhibit 2.6).

Johnson & Johnson achieved this El Dorado of accounting through the stages just listed. The company quickly got to day 3 reporting by following these steps:

- All management was made aware of the problem.
- Buy-in was obtained from management.

EXHIBIT 2.6 J&J Month-End Reporting
Time Scales

At start—eight days
6 months later—three days
12 months from start—two days
24 months from start—one day

- A multifunctional project team was set up (reporting, marketing, operations, information technology [IT], production planning).
- The project team was empowered to make decisions.
- The focus was on continuous improvement and teamwork.
- Deadlines were adhered to.

At day 3, the company hit the wall; improvement now required a complete paradigm shift by the finance group. The group needed to reengineer the process, so it:

- Identified nonvalue tasks, such as: posting of automated journals on day 1, journals had to be reviewed before entry into system, period production not finalized until day 2, allocations not made until end of day 2, inventory movement entries not made until day 3.
- Applied the Pareto principle (80/20) rigorously, focusing on the big numbers. Materiality levels were established—manual journal entry line items were reduced by 80 percent.
- Eliminated all interdepartmental corrections at month-end.
- Eliminated management review as budget holders now had responsibility to resolve issues.
- Condensed the management report into one page of key indicators plus one page on the business unit's performance.
- Used estimates to avoid slowing down the process. (The difference between estimate and actual was found never to be significant.)
- Communicated changes to month-end reports far in advance.
- Ensured budget holders tracked activity throughout the month, eliminating the usual surprises found during the closing process.
- Processed allocations without reviewing departmental spending.
- Moved preparations for month-end close to before period-end instead of after.
- Replaced reconciled accounts in days 1 and 2 with variance analysis.
- Manually entered the last day's debtors and cash receipts as total and the details were handled later.

EXHIBIT 2.7 Time Scale of Change

14 to 7 days in 12 months
7 to 4 days in 12 months
4 to 2 days in 12 months

J&J streamlined all processes by following three principles—(1) eliminate what you can, (2) simplify what is left, and (3) consolidate similar
activities or information—and in so doing reached the El Dorado of
accounting day one reporting.

Case Study: A Distributor and Seller of Alcoholic Beverages

Originally this company's month-end reporting process took approximately
14 days. Like J&J, the company brought this down quickly (see Exhibit
2.7).

The company achieved day 2 reporting by following the stages just
discussed. The outcome of quick reporting for this company was that
financial information became an integral part of decision making and strategy setting for the future months of business activities.

The company quickly got to day 4 reporting by:

- Creating focus and vision, and setting goals for the project.
- Communicating achievements constantly.
- Commencing restructuring of the finance team from processing to
  value-added activities.
- Mapping all processes and dependencies.
- Tightening up accounts payable and accruals.
- Interviewing key users to determine information requirements.
- Developing concise decision-based reports.
- Ceasing to issue large computer printouts.
- Upgrading systems to be online real time.
- Removing duplicate data entry and manual reconciliations.
- Training, encouraging, and telling budget holders to analyze their
  figures during the month and take corrective action for mispostings,
  and so on.
- Placing management accountants in key departments outside of finance.
- Changing accounting team makeup, with more professional accoun-
  tants being added to replace clerical staff.

The move from day 4 to day 2 involved bringing management meetings to the third working day after month-end, effectively locking in the

benefit. The company continued to focus on process improvement, which helped the teams with their understanding of the business.

Case Study: Motorola—"12 Nonevents a Year"

Motorola, a huge company by any standards, had six operating sectors, each containing multiple divisions over 30 nations, with over 40 balance sheets. It moved from an eight-day close to a two-day close quickly by:

- Adopting world-class "better practices."
- Looking for ways to change, not saying. "no, it can't be done."
- Allowing natural competition between sectors to reduce errors (nobody likes being on the bottom).
- Counting the processing errors, which moved from 10,000 errors for every 700,000 transactions to 1,000 errors per 2 million transactions (5 SIGMA) with a target of only three errors per million (6 SIGMA).
- Eliminating time costly errors.
- Using "Post-it" reengineering (see section later in the chapter).
- Allowing sectors to have their own accounting systems.
- Looking for hundreds of small (1 percent) improvements.

The financial impact of this change was amazing, with the worldwide finance costs falling from 2.4 percent of annual revenue to about 1 percent (a reported savings of greater than $10 million per year). Motorola found that its final reports were virtually error free. In other words, by being quicker, the company also successfully tackled the error rate. The month-ends were drama free, with less anxiety and higher morale in the accounting team. What was also unbelievable was that the company stated that the finance team management even had more time for analysis within this day 1 reporting regime than it had previously in the error-prone, eight-day close.

Research on Quick Month-Ends

There has been much research on quick month-ends, and an Internet search using the string "month-end" + "quick" + "reporting" will find much information.

Implementing Quick Month-End Reporting

Exhibit 2.8 is a draft implementation plan that should be used in conjunction with the quick month-end reporting implementation checklist in Appendix B. Both are available electronically on www.davidparmenter.com.

Project weeks	pre	1	2	3	4	5	6	7	8	9	10	11	12	13
Create focus and vision for initiatives														
1 Make all management aware of the problem.	X													
2 Sell change to the accounting team.		X												
3 Sell change to the senior management team (SMT) and budget holders.			X											
4 Establish multifunctional project team (reporting, marketing, operations, IT, production planning).			X											
5 SMT to empower project team to make decisions.			X											
Post-it reengineering workshop with accounting team and selected budget holders														
6 Assess what changes need to be made within existing system constraints. Work to:														
Identify all non-value tasks and reschedule (e.g., posting of automated journals, allocations, inventory movement entries)			X											
Establish levels of relevancy (materiality levels)														
Reduce manual journal entry line items by >75%					X	X								
Eliminate all interdepartmental corrections at month-end					X	X								
Ascertain where estimates can be used to avoid slowing down process and implement.										X	X			
Communication														
7 Implement quick wins to get the SMT excited and more committed.							X	X						
8 Develop an intranet-based newsletter that spreads the good news of achievements.						X	X							
Report redesign														
9 Interview key users to determine information requirements.				X										
10 Condense budget holder's management report into one page. Develop flash report to be issued to CEO by 5 PM day ones of key indicators plus one–page financial report.				X	X									
11 Cease issuing large paper-based reports.			X											
12 Develop flash report to be issued to CEO by 5 PM day one.						X	X							
Training of budget holders to reduce their reporting requirements														
13 Send letter to relevant budget holders from CEO about attendance.										X				
14 Deliver training.									X					
Reducing month-end time frames														
15 Month-end reports by day 4.					X									
16 Month-end reports by day 3.										X				
17 Month-end reports by day 3. with reduced budget holder month-end reports.														X
Ascertain system requirements														
18 Ascertain what system upgrades are required to avoid duplication of data entry and to provide online real-time information to budget holders.														X
19 Scope planning tool for reporting and forecasting purposes.													X	X
20 Aim for automatic generation of user-friendly management reports requiring only limited analysis and insightful comments.													X	X

EXHIBIT 2.8 Implementation Plan for an Organization with over 600 Full-Time Employees

Suggested Implementation Plan

The suggested steps in Exhibit 2.8 incorporate the key stages that an organization with over 1,000 employees would need to go through. Each organization will need to tailor its plan to suit its own needs. It is important to
first remodel month-end reporting within system constraints. In the plan,
it is suggested that within 13 weeks, you will be able to achieve day 3
reporting. At that stage, it is worth looking at system requirements to ascertain what you will need and whether you can afford it.

Run a Workshop to "Post-it" Reengineer Month-End Reporting Processes

Reengineering month-end can be a complex and expensive task or a relatively easy one; the choice is yours. Many organizations start by bringing
in consultants to process map the existing procedures. This is a futile exercise; why spend a lot of money documenting a process you are about to
radically alter? After all, when it is done, only the consultants will understand the resulting data-flow diagrams.

The answer is to Post-it reengineer your month-end procedures in a
workshop. Doing so will revolutionize the finance team's effectiveness and
efficiency (see Exhibit 2.9). Obtain different-colored Post-it pads, one for
each team involved in the process, and ask the staff to write down on separate
Post-its each action they undertake. Make sure they understand to write in
big letters using a felt-tip pen as the stickers will need to be seen from 15 feet.

Hold a workshop with all teams attending and stick all the Post-its on
one wall in time bands. Then ask the team members to look at removing
various activities. The three questions that need to be asked are:

EXHIBIT 2.9 Post-it Reengineering on a Whiteboard

- Do we need to do this action?
- Can it be done earlier?
- Can it be done differently?

All procedures that are deemed surplus to requirements are removed and stuck on another wall. Each such action should be celebrated as it represents a substantial saving (see Exhibit 2.10 for an outline of the workshop).

EXHIBIT 2.10 Outline of Workshop on Implementing Quick Monthly Reporting within Existing System Constraints

---

Reengineering Month-End
Agenda for Workshop

Date & Time: xxxxxx

Location:

Suggested Attendees: All those involved in month-end, including accounts payable, financial and management accountants, representatives from teams interfacing with month-end routines (e.g., someone from IT, payroll, etc.)

Learning Outcomes: After this workshop, attendees will be able to:
- Discuss and explain why xxxxxxxx should have quicker month-end reporting.
- Implement the steps required to move month-end reporting back to day 3 or less.
- Describe better practice month-end routines.
- Recall all agreements made at the workshop. (These will be documented.)

9:00 A.M.   Welcome by Financial Controller

9:10   **Setting the scene**—a review of better practices among accounting teams that are delivering swift reporting; topics covered include:
- what is quick reporting
- benefits of quick reporting to management and the finance team
- better practice month-end procedures—stories
- the current performance gap between xxxxxxxxx and better practice
- precision versus timeliness
- latest developments—day 1 reporting and virtual closing

Senior management and a selection of budget holders (who are based locally) will be invited to attend this "setting the scene" session.

(Continued)

EXHIBIT 2.10 (*Continued*)

9:50	**Agreement on the current key bottlenecks of month-end reporting presented by the Financial Controller** (the current cost estimate of month-end reporting, the human costs, what we are doing well, we need to work within existing systems, goal is "12 nonevents" each year, etc.)
10:05	**Workshop 1 on when activities should start and finish,** where separate teams look at the different issues (we will cover month-end close-off of the various teams, listing bottlenecks within and between teams, reporting and forecasting issues, reconciliation issues, etc.)
10:30	Morning break
10:45	**Workshop 1** continues
11:00	Feedback from work groups and action plan agreed (date and responsibility)
11:20	**Workshop 2 to analyze the month-end procedures using Post-its** (AP—Yellow, Accounts Receivable—Green, Production—Red, Financial Accountants Team—Blue, MA Team—Etc.)
12:30 P.M.	Lunch
1:15	**Workshop 2** to analyze the month-end procedures using Post-its continues
2:00	Feedback and pulling it together, where participants will document agreed changes and individuals will be encouraged to take responsibility for implementing the steps
2:30	Afternoon break
2:45	Implementing a quick month-end—the implementation plan, the issues to look at
3:00	**Workshop 3 to set out the appropriate implementation steps to implement quick reporting.** Each team prepares a short presentation of the key steps it is committed to making (teams will use PowerPoint on laptops).
4:00	Each team presents reports to the group on what changes it is going to implement and when. Teams also can raise any issues they still have. **Those SMT and budget holders who attended the first session will be invited to attend this session.**
4:45	Wrap-up of workshop by Financial Controller
5:00	Finish

EXHIBIT 2.11 Post-it Reengineering Instructions to Be Sent Out to Attendees a Week Prior to the Workshop

You have been asked to attend a workshop on reengineering month-end processes. In order to do this, we need you to prepare a list of all the processes you undertake as a team at month-end.

This process is quite simple; all it requires is:

- Each team to list all its processes on the Post-it stickers allocated to them prior to the workshop and to document each process with a whiteboard marker pen as set out in the example below. It is important that these stickers can be read from 4 to 5 yards.

+2 Close off

Accounts

Payable

- One procedure/process per Post-it. (Please note, every Excel spreadsheet is a process.)
- State when it is done—time scale is −2, −1 (last working day), +1 (first working day), +2, etc.

You will need to send out instructions to teams to prepare their Post-it stickers (see Exhibit 2.11).

Some Tips on Running a Post-it Reengineering Session

Set up a schedule to ensure that all the main teams have a unique color of Post-it sticker. Check up on teams the week prior to the workshop to ensure they have one procedure per Post-it and are writing in felt-tip pen and in big letters.

In the workshop, each team will place its Post-its in time order under column headings Day −2, Day −1, Day +1, Day +2, and so forth, using a whiteboard.

When all the Post-its are on the board, ask the three questions stated earlier, in turn, not moving forward until you are satisfied that the attendees have thought long enough on each question.

Buy a dozen movie vouchers, and give one to each attendee who points out a process that can be removed as it is not necessary (they were done because they were done last month)—each procedure that is removed is like finding gold because it means less work and fewer steps.

Reorganize the key processes and bottlenecks based on better practice (e.g., accounts payable close-off occurring at noon on the last working day), and reschedule tasks that can be done earlier. You will find it hard to justify any task that needs to be done after day 3.

Look at day −1 steps, as you may have too many. Move the non-time-critical ones between day −2 and day +1 to better spread the workload.

(View my video demonstration on Post-it reengineering on www .davidparmenter.com.)

Some Case Studies that Used the Post-it Re-engineering

Organizations in both public and private sectors have improved their month-end reporting using the Post-it reengineering workshop.

The CFO of a famous entertainment center in Australia brought 20 of his team to a training session one September. They all went back and reengineered their month-end. Six weeks later, the CFO announced that his team had the final accounts in his hand—day 3 reporting within six weeks! The CFO had for years been used to very quick reporting with a U.S. company, so you can imagine his frustration when he first arrived at his new position. The Post-it reengineering process unlocked the potential he knew was there.

A CFO of a radio station conglomerate flew all her management accountants from around the country for a one-day Post-it reengineering workshop. For some it was the first time they had met. The workshop was a fun day, and members could laugh at the bottlenecks that they, in some cases, had created. Excel spreadsheets were tossed out along with other low-value, month-end activities. Two weeks after the end of their training, the CFO was asked how the month-end was going. She replied, "What do you mean going, it is finished." She achieved day 2 month-end reporting, down from day 8, in two weeks.

The financial controller at Uecomm attended a workshop that covered quick month-end reporting and then sent his accounts payable team and management accountants for training. They then ran the Post-it reengineering workshop by themselves and within one month were reporting on working day 3 month-end.

Selling the Need for Quick Month-End Reporting

Remember, nothing was ever sold by logic. You sell through emotional drivers (e.g., your last car purchase). Thus we need to radically alter the way we pitch this sale to the SMT and the board. We have to focus on the emotional drivers that matter to them:

- Budget holders and SMT working late on a task that is not adding value.
- The lost evenings/weekends producing meaningless variances comments.
- The huge costs (e.g., estimate on the high side!—costs motivate boards).
- Gather a copy of every month-end report—yes, I mean every month-end report. Draft a memo to the CEO. In some organizations the pile will be over four feet high. Put it in a clear plastic column. Now make a plastic column a quarter of the size and say that is the total amount of month-end reporting allowed.
- Point out that modern companies are reporting within three days and some by day 1.

Budget holders will need to understand how quick month-end processes are going to help them manage their business and be more efficient.

We also need to sell quick month-end reporting to the accounting team, especially the management accountants who may, in the past, have been wedded to detail.

Key Month-End Activities on a Day 3 Month-End

The key activities in a day 3 month-end are set out in Exhibit 2.12. As the finance team gains more confidence, the quality assurance steps in days 2

EXHIBIT 2.12 Key Activities of a Month-End

Day −3 and earlier	Day −2	Day −1	Day +1	Day +2 and 3
Payroll accrual finalized	Close off accruals	Close off AP, AR, work in	Flash report by 5 P.M. to	Draft report Quality
Depreciation finalized	DBR	progress (WIP), WIP to finished	CEO Second close of G/L	assurance procedures
Daily bank a/c reconciliation (DBR)		goods, production for last day, time sheets by noon	Budget holders complete two-page	Report preparation Issue report DBR
		First close of G/L Numbers available to budget holders by 5 P.M. DBR	report DBR	

and 3 are truncated until they eventually issue the flash report to the CEO, at close of business on the first working day, and say, "That is it." Well, not quite, as the CEO would want a few more pages to accompany the one-page flash report.

Notes

1. David Parmenter, "Quick Monthly Reporting—By Day 3 or Less!" www. davidparmenter.com, 2010.
2. Jeremy Hope, *Reinventing the CFO: How Financial Managers Can Transform Their Roles and Add Greater Value* (Boston: Harvard Business School Press, 2006).

CHAPTER 3

Make the Monthly Reports Worth Reading

Many management reports are not management tools; they are merely memorandums of information. As management tools, management reports should encourage timely action in the right direction, by reporting on those activities the board, management, and the staff need to focus on. The old adage "what gets measured gets done" still holds true.

This chapter is an extract from a white paper[1] I deliver around the world that has revolutionized how many finance teams report. Due to space constraints, I have highlighted the main issues. For further information, it may be worth accessing this white paper.

Foundation Stones on Month-End Reporting

What is good monthly reporting? A good month-end finance report should:

- Be completed quickly—following the rules set out in Chapter 2.
- Be consistent—between months, judgment calls, format.
- Be a true and fair view and error free.
- Be concise—less than nine pages.
- Have a separate reporting line only if category is over 20 percent of total revenue or expenditure, whichever is relevant; thus the report will have only 10 to 15 lines.
- Have an icon system to highlight major variances.
- Do away with the essay in front of the financial statements; merely merge numbers, graphs, and comments on the one page.

- Have graphs that say something—a title that describes the main issue, and following the rules set by Stephen Few,[2] an expert on data visualization.
- Avoid reporting unnecessary detail, such as Sales of $23,456,327— surely $23.5m is much easier to read.
- Show a trend going back at least 15 months so that you show the same month as last year along with some of the preceding months.
- Be made available to the entire finance team once it has been issued.

Board members and the senior management team have complained for years that they are sent too much information, yet we still insist on preparing 20+—page month-end financials. The cost of preparing, analyzing, and checking this information is a major burden on the accounting function, creating significant time delays and consequently minimizing the information's value.

Have a separate reporting line if a category is over 20 percent of total revenue or expenditure, whichever is relevant (e.g., show revenue line if revenue category is over 20 percent of total revenue). If a category is between 15 to 20 percent, look at it and make an assessment as to whether a separate reporting line is merited.

Set up an icon system to highlight variances, as shown in Exhibit 3.1. A suggested way is to ignore all variances less than a certain amount. For all variances over this amount, allow a tolerance of, say, plus or minus 10 percent and show an icon for this, and then show as a positive or negative any variance over 10 percent. For example, if the threshold is $10,000, then an $8,000 negative variance would not have an icon; if a variance is $15,000 overspent but it is only 6 percent of total expected, then it is flagged with a "within tolerance" icon; if a variance is $15,000 overspent and is 12 percent of total expected, it is flagged with a "negative" icon.

Reporting a Business Unit's Performance

A business unit's report should be limited to one page and be able to be completed in 20 to 30 minutes. Nobody wants a dissertation, and nobody will read it. If the business unit manager is having problems, it is far too late to bring them up in the monthly report. The finance team should have alerted senior management during the month, and discussions should have been held then on what best to do.

Exhibit 3.1 is an example of a business unit's report. The profit and loss statement (P&L) is summarized in 10 to 15 lines. Two graphs are shown; one looks at the trend of the major expenditure items and the other looks at revenue if a profit center, or a graph may contrast financial and nonfinancial numbers, in this case tourist numbers against personnel costs.

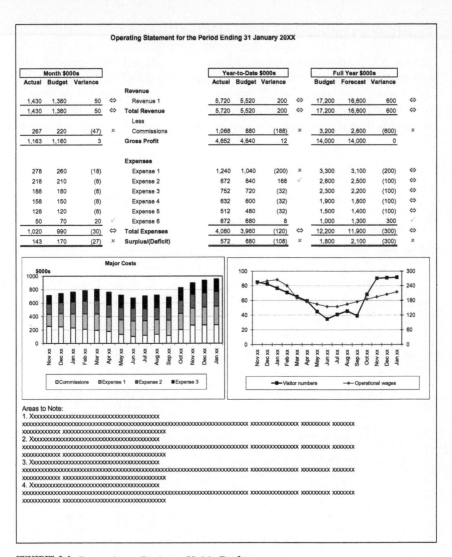

Operating Statement for the Period Ending 31 January 20XX

Month $000s				Year-to-Date $000s				Full Year $000s			
Actual	Budget	Variance		Actual	Budget	Variance		Budget	Forecast	Variance	
			Revenue								
1,430	1,380	50	⇔ Revenue 1	5,720	5,520	200	⇔	17,200	16,600	600	⇔
1,430	1,380	50	⇔ Total Revenue	5,720	5,520	200	⇔	17,200	16,600	600	⇔
			Less								
267	220	(47)	✕ Commissions	1,068	880	(188)	✕	3,200	2,600	(600)	✕
1,163	1,160	3	**Gross Profit**	4,652	4,640	12		14,000	14,000	0	
			Expenses								
278	260	(18)	Expense 1	1,240	1,040	(200)	✕	3,300	3,100	(200)	⇔
218	210	(8)	Expense 2	672	840	168	✓	2,600	2,500	(100)	⇔
188	180	(8)	Expense 3	752	720	(32)		2,300	2,200	(100)	⇔
158	150	(8)	Expense 4	632	600	(32)		1,900	1,800	(100)	⇔
128	120	(8)	Expense 5	512	480	(32)		1,500	1,400	(100)	⇔
50	70	20	✓ Expense 6	672	680	8		1,000	1,300	300	✓
1,020	990	(30)	⇔ **Total Expenses**	4,080	3,960	(120)	⇔	12,200	11,900	(300)	⇔
143	170	(27)	✕ **Surplus/(Deficit)**	572	680	(108)	✕	1,800	2,100	(300)	✕

Areas to Note:
1. Xxxxxxxxxxxxxxxxxxxxxxxxxxxxxxxxxxxxxxxxxxx
xxxxxxxxxxxxxxxxxxxxxxxxxxxxxxxxxxxxxxxxxxxxxxxxxxxxxxxxxxxxxxxxxxxxxxxxxxx xxxxxxxxxxxxxx xxxxxxxx xxxxxx
xxxxxxxxxxxx xxxxxxxxxxxxxxxxxxxxxxxxxxxxxxxxxxxx
2. Xxxxxxxxxxxxxxxxxxxxxxxxxxxxxxxxxxxxxxxxxxx
xxxxxxxxxxxxxxxxxxxxxxxxxxxxxxxxxxxxxxxxxxxxxxxxxxxxxxxxxxxxxxxxxxxxxxxxxxx xxxxxxxxxxxxxx xxxxxxxx xxxxxx
xxxxxxxxxxxx xxxxxxxxxxxxxxxxxxxxxxxxxxxxxxxxxxxx
3. Xxxxxxxxxxxxxxxxxxxxxxxxxxxxxxxxxxxxxxxxxxx
xxxxxxxxxxxxxxxxxxxxxxxxxxxxxxxxxxxxxxxxxxxxxxxxxxxxxxxxxxxxxxxxxxxxxxxxxxx xxxxxxxxxxxxxx xxxxxxxx xxxxxx
xxxxxxxxxxxx xxxxxxxxxxxxxxxxxxxxxxxxxxxxxxxxxxxx
4. Xxxxxxxxxxxxxxxxxxxxxxxxxxxxxxxxxxxxxxxxxxx
xxxxxxxxxxxxxxxxxxxxxxxxxxxxxxxxxxxxxxxxxxxxxxxxxxxxxxxxxxxxxxxxxxxxxxxxxxx xxxxxxxxxxxxxx xxxxxxxx xxxxxx
xxxxxxxxxxxx xxxxxxxxxxxxxxxxxxxxxxxxxxxxxxxxxxxx

EXHIBIT 3.1 Reporting a Business Unit's Performance

The notes are the main highlights and action steps to take. No other commentary is provided on the business unit's P&L. The business unit manager can discuss other issues in person with the CEO.

Each business unit may have up to five different graphs, and the two that show the most pertinent information are shown in that month's report. Each business unit report will look slightly different. The titles of the key lines and graphs may be different.

Reporting a Consolidated Profit and Loss Account

Exhibit 3.2 is an example of reporting a consolidated P&L account. This report summarizes the P&L in 10 to 15 lines. Instead of looking at consolidated costs, such as personnel, premises, and so forth, the report summarizes the expenditures of the divisions/business units. The graphs look at the trends in major revenue and expenditure. A number of different graphs

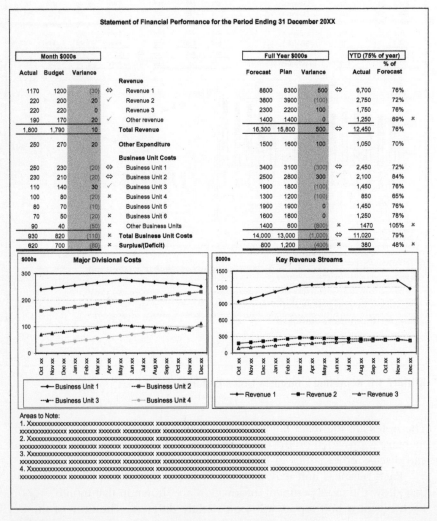

EXHIBIT 3.2 Reporting a Consolidated Profit and Loss Account

will be maintained, and the most pertinent ones will be shown. The notes are the main highlights and action steps to take. There is no other commentary on the P&L. The icons are fully automated based on preset criteria.

One-Page Summary to the CEO

All CEOs like a great summary page where they can see the whole picture. In my research I came across this one-pager that I believe is an excellent example of clever reporting. On one A3 page (U.S. standard fanfold), the finance team has summarized the areas to note, referred to the last end-of-year forecast, reviewed the major business units, and commented on the summary P&L and balance sheet (see Exhibit 3.3).

The concept here is to give the CEO a summary of the financial report that is easier to read than the full finance report. Once you have designed this carefully, you will find, I am sure, that this page becomes the main report. Both sides of the page can be used. The back side of the page could include summary business unit performance, or ranking tables for retail branches, or a dashboard summarizing financial and nonfinancial information. These are illustrated in Chapter 19.

Whatever you include on the back side, ensure you do not go below a 10-point font size.

Reporting the Balance Sheet

Exhibit 3.4 is an example of a summary balance sheet with rounded numbers in millions, more rounded than the numbers in the P/L. Surely the key is to give management a clear view of the relative sizes of the major assets and liabilities rather than precision (e.g., tell management debtors owe $28 million rather than $27,867,234; I can assure you, they will remember $28 million but forget the other number). The detailed trial balance, balanced to the cent, should be left to the accountants' working papers.

The balance sheet should have no more than 10 categories following the 10 percent rule discussed earlier. Each additional category in the balance sheet serves to confuse management and benefits only the accountants. If you can draft the balance sheet in fewer than 10 categories, all the better.

The graphs focus on main balance sheet issues such as debtors' aging, stock levels, and cash. The notes cover the main highlights and action steps to take. There would be no other commentary about the balance sheet.

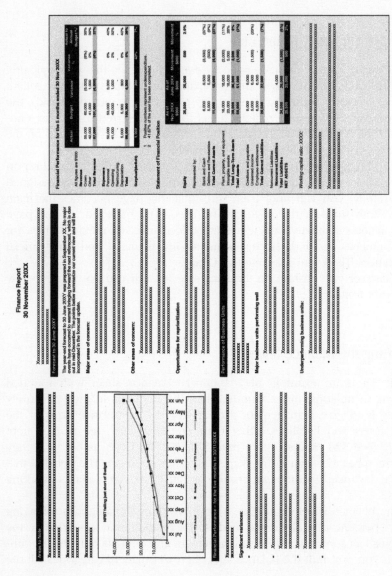

EXHIBIT 3.3 Summary Report for the CEO

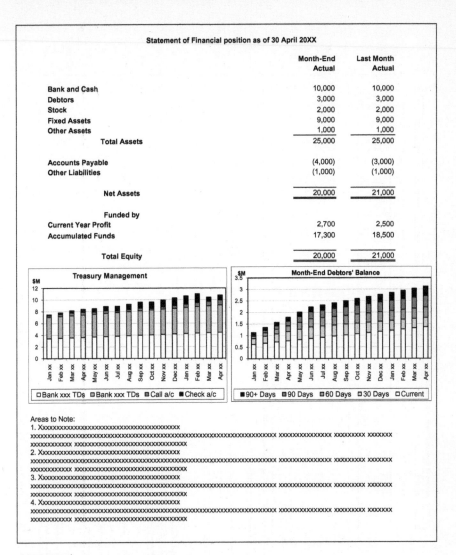

Statement of Financial position as of 30 April 20XX

	Month-End Actual	Last Month Actual
Bank and Cash	10,000	10,000
Debtors	3,000	3,000
Stock	2,000	2,000
Fixed Assets	9,000	9,000
Other Assets	1,000	1,000
Total Assets	25,000	25,000
Accounts Payable	(4,000)	(3,000)
Other Liabilities	(1,000)	(1,000)
Net Assets	20,000	21,000
Funded by		
Current Year Profit	2,700	2,500
Accumulated Funds	17,300	18,500
Total Equity	20,000	21,000

EXHIBIT 3.4 Balance Sheet Example

Reporting a Quarterly Rolling Accrual Forecast

The update of the year-end forecast should occur once a quarter, as explained in Chapters 2 and 15. Exhibit 3.5 shows a number of features worth discussing:

- Only show monthly data for the next six months; after that, quarterly is better.

Summary of Forecast Profit and Loss for the Period Ending xxxxxx

| | 9 months to 31/12 * | Quarter 1 | | | Y/E Forecast | Quarter 2 | | | Quarter 3 | Quarter 4 | Quarter 5 | Quarter 6 |
		Jan	Feb	Mar		Apr	May	Jun	Jul–Sept	Oct–Dec	Jan–Mar	Apr–Jun
INCOME												
Income 1	58,500	6,300	6,500	6,700	76,000	6,300	6,100	6,300	18,200	18,400	18,600	18,200
Income 2	35,200	3,900	4,100	4,300	47,500	3,900	3,700	3,900	11,000	11,200	11,400	11,000
Income 3	22,700	2,500	2,700	2,900	30,800	2,500	2,300	2,500	6,800	7,000	7,200	6,800
Total Revenue	114,400	12,700	13,300	13,900	154,300	12,700	12,100	12,700	36,000	36,600	37,200	36,000
EXPENDITURE												
Cost category 1	35,400	4,600	4,700	4,600	49,300	4,800	4,900	4,800	12,400	14,400	14,600	12,000
Cost category 2	15,900	2,000	2,100	2,200	22,200	2,200	2,300	2,400	6,700	6,600	6,800	7,000
Cost category 3	9,500	1,100	1,200	1,100	12,900	1,300	1,400	1,300	4,000	3,900	4,100	3,600
Cost category 4	5,700	600	500	600	7,400	800	700	800	2,300	1,800	2,000	2,100
Cost category 5	4,300	500	600	500	5,900	700	800	700	2,200	2,100	2,300	1,800
Cost category 6	4,100	500	400	500	5,500	700	600	700	2,000	1,500	1,700	1,800
Other operational costs	8,100	900	1,000	900	10,900	1,100	1,200	1,100	3,400	3,300	3,500	3,000
Total Expenditure	83,000	10,200	10,500	10,400	114,160	11,600	11,900	11,800	33,000	33,600	35,000	31,300
Management overview					–200							
Net Profit	$31,400	$2,500	$2,800	$3,500	$40,000	$1,100	$200	$900	$3,000	$3,000	$2,200	$4,700

* Includes estimate for December

Areas to Note:

1. xxxxxxxxxxxxxxxxxxxxxxxxxxxxxxxxxxxxxxxxxxxxxx

2. xxxxxxxxxxxxxxxxxxxxxxxxxxxxxxxxxxxxxxxxxxxxxxxxxx

3. xxxxxxxxxxxxxxxxxxxxxxxxxxxxxxxxxxxxxxxxxxxx

4. xxxxxxxxxxxxxxxxxxxxxxxxxxxxxxxxxxxxxxxxxxxxxxxxx

Key Income Streams

Rev 1—Actual / Rev 1—Forecast / Rev 2—Actual / Rev 2—Forecast / Rev 3—Actual / Rev 3—Forecast

Key Expenditure Lines

Cost 1—Actual / Cost 1—Forecast / Cost 2—Actual / Cost 2—Forecast / Cost 3—Actual / Cost 3—Forecast

EXHIBIT 3.5 Quarterly Rolling Forecast to the Senior Management Team

- Only forecast at category status, never at account code level.
- Forecast each category line to the level of accuracy the CEO would expect; for example top line of revenue to nearest $0.5m, next revenue line to $0.1m.
- Forecast 18 months forward.
- The expenditure graph looks at the three main expenditure lines and highlights where budget holders are playing the old game of hiding funds in case they might be needed.
- The revenue graph highlights the reasonableness of the sales teams' projections.
- Commentary is restricted to bullets points.

Chapter 15 explains the reasoning and the 10 foundation stones of a rolling forecasting process.

Snapshot of All Projects Currently Started

Project reporting can be a huge burden on a project team, consuming significant amounts of time and creating documents that are too long, poorly structured, and often lacking quick reference action points.

Project management software was first designed for very complex projects, such as putting a man on the moon. Project managers charging in excess of $200 per hour for their time can spend it completing endless progress schedules. As a rule of thumb, if more than 5 percent of the project time is spent on reporting, balance has been lost. Project reporting is best managed by progressively updating a PowerPoint presentation. This means that at any time the project team can give an interesting and informative progress update.

It is worthwhile measuring metrically—that is, measuring accurately, without estimate—only those performance measures that are so fundamental to the organization that they affect nearly every aspect of its operation (e.g., the key performance indicators, which are explained in a later section).

"Project progress" certainly does not fit into this category. Hence I promote two simple types of project reporting, as shown in Exhibits 3.6 and 3.7. One gives a snapshot of all projects currently started and one focuses on the progress of the top 10 projects.

Using this report enables management and the senior management team to see the overall picture and answer the questions: Have we got too many projects on the go? What projects are running late? What projects are at risk of noncompletion?

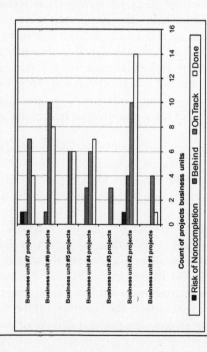

EXHIBIT 3.6 Project Report Example

48

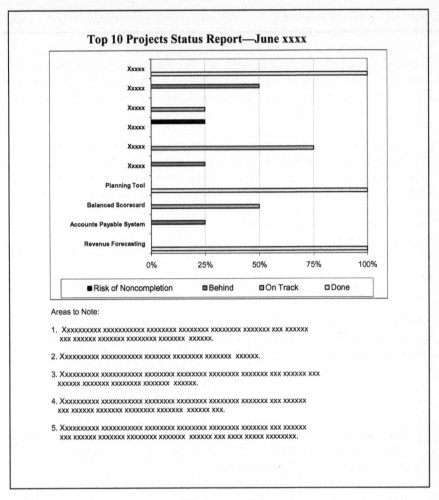

EXHIBIT 3.7 Top 10 Projects Report Example

Reporting Progress of the Top 10 Projects

To minimize the time spent reporting progress, I promote a five-band and four-color project progress status. Using this method, a project is 0, 25, 50, 75, or 100 percent complete, and it is at risk of noncompletion, behind, on track, or finished.

A project that is 15 percent complete would be shown as 25 percent complete, and next month when it might be 30 percent complete, it would still stay at the 25 percent band. Project managers are asked simply which quadrant and what color best reflect progress to date.

Managers at first may try to hide lack of progress. This soon becomes apparent when a project has been at the 25 percent band for three months and supposedly is still on track. This method applies Pareto's 80/20 principle and also acknowledges that progress reports, by their very nature, are arbitrary, and no two project managers would come up with the same progress evaluation.

The key message for projects in the last quadrant is to finish the project no matter what the sunk cost is. It is thus not particularly helpful for the accounting team to constantly focus on the overrun. It would be far better to focus on the remaining costs and compare them against the benefits of finishing. After the project is the time for postmortems. This will help reduce the tendency for staff to move from a project with overruns to a project with a new budget.

Cash Flow Forecasting

Cash flow forecasting is error prone for many of us. It is very hard to get right for the following reasons: lack of information—we do not know when major customers are paying us; no historic analysis of daily cash flows; no historic tracking of the large receipts; a lack of use of electronic receipts and payments; and often a lack of understanding and coordination with the organization's buyers and sales staff.

> *The most important part of a forecast is not the prediction of what is likely to happen, but the strength of the logic behind the forecast—even a broken clock is right twice a day.*
>
> *The best way to gauge the present against the future changes is to look back twice as far as you look forward.*
>
> Paul Saffo, Institute of the Future

The building blocks of a better practice daily cash flow forecast process include:

Enter the certain figures first	■ Rent, rates, leases, loan repayments, loan interest, payroll, taxes are all certain payments.
	■ Track cash flow of major customers; they are more certain.

	■ Track cash flow of all other customers who have signed up for a direct debit (DD)—offer continuing discounts to customers to go onto direct debits.
	■ Track payment of major suppliers paid by DD or direct credit (DC).
	■ Track payment of minor suppliers paid by DC.
Trap the history of your daily cash flows	■ Need at least last 24 months of cash flows data in the same categories that you are forecasting in—the best place for storing this historic data is in a forecasting application.
	■ Use trend graphs in your forecasting application to help understand seasonal fluctuations—remember, you need to go back twice as far as you look forward.
Appropriate time frame	■ Look forward at least to week 5 in working days and to week 13 in weeks—the month-end is irrelevant for cash flow forecasting, as a cash flow crisis comes at any time.
	■ It is normally okay to cash flow model in months from month 4 onward—this modeling can be automated from the accrual forecasting model and in some cases is taken out a rolling 24 months.
Automatic feeds to the cash forecasting application	■ Use daily major receipts from accounts receivable.
	■ Tax payment calculations can be automated.
	■ For key customers, cash flows can be accurately predicted in the short term.
Cash flow forecast on a planning application, not Excel	■ Put the cash flow on an appropriate forecasting application—Excel is best left to noncore activities, for example, designing a report template or one-off diagrams.

Exhibits 3.8 and 3.9 show the short-term cash flow predicted by day and the longer-range one going out in months, which typically would be generated from the accrual forecast via standard timing amendments.

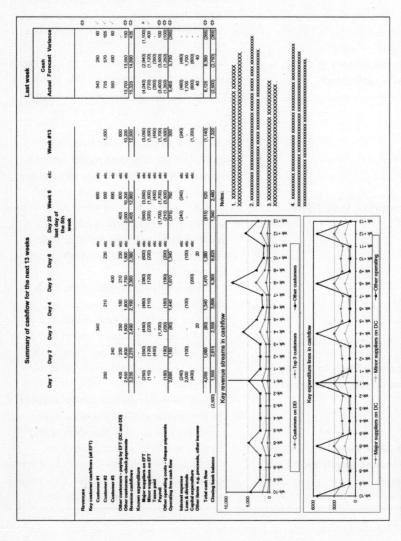

EXHIBIT 3.8 Short Range Cash Flow Example

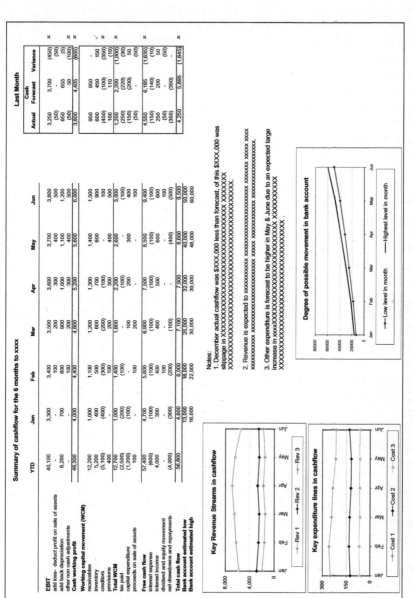

Summary of cashflow for the 6 months to xxxx

	YTD	Jan	Feb	Mar	Apr	May	Jun	Actual	Cash Forecast	Variance	
									Last Month		
EBIT	40,100	3,300	3,400	3,500	3,600	3,700	3,800	3,250	3,700	(450)	x
add loss- deduct profit on sale of assets	-	-	100	200	300	400	500	(50)	-	(50)	x
add back depreciation	8,200	700	800	900	1,000	1,100	1,200	650	655	(5)	x
other non cash adjustments	-	-	100	200	300	400	500	(50)	50	(100)	x
Cash working profit	48,300	4,000	4,400	4,800	5,200	5,600	6,000	3,800	4,405	(605)	x
Working capital movement (WCM)											
receivables	12,200	1,000	1,100	1,200	1,300	1,400	1,500	950	950	-	>
inventory	5,200	400	500	600	700	800	900	600	450	150	x
creditors	(5,100)	(400)	(300)	(200)	(100)	-	100	(450)	(100)	(350)	x
provisions	400	-	100	200	300	400	500	100	110	(10)	x
Total WCM	12,700	1,000	1,400	1,800	2,200	2,600	3,000	1,200	2,200	(1,000)	x
tax paid	(2,500)	(200)	(100)		(100)		(100)	(250)	(220)	(30)	x
capital expenditure	(1,200)	(100)	(100)	100	(100)	300	400	(150)	(200)	50	
proceeds on sale of assets	100	-	100	200	-	-	100	(50)	-	(50)	
Free cash flow	57,400	4,700	5,800	6,900	7,500	8,500	9,400	4,550	6,185	(1,635)	x
interest expense	(600)	(100)	(100)	(100)	(100)	(100)	(100)	(150)	(140)	(10)	
interest income	4,000	300	400	400	500	600	600	250	200	50	
dividend and equity movement	-	-	100	100	-	-	100	(50)	-	(50)	
net drawdowns and repayments	(4,000)	(300)	(200)	(100)	-	(400)	(500)	(350)	(350)	-	
Total cash flow	56,800	4,600	6,000	7,100	7,900	8,600	9,500	4,250	5,895	(1,645)	x
Bank account estimated low		13,000	18,000	25,000	32,000	40,000	50,000				
Bank account estimated high		16,000	22,000	30,000	39,000	48,000	60,000				

Notes:
1. December actual cashflow was $XXX,000 less than forecast, of this $XXX,000 was slippage in XXXXXXXXXXXXXXXXXXXXXXXXXXXXXXXXXXXXXXX XXXXXXX XXXXXXXXXXXXXXXXXXXXXXXXXXXXXXXXXXXXXXX.

2. Revenue is expected to xxxxxxxxxxxxxxx xxxxxxxxxxxxxxxxxxxxxxxxx xxxxx xxxx xxxxxxxxxxxxxxxxxxxxxxxxxxxxxxxxxx xxxxx xxxx.

3. Other expenditure is forecast to be higher in May & June due to an expected large increase in xxxxXXXXXXXXXXXXXXXXXXXXXXX XXXXXXXXXX XXXXXXXXXXXXXXXXXXXXXXXXXXX

Key Revenue Streams in cashflow

Key expenditure lines in cashflow

Degree of possible movement in bank account

EXHIBIT 3.9 Longer Range Cash Flow Forecasting Example

CAPEX Reporting

There are two main issues with reporting capital expenditure (CAPEX). First and most important, there will be CAPEX slippage. Worse still is the fact that the aim of CAPEX was to improve working conditions, improve quality of products/services, increase profitability, and so on. If an office renovation has been approved, why is it completed in the last month of the year? Surely it would have been better for it to have been completed in the first couple of months, as the staff would have the benefit of it. We therefore need a report (see Exhibit 3.10) that contrasts the percentage of capital spent on key projects against the percentage of the year gone. The aim is for status of the CAPEX projects to beat the year-gone progress bar.

Second, it is important to control the CAPEX approval process. During the life of a CAPEX project, there may be signs that it may be going over budget. Normally this is hidden from the board until management is sure there is a problem. If you have a process whereby the board is informed about the possibility of CAPEX exceeding the budget as soon as it recognized, it gives the Board a choice. They can make the decision as to whether they want a formal application for the additional expenditure or decide to defer and wait until more information is known about the magnitude of the overexpenditure. In Exhibit 3.11 the Board would hold off as there is still half the project to go so the overexpenditure may not eventuate. They may flag that a progress brief is required by the project manager for the next meeting or request a new CAPEX approval application.

The One-Page Investment Proposal

One of the important principles that make Toyota so successful is the need for transparency. This view is carried through to its investment proposals. All proposals have to fit on an A3 page (U.S. Standard Fanfold; see Exhibit 3.12). Condensing a major investment into an A3 page is a very difficult task. The one-page summary ensures clarity of thought and reduces the possibility that the proposal will be 50 pages because it represents a $500 million investment. Toyota has recognized that a large investment document will not be read or fully understood by all the decision makers. In fact, the larger the document, the less there is "clarity" for decision making. A must-read book to understand the guiding principles of Toyota is *The Toyota Way*.[3]

Capital Expenditure for the period ending 31 December 20XX

	% spent	YTD Actual	Annual Budget	Outstanding
Div 1	50%	45	90	45
Div 2	31%	25	80	55
Div 3	70%	63	90	27
Div 4	72%	93	130	37
Div 5	56%	25	45	20
Other Divs	58%	105	180	75
Average	56%			
% of Year gone	75%			
Total		356	615	259

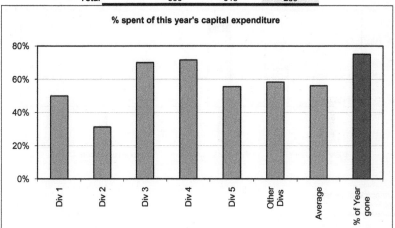

Areas to Note:

1. xxxxxxxxxxx xxxxxxxxxxxxxxx xxxxxxxx xxxxxxxxxxx xxxxxxxxxxxxxx
xxxxxxxxxxxxxxxxxxxxxx xxxxxxxxxxxxxxx xxxxxxxxxxxxxxxxxxxxxxxxxx
xxxxxxxxxxxxxxxxxxx xxxxxxxxxxxxxx xxxxxxxxxxxxxxxxxxxxxxxxxxx.

2. xxxxxxxxxxx xxxxxxxxxxxxxxxxxxxxxxxx xxxxxxx xxxxx xxxx xxxxxxxxxxx
xxxxxxxxxxxxxxxxxxxxxxxxxx xxxxx xxxxxxxxxxxxx xxxxxxxxxxxxxxxxxxxx.

3.xxxxxxxxxxx xxxxxxxxxxxxxxx xxxxxxxx xxxxxxxxxxx xxxxxxxxxxxxxx
xxxxxxxxxxxxxxxxxxxxxx xxxxxxxxxxxxxxx xxxxxxxxxxxxxxxxxxxxxxxxxxxxx.

4. xxxxxxxxxxx xxxxxxxxxxxxxxx xxxxxxxx xxxxxxxxxxx xxxxxxxxxxxxxx
xxxxxxxxxxxxxxxxxxxxxx xxxxxxxxxxxxxxx xxxxxxxxxxxxxxxxxxxxxxxxxx
xxxxxxxxxxxxxxxxxxx xxxxxxxxxxxxxx xxxxxxxxxxxxxxxxxxxxxxxxxxx.

EXHIBIT 3.10 CAPEX Slippage Report

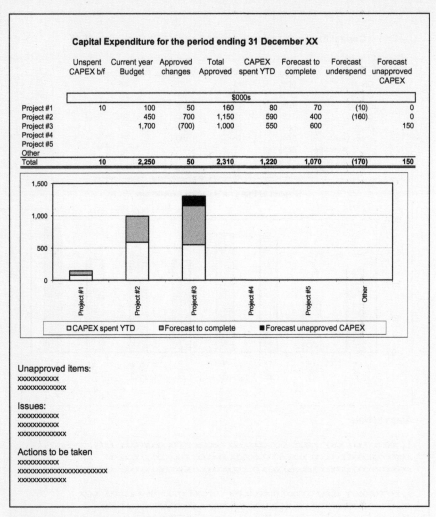

Capital Expenditure for the period ending 31 December XX

	Unspent CAPEX b/f	Current year Budget	Approved changes	Total Approved	CAPEX spent YTD	Forecast to complete	Forecast underspend	Forecast unapproved CAPEX
				$000s				
Project #1	10	100	50	160	80	70	(10)	0
Project #2		450	700	1,150	590	400	(160)	0
Project #3		1,700	(700)	1,000	550	600		150
Project #4								
Project #5								
Other								
Total	10	2,250	50	2,310	1,220	1,070	(170)	150

Unapproved items:
xxxxxxxxxxx
xxxxxxxxxxxxx

Issues:
xxxxxxxxxxx
xxxxxxxxxxx
xxxxxxxxxxxxx

Actions to be taken
xxxxxxxxxxx
xxxxxxxxxxxxxxxxxxxxxxxxx
xxxxxxxxxxxxx

EXHIBIT 3.11 CAPEX Approval Report

Reporting the Strategic Objectives/Risks/Costs Pressures

Finance teams are realizing that the finance report needs to also focus on strategic issues. If the finance team do not do this, another team will do it. The following reporting is recommended:

- Monthly reporting of progress against the strategic objectives/themes and the initiatives within them. The example in Exhibit 3.13 uses a simple traffic light display.

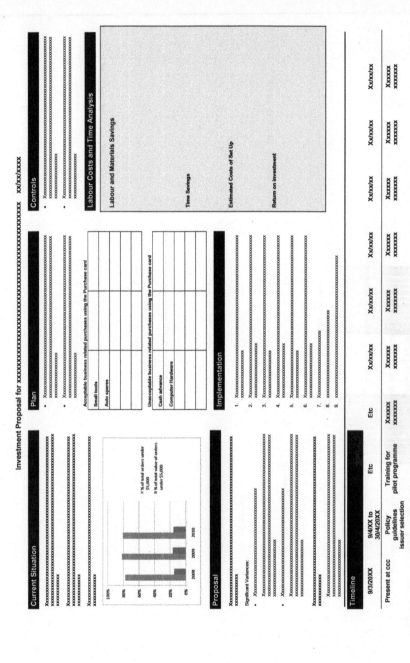

EXHIBIT 3.12 The One-Page Investment Proposal

57

Progress Against Strategy

Status as 30 June xx

● Warning: little progress made
◐ Some progress but behind schedule
○ On track or finished

Comments (required action if amber or red)

Strategy one xxxxxxxxxxxxxxxxxxxxxxx

A1	Initiative xxxx xxxx xxxx xxxxxxx xxx xxx	○ Completed in third week of May
A2	Initiative xxxx xxxx xxxxxxx xxx xxx	● xxxxxxx xxxxxxx xxx xxx xxxx xxxx xxxxx xxxx xxxxxx xxxxxxx xxxx xxxx x xxxxxx x xxxxxx xxxxxxx xxxx xxxx
A3	Initiative xxxx xxxx xxxxxxx xxx xxx	◐

Strategy two xxxxxxxxxxxxxxxxxxxxxxx

B1	Initiative xxxx xxxx xxxxxxx xxx xxx	◐ xxxxxxxxxx xxxxxxx xxx xxxx xxxx xxxxx xxxx xxxxxx xxxxxxx xxxx xxxx x xxxxxx x xxxxxx xxxxxxx xxxx xxxx
B2	Initiative xxxx xxxx xxxxxxx xxx xxx	○ Completed in March
B3	Initiative xxxx xxxx xxxxxxx xxx xxx	○ On track, completion date mid Sept

Strategy three xxxxxxxxxxxxxxxxxxxxxxx

C1	Initiative xxxx xxxx xxxxxxx xxx xxx	○ Completed in third week of May
C2	Initiative xxxx xxxx xxxxxxx xxx xxx	◐ Completed in third week of May
C3	Initiative xxxx xxxx xxxxxxx xxx xxx	○ On track, completion date end Dec

Strategy four xxxxxxxxxxxxxxxxxxxxxxx

D1	Initiative xxxx xxxx xxxxxxx xxx xxx	● xxxxxxxxx xxxxxxx xxx xxxx xxx xxxx xxxxx xxxx xxxxxxx xxxx xxxxx xxxx xxxx x xxxxxx x xxxxxx x xxxxxx xxxxxxx xxxx xxxx
D2	Initiative xxxx xxxx xxxxxxx xxx xxx	◐
D3	Initiative xxxx xxxx xxxxxxx xxx xxx	○ Completed in third week of May

EXHIBIT 3.13 Reporting Progress against Strategy

Major Risks

Status as 30 June xx of all risks with a potential cost of over $xm

Legend:
- ● Major risk
- ◐ Some risk
- ○ Little or no risk

	$m				Risk Level	Mitigation action
	20X0	20X1	20X2	20X3		
CAPEX shortfall	-4	-6	1	-8	○	xxxxxxxxxx xxxx xxx xxxxx xxxxx xxxxx xxxxxxx xxxxxxxx xxxx xxxx x xxxxxxx x xxxxxx xxxxxxxx xxxx xxxx
Loss of customer XYZ	-13	-15	-23	-23	◐	xxxxxxxxxx xxxxxxx xxxx xxxx xxxx x xxxxxx xxxxxxxx xxxx xxxx xxxxx xxxxx xxxxx xxxxxxx xxxxxxxx xxxx xxxx x xxxxxxx x xxxxxx
Loss of xxxxxxxxxxxxxxxxxxxx	-6	-5	-7	9	○	xxxxxxxxxx xxxxxxx xxxx xxxx xxxx x xxxxxx xxxxxxxx xxxx xxxx xxxxx xxxxx xxxxx xxxxxxx xxxxxxxx xxxx xxxx x xxxxxxx x xxxxxx
With drawing product xxxxxxxxxxxx	-2	-8	-4	-3	○	xxxxxxxxxx xxxxxxx xxxx xxxx xxxx x xxxxxx xxxxxxxx xxxx xxxx xxxxx xxxxx xxxxx xxxxxxx xxxxxxxx xxxx xxxx x xxxxxxx x xxxxxx
Payroll increase over current year costs	-13	-15	-23	-23	◐	xxxxxxxxxx xxxxxxx xxxx xxxx xxxx x xxxxxx xxxxxxxx xxxx xxxx xxxxx xxxxx xxxxx xxxxxxx xxxxxxxx xxxx xxxx x xxxxxxx x xxxxxx
Pension funding shortfall	-20	-25	-30	-35	●	xxxxxxxxxx xxxxxxx xxx xxx xxxxx xxxxx xxx xxxxxx xxxxxxxx xxxx xxxx xxxxx xxxxx xxxxx xxxxxxx xxxxxxxx xxxx xxxx x xxxxxxx x xxxxxx
Anticipated lease agreement increases over current year costs	-3	-25	-25	-25	●	xxxxxxxxxx xxxxxxx xxxx xxxx xxxxx xxxxx xxxxx xxxxxxx xxxxxxxx xxxx xxxx x xxxxxxx x xxxxxx
Increase costs over current year levels	-36	-65	-78	-83	●	
Offset by additional revenue					○	xxxxxxxxxx xxxxxxx xxxx xxxx xxxx x xxxxxx xxxxxxxx xxxx xxxx xxxxx xxxxx xxxxx xxxxxxx xxxxxxxx xxxx xxxx x xxxxxxx x xxxxxx
Extra profit due to price increases creating greater margin over current year levels	25	28	31	34	○	xxxxxxxxxx xxxxxxx xxxx xxxx
Extra profit due to new product revenue	10	15	20	25	○	xxxxxxxxxx xxxxxxx xxx xxxxx xxxxx xxxxx xxxxxxx xxxxxxxx xxxx xxxx x xxxxxxx x xxxxxx xxxxxxxx xxxx xxxx
Net operating shortfall to manage	-1	-22	-27	-24	◐	

EXHIBIT 3.14 Reporting on Major Risks

■ Quarterly look at costs pressures as they are going to affect this and the next three to four years (see Exhibit 3.14). It is too late to address these at the strategic planning phase.

Designing Graphs and Dashboards

A must visit for all corporate accountants is Stephen Few's website where he has lodged many high-quality white papers on the topic of graphical displays (www.perceptualedge.com/articles).

He has come up with a very useful list of common pitfalls in dashboard design:

1. Exceeding the boundaries of a single screen (where managers have a choice as to what they can see; in other words, the designer has not determined what is important)
2. Supplying inadequate context for the data (graphs that do not clearly show what is good or bad performance)
3. Displaying excessive detail or precision (not rounding enough—why do we need to show 23.4% when 23% would suffice? why show $23,453,567 when $23.5 m or $23 m would suffice?)
4. Expressing measures indirectly (Few prefers, on occasion, to hold one data series as a constant and express the other as a percentage deviation.)
5. Choosing inappropriate media of display (choosing the wrong graph, especially a pie chart; using a graph when a table would be better, etc.)
6. Introducing meaningless variety (using a myriad of different graphs on one page, just because we can do them)
7. Using poorly designed display media (lack of thought regarding the real issues)
8. Encoding quantitative data inaccurately (by setting the starting scale away from zero)
9. Arranging the data poorly (by not linking issues together and not positioning graphs on the same point together)
10. Templates for reporting performance measures
11. Not highlighting what is important (all data competing for attention)
12. Cluttering the screen with useless decoration (too many rocket scientists' toys)

Each one of these pitfalls is explained in detail in his white paper on the topic, "Common Pitfalls in Dashboard Design" on www.perceptualedge .com/articles.

Notes

1. David Parmenter, *Decision based reporting* www.davidparmenter.com 2010.
2. Stephen Few's work is accessible from www.perceptualedge.com
3. Jeffrey K. Liker, *The Toyota Way*, McGraw-Hill, 2003.

CHAPTER 4

Limit the Time Invested in Board Reporting

It must be one of the classic catch-22 situations: Boards complain about getting too much information too late, and management complains that nearly 20 percent of its time is tied up in the board reporting process. Boards obviously need to ascertain whether management is steering the ship correctly, and the state of the crew and customers, before they can relax and strategize about future initiatives. The process of reporting the current status of the organization, last month's board report, is where the principal problem lies. This process needs to occur more efficiently and effectively for both the board and management.

Selling Change to the Board

We need to see why selling change to the board has not worked in the past. As accountants, we are commonly selling by logic as we are thinking and judgmental people, in Myers-Briggs[1] terms. We need to sell change by the board's emotional divers, a concept that is covered in the Introduction.

The corporate accountants should work with the CEO and the board to carry out these tasks:

- Commence an education process regarding the cost versus benefit of the board reporting process; start with costing out each board paper, and the board will be the first to complain about the waste.
- Ensure all requests for information are properly scoped and costed first.
- Instigate an empowerment program so reports are not rewritten unless absolutely necessary.

- Table board papers electronically, using some of the innovative applications designed for this purpose.
- Release papers to the board as they become available.
- Bring the board meeting forward to the tenth working day.
- Refocus "variance to budget" reporting to the year-to-date numbers.
- Work with the chairperson to constantly purge the number of board papers.
- Report key result indicators in a dashboard to the board.

Costing the Preparation of Board Papers

Board papers can reach mammoth proportions, tying up vast amounts of management time in preparation. In some organizations one week a month is written off by the senior management team (SMT). The result of these excesses often is late board meetings, with the papers being sent to the directors only a day or two before the meeting. The board meetings themselves can then be sidetracked by the detail, with the strategic overview inadequately addressed.

Directors themselves are often guilty parties, requesting changes to board report formats, or additional analysis without first finding out what the exercise will involve, or giving staff guidelines as to how much detail is required.

What amount of SMT time is absorbed by the monthly reporting process? It is important to cost this out and report it to the board. They will be horrified. All you need do now is cost out each request; this will soon rein in the scope of changes to the board pack. Use the costing approach set out in the monthly reporting Chapter 2.

Scoping of the Information Requests

A request for information from the board often can take on a life of its own. A simple request soon adopts "Charge of the Light Brigade" characteristics as the request is passed down the management tree. Often the director who asked the question had visualized a 30-minute job, and now the staff member embarks on a massive exercise. How often has the board received a lengthy report only to glance cursorily at it after over $20,000 of time has been invested?

There needs to be more direct communication between the directors and the staff who are going to research the request. A discussion among the director, the researcher, and a general manager will probably scope the exercise and ensure the likely investment is worthwhile. Failing that, all directors should be asked by the chairperson to scope their requests.

"I would like to know about xxxxxxx. I suggest we invest no more than x days and $x,xxx on this."

Avoiding Rewrites of Board Reports

Some organizations have made a major cultural change to board report writing, obtaining commitment from the board, CEO, and SMT that the original report can be sent, unaltered grammatically, to the board, thus avoiding expensive rewrites. The board no longer considers the quality of the board papers as a reflection of the CEO's performance. The organizations have learned to delegate and empower their staff so that SMT and board papers are being written with limited input from senior managers and are being tabled with few amendments provided that the SMT agree with the recommendations. The CEO can choose to put a caveat on each report: "While I concur with the recommendations, the report was written by XXX."

The board understands that the report is not written in SMT-speak. Board members are encouraged to comment directly to the writer about strengths and areas for improvement in report writing. The writers are also the presenters, where necessary. The organization thus has a much more relaxed week leading up to the board meeting, having largely delegated the report writing and the associated stress. The rewards include motivated and more competent staff, and general managers being free to spend more time contributing to the bottom line.

Tabling Board Papers Electronically

Many of the procedures that support a board meeting have changed little since Charles Dickens's time. Board members would receive large board papers that they had difficulty finding the time or inclination to read. In the 21st century we should be using technology.

The financial report should be made available as soon as it has been completed via a secure area of the organization's intranet. Other board papers likewise can be read as and when they are ready, instead of the last paper determining when all the rest are available.

The executive information system (EIS) also offers an answer to the question, "How can we reduce the ridiculous size of the board papers?" Imagine an environment where board members would receive a 20-page document with pointers to relevant pages in the EIS. Board members then could arrive before the meeting and examine those areas of particular interest. Some queries could be dealt with during the board meeting. One manufacturing participant has such a system and comments that board meetings are now more strategic, the board papers are brief, the nonexecutive directors have access to the EIS, and management has better control over the business.

More Timely Board Meetings

The longer the period of elapsed time you allow for a task to be completed, the greater the chance of its being completed inefficiently. Thus, a prompt board meeting will ensure a more efficient one. Some boards are meeting within 10 working days of month-end. Why is yours not?

In some cases management is meeting with the board six weeks after month-end. There is, of course, another month-end in between so they have to be careful to talk about the correct month. This situation is ridiculous.

Board Meeting Less Frequently than Once a Month

Seek to restructure the operations of the board, setting bimonthly meetings, with the board members' investing the saved time elsewhere, such as:

- Sitting on subcommittees that are looking at improvements in key areas of the business.
- Assisting the organization with specialist know-how by presenting on topics to management and staff.
- Helping the company by opening doors to new markets.

Since board meetings are to be strategic, there is no need for monthly meetings, and enlightened companies now have bimonthly meetings or at most eight board meetings a year.

Continually Purging the Board Papers

Does it take a 200-page board paper package to run a business? Are the key decisions a direct result of board papers or the collective experiences of the board members? Increasingly today Microsoft PowerPoint is used to deliver presentations to the board. A major time saving can be achieved if board members are given a copy of the slides plus notes rather than a written report. The benefit to the board is that management has less space to cloud a problem. Management has to set out the issues clearly and concisely.

EXHIBIT 4.1 Board Meeting Efficiency Rating (days since month-end)

Exceptional	Above average	Average	Below average
<5 working days	6–10 working days	11–15 working days	>15 working days

Timeliness of Board Meetings

While boards do not need to sit every month—some sit six, others eight times a year—when they do sit, it is important that there is not a large period of time between the month-end and the board meeting, if we are after efficient and cost-effective board papers.

Exhibit 4.1 shows an efficiency scale in the holding of board meetings after the month-end in question.

Reporting Key Result Indicators in a Dashboard to the Board

There is a major conflict in most organizations that have boards, as to what information is appropriate for the board. Since the board's role is clearly one of governance and not of management, it is inappropriate to be providing the board with key performance indicators (KPIs) unless the company is in trouble and the board needs to take a more active role. KPIs are the very heart of management, and used properly, many of them are monitored 24/7 or at least weekly. Certainly they are not measures to be reported monthly or bimonthly to the board.

We need indicators of overall performance that should be reviewed only on a monthly or bimonthly basis. These measures need to tell the story as to whether the organization is being steered in the right direction at the right speed; whether the customers and staff are happy; and whether the organization is acting in a responsible and environmentally friendly way.

In Chapter 19 these measures are called *key result indicators* (KRIs). These KRIs help the board focus on strategic rather than management issues.

A good dashboard, with the KRIs going in the right direction, will give the board confidence that management knows what it is doing and the ship is being steered in the right direction. The board can then concentrate on what it does best: focusing on the horizon for icebergs or looking for new ports of call and coaching the CEO, as required. This is instead of directors parking themselves on the bridge and getting in the way of the captain who is trying to perform important day-to-day duties.

A dashboard should be a one-page display such as the two examples in Exhibit 4.2 and 4.3. The commentary should be included on this page.

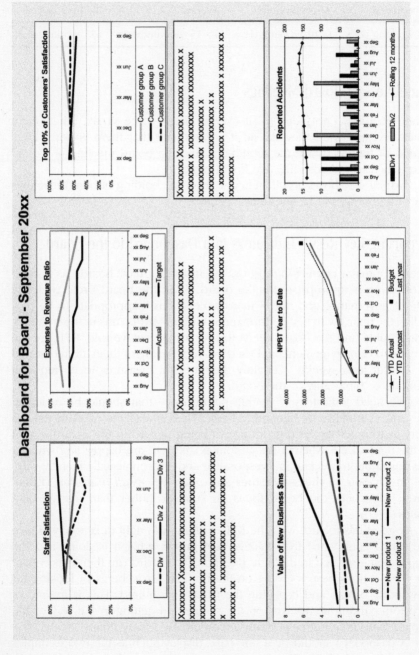

EXHIBIT 4.2 Six-KRI Dashboard for a Board

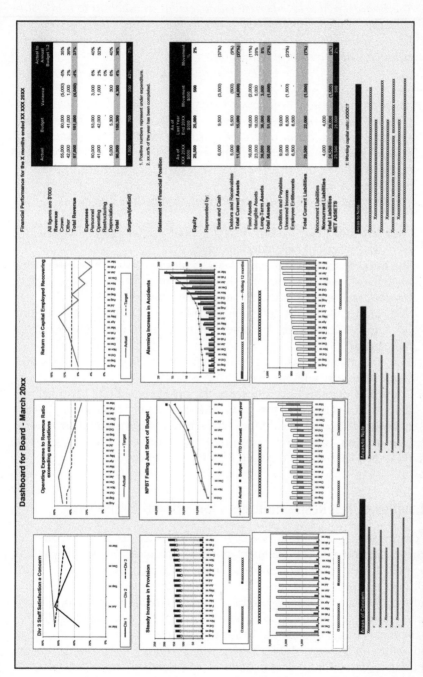

EXHIBIT 4.3 Board Dashboard on an A3 Page (U.S. Fanfold)

The Board's role is to supervise management as much as to think stra-
tegically. You can't point them away from the KPIs; otherwise you will
hit the icebergs. They need to challenge and measure performance in
balance with the strategic direction.

                                   CFO with blue chip international experience

Author's response: I understand this point of view and agree that
once the ship is in dangerous waters, the board will want to see and
should see more detail. However, if sailing on flat calm water, wind
behind, with the sun setting, there should be no need for the board to
see the KPIs.

The key features of these two example dashboards include:

- They are one-page documents with brief commentary covering the issue and what is being done about it.
- The trend analysis goes back at least 15 months (some businesses need to go back a rolling 18 months). Remember that business has no respect for your year-end; it is merely an arbitrary point in time.
- You can use the title of the graph to explain what is happening. "Return on Capital Employed." becomes "Return on Capital Employed Is Increasing."
- You may need to maintain somewhere between 8 to 12 graphs and report the most relevant ones to the board.
- These KRI measures need to cover the progress made in the organization's critical success factors and at the same time cover the six perspectives of a balanced scorecard. (See Chapters 18 and 19 for more information).
- You need to ascertain the organization's critical success factors first as these will lead you to the right KPIs (See Chapter 18).[2]

Examples of Key Result Indicators for a Board Dashboard

A dashboard should be a one-page display, such as the examples in Exhibits 4.2 and 4.3. The commentary should be included on this page. A good dashboard, with the key result indicators going in the right direction, will give the board confidence that management knows what it is doing and that the ship is being steered in the right direction. The directors can then concentrate on what they do best: focusing on the horizon for icebergs in the first-class lounge instead of parking themselves on the ship's bridge and getting in the way of the captain, who is trying to perform the important day-to-day duties. Ten examples of KRI board dashboard graphs can be found in Exhibit 4.4.

EXHIBIT 4.4 KRIs for a Board Dashboard

Staff satisfaction:

No different or less important than customers. As one person said, happy staff make happy customers that make a happy bottom line. If you believe in this connection, run a survey now. A staff satisfaction survey need not cost the earth and should never cover all staff; instead it should be replaced by a rolling survey. See article "How You Can Seek Staff Opinion for Less than $6,000" on www.davidparmenter.com.

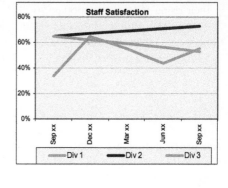

Expenses to revenue as a ratio:

The board should be interested in how effective the organization has been in utilizing technology and continuous improvement to ensure cost of operations is tracking well against revenue.

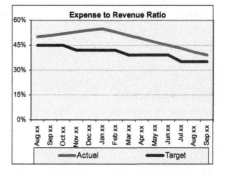

Customer satisfaction:

This needs to be measured at least every three months. By using statistical samples and focusing on your top 10 to 20 percent of customers (the ones who are generating most if not all of your bottom line), you can keep this process from being overly expensive. If you think once a year is adequate for customer satisfaction, stick to running a sports club as you are not safe in the public or private sector.

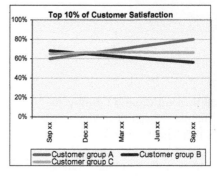

(Continued)

EXHIBIT 4.4 (*Continued*)

Value of new business:

All businesses in the private sector need to focus on the growth of their rising stars. It is important to monitor the pickup of this new business, especially among the top 10 to 20 percent of customers.

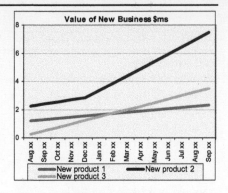

Net profit before tax (NPBT):

Since the board will always have a focus on the year-end, it is worthwhile showing the cumulative NPBT. This graph will include the most recent forecast, which should be updated on a quarterly basis bottom-up.

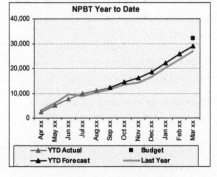

Health and Safety:

All boards are interested in this area, as the well-being of staff is a much higher priority these days.

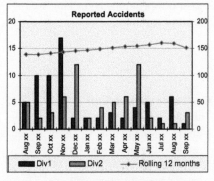

Return on Capital Employed:

The old stalwart of reporting. The difference now that it is no longer a KPI but a KRI. This graph needs to be a 15- to 18-month trend graph.

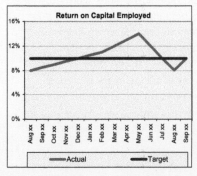

EXHIBIT 4.4 *(Continued)*

Cash Flow:
This would be projected out at least six months forward.

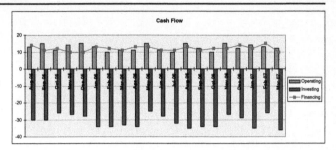

Capacity:
This monitors the capacity of key machines and plant. It would go forward at least 6 to 12 months. The board needs to be aware of capacity limitations, and such a graph will help focus it on new capital expenditure requirements.

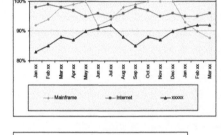

Operational Efficiency:
This is a composite index based on a variety of statistics, such as delivered in full on time and portion of idle machine time (measuring key machines only).

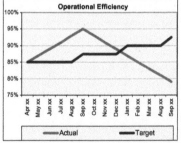

Notes

1. Visit www.myersbriggs.org.
2. See David Parmenter, *Key Performance Indicators: Developing, Implementing, and Using Winning KPIs*, 2nd ed. (Hoboken, NJ: John Wiley & Sons, 2010).

CHAPTER 5

Timely Annual Planning Process:
Ten Working Days or Less!

This sounds impossible, yet it is achieved. It takes good organization and recognition that the annual planning process is not adding value; instead it is undermining an efficient allocation of resources, encouraging dysfunctional budget holder behavior, negating the value of monthly variance reporting, and consuming huge resources from the board, senior management team (SMT), budget holders, their assistants, and of course the finance team. When was the last time you were thanked for the annual planning process? You have a situation where, at best, budget holders have been antagonized; at worst, budget holders now flatly refuse to cooperate.

The future for your organization is quarterly rolling planning, which is covered in Chapters 14 and 15 in this book. However, it will take upward of nine months to implement, and your annual planning cycle may be just around the corner.

This chapter is an extract from a white paper[1] I deliver around the world that has revolutionized how many finance teams manage the annual planning process. Due to space constraints I have highlighted the main better practices that will also be carried over into quarterly rolling planning and forecasting. For further information it may be worth accessing this white paper.

Sell the Change through Emotional Drivers

It is important to sell to management why a quick annual plan is a good annual plan. This is not particularly difficult because it is rare to find a manager who enjoys the process or finds it rewarding and worthwhile. The difficulty is that while managers will concur with the concept, getting them to change old and embedded bad practices requires a culture change.

To start the process off, we need to sell the change using emotional drivers rather than selling by logic, as already discussed in the introduction.

The following are some of the emotional drivers you would use to sell the need to streamline the annual planning process to the SMT:

- The monthly budgets from the annual plan create meaningless month-end reports (e.g., "it is a timing difference").
- Lost months and lost weekends with family producing the annual plan.
- Huge cost associated with the annual plan—estimate on the high side, as costs motivate the SMT and the board.
- Time spent by the board and SMT second-guessing the next year—it is more efficient on a rolling quarterly basis.
- It is a best practice to implement quarterly rolling forecasting and planning (e.g., 80 percent of major U.S. companies expect to be doing quarterly rolling forecasts, etc.).

The emotional drivers to create change in an annual planning process within the finance team include:

- In the weeks before the annual planning process commences, are you already depressed about the evenings you will be spending at work and the family time you will be missing?
- Are you frustrated by going down the same annual planning process just like a laboratory rat?
- Are you and your team held prisoner for three months by the annual planning process, which creates yardsticks that are out of date before the ink dries?
- Are you concerned about the reliability of the spreadsheets that are generating your budgets?
- Do your in-house clients get frustrated about your unavailability during this period?
- Are you dismayed at the lack of value this annual process adds?
- Are you frustrated with the same "it's a timing difference" commentary derived from the inappropriateness of the monthly budgets?

Foundation Stones of an Annual Planning Process

There are a number of foundation stones that need to be laid before we can commence a project on reducing the annual plan to two weeks. When building a house, you need to ensure that all of the structure is built on the foundations. This project has a number of foundation stones that should never be undermined. These are:

- Set strategic targets prior to the annual plan.
- Never budget at account code level; use the 10 percent rule.
- Avoid monthly phasing the annual budget.
- The annual plan does not give an annual entitlement to spend; that is given each quarter during the quarterly rolling planning update.
- Have the budget committee commit to a lock-up in the second week of the annual planning process.
- The CEO must make the two-week time frame nonnegotiable.

Bolt Down Your Strategy Beforehand

Leading organizations always have a strategic workshop out of town. This session should be anticipated with a positive attitude. Normally board members will be involved, as their strategic vision is a valuable asset. These retreats are run by an experienced external facilitator. The key strategic assumptions thus are set before the annual planning round starts, and board members also can set out what they are expecting to see.

It is important that the board and management separate out in their minds the difference between a target—for example, the board wants a $200m net profit next year—and the annual plan forecast of $180m. It serves no purpose to lie to the board by fixing the annual plan to come up with $200m when you know it cannot be achieved. This is hiding the performance gap. This point is discussed more in Chapter 15.

Never Budget at Account Code Level; Use the 10 Percent Rule

As accountants, we never needed to set budgets at account code level. We simply have done it because we did it in the previous year's plans. Do you need a budget at account code level if you have good trend analysis captured in the reporting tool? I think not. We therefore apply Pareto's 80/20 and establish a series of category headings that include a number of general ledger (G/L) codes.

Some rules to follow include:

- Limit the number of categories in a budget holder's budget to no more than 12. Have a budget line if the category is over 10 percent of total (e.g., show revenue line if revenue category is over 10 percent of the total revenue). If the category is under 10 percent, consolidate with other categories.
- Map the G/L account codes to these categories—a planning tool can easily cope with this issue without the need for a revisit of the chart of accounts. (See Exhibit 5.1 for an example of how to map these changes.)

EXHIBIT 5.1 How Forecasting Model Consolidates Account Codes

Forecasting at Account Code Detail		Forecasting by Categories		Notes
Stationery	4,556			
Uniforms	3,325			
Cleaning	1,245			
Miscellaneous	7,654			No detail required
Consumables	2,367			
Tea & Coffee	2,134			
Kitchen Utensils	145			
	21,426	Consumables	21,400	
Salaries and Wages	25,567,678	Salaries and Wages	27,400,000	Budget holder calculates salaries and wages to nearest $100k
Taxes	2,488,888	Taxes	2,900,000	Model automatically calculates taxes
Temporary Staff	2,456,532	Other Employment Costs	4,200,000	This number is the balancing item
Contract Workers	2,342,345			
Students	234,567			
	33,090,010	Employment Costs	34,500,000	Budget holder estimates costs to nearest $0.5m

Avoid Monthly Phasing the Annual Budget

As accountants, we like things to balance. It is neat and tidy. Thus it appeared logical to break the annual plan down into 12 monthly breaks before the year started. We could have been more flexible. Instead we created a reporting yardstick that undermined our value to the organization. Every month we make management, all around the organization, write variance analyzes that I could do just as well from my office in New Zealand. "It is a timing difference," "We were not expecting this to happen," "The market conditions have changed radically since the plan," and so forth.

The monthly targets should be set a quarter ahead using a quarterly rolling forecasting process, which is discussed in Chapter 15. This change has a major impact on reporting. We no longer will be reporting against a monthly budget that was set, in some cases, over 12 months before the period being reviewed.

Annual Plan Does Not Give an Annual Entitlement to Spend

The annual plan should not create an entitlement; it should be merely an indication, with the funding based being allocated on quarterly rolling regime, a quarter ahead each time (see Chapter 15).

Asking budget holders what they want and then, after many arguments, giving them an "annual entitlement" to funding is the worst form of management we have ever presided over.

Budget Committee Commits to a "Lock-up"

Most organizations have a budget committee comprised of a CEO, CFO, and two general managers. You need to persuade this budget committee that a three-day lock-up, whereby the committee sits for up to three days, is more efficient than the current scenario that stretches over months.

During the three-day lock-up, each budget holder has a set time to:

- Discuss their financial and nonfinancial goals for the next year.
- Justify their annual plan forecast.
- Raise key issues (e.g., the revenue forecast is contingent on the release to market and commissioning of products X and Y).

CEO Makes the Two-Week Time Frame Nonnegotiable

The CEO needs to make a fast time frame nonnegotiable in all communication with staff.

From the memo that goes out to invite budget holders to the first annual planning workshop, the address of the attendees at the workshop, and the daily chasing up of the laggards during the three days budget holders have to complete their annual plan, the message is clear: We want a fast, light-touch annual plan. "Fast" in that the annual plan is completed in less than two weeks, and "light touch" in that unnecessary detail is avoided.

As part of this foundation stone, common templates are established to replace the myriad of spreadsheets. One such common template is the payroll worksheet that shows budget holders all their staff and their salaries, start date, leaving date if known, and so on (see Exhibit 5.2).

EXHIBIT 5.2 Payroll Calculation Worksheet

Employee Name	Position Grade	Department	Std Annual Salary	Override Salary	Start Month	End Month
Jump, John	Junior	Sales team 1	35,000	40,000	June	
Host, Chris	Sales	Sales team 1	70,000			
Big, Terry	Sales	Sales team 1	68,000			August
Etc.	Sales	Sales team 1				

Efficient Annual Planning Processes

The foundations stones already mentioned and the processes that you need to adopt, set out next, need to be understood, developed, and implemented. Due to space constraints I briefly outline only the key processes. For further information, see the white paper "Timely Annual Planning Process in Two Weeks or Less" on www.davidparmenter.com.

Sell the Change and Get Buy-in (SMT and the Board)

You start this process by sending a memo to the CEO; see Appendix J for a suggested draft.

When you get an audience, you present a compelling argument in a 20-minute presentation (see www.davidparmenter.com). I recommend that you practice this in front of a public relations expert who will fine-tune the way you are selling through the emotional drivers of your intended audience.

Hold a Focus Group Workshop

A focus group needs to be formed; see Exhibit 5.3 for a workshop agenda. The workshop is important for a number of reasons:

- Many people will doubt our ability to move from four months to two weeks, and we need to ensure that all likely objections are covered in the annual planning workshop.
- We need to reengineer the annual plan process using Post-it Notes, as discussed in Chapter 2.
- A green light from the focus team will help sell this concept to the SMT.
- The focus group will give valuable input as to how the implementation should best be done to maximize its impact.

EXHIBIT 5.3 Focus Group Workshop Agenda

Location: xxxxxxxxxxxxx

Date and Time: xxxxxx

Suggested attendees: Budget committee, selection of business unit heads, all management accountants, and a selection of budget holders

Prework: Attendees to document forecasting procedures on Post-it Notes. One procedure per Post-it. Each team to have different color Post-its.

Requirements: Event secretary, two laptops, data show, two whiteboards

8:30 A.M.	Welcome by CFO, a summary of progress to date at xxxxxx, an outline of the issues, and establishing the outcome for the workshop.
8:40	**Setting the Scene**: topics covered include:

- Why we cannot afford the current annual planning process
- Better practice stories
- Some of the major flaws with the annual planning process
- Proposed two-week process
- The new rules

9:40	**Workshop 1: Analyzing the New Rules.** Separate teams look at the proposed new rules and comment on changes required.
10:15	Morning break.
10:30	**Workshop 2: Workshop on Post-it Reengineering of the Annual Planning Process.** During the workshop we analyze the bottlenecks of the forecasting process. In this workshop we use Post-its to schedule the steps during the forecast (e.g., yellow— budget holder activities, red—forecasting team activities, blue— budget committee activities).
12:00 P.M.	Feedback from work groups on both workshops and action plan agreed (document deadline date and who is responsible). Individuals will be encouraged to take responsibility for implementing the steps.
12:30	Lunch at venue.
1:30	Delivery of the proposed "selling" presentation.
2:00	**Workshop 3: Feedback on the Presentation.** Separate work groups look at different parts of the presentation.
3:00	The team presents reports to an invited audience on what changes they would like to implement and when. They can also raise any issues they still have. Suggested audience: all those who attended the setting the scene morning session.
4:00	Wrap-up of workshop.

EXHIBIT 5.4 Post-it Notes

Week −1
Finalize Sales Forecast

The Post-it reengineering exercise is the same as the month-end process reengineering. Please see the section on some tips on running a Post-it reengineering session in Chapter 2. The only difference is:

- The time scale is week −2, week −1 (last week before annual planning kick-off workshop), week +1 (first week of annual plan), week +2 etc. instead of day −2, day −1 etc. See Exhibit 5.4.
- There will be different attendees at the workshop.
- The invite to attend comes from the CEO with a career-limiting nonattendance warning. See Appendix J for a suggested draft.

New Sales Model Developed to Look at Demand from Major Customers by Major Products

If you have 200 products and 2,000 customers, how do you get to a reasonably accurate forecast? The answer lies in applying Pareto's 80/20 rule to the sales forecasting process. Sales need to be forecast by major customers and major products. The rest of the customers and rest of the products should be put into meaningful groups and modeled based on the historic relationship to the major customers' buying patterns. See Exhibit 5.5 for a suggested format.

Many organizations liaise with customers to get demand forecasts only to find them as error prone as the forecasts done in-house. The reason is that you have asked the wrong people. You need to get permission to meet with the staff who are responsible for ordering your products and services.

For example, one financial team decided to contact its major customers to help with demand forecasting. Naturally, the team was holding discussions with the major customers' "headquarters" staff. On reflection, the financial team found it better but still error prone, so its members went back and asked, "How come these forecasts you supplied are so error prone?" "If you want accurate numbers, you need to speak to the procurement managers for our projects" was the reply. "Can we speak to them?" "Of course, here are the contact details of the people you need to meet around the country." A series of meetings were then held around the country. The team found that these managers could provide very accurate

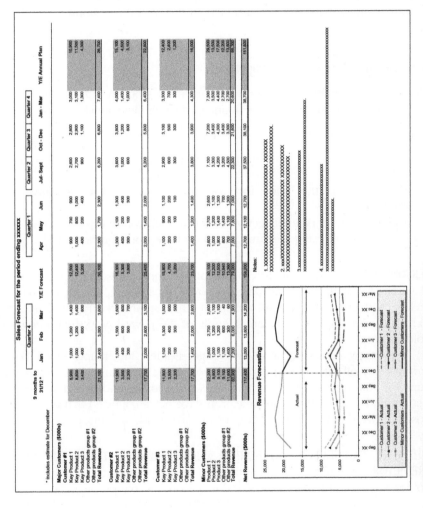

EXHIBIT 5.5 Suggested Sales Forecast Model

information and were even prepared to provide it in an electronic format. The sales forecast accuracy increased sevenfold due to focusing on getting the demand right for the main customers.

The lesson to here is that you want to forecast revenue more accurately by delving into your main customers' business, ask them, on a quarterly basis, "Whom should we speak to in order to get a better understanding of your likely demand for our products in the next three months and the next five quarters?"

Prework: On the Annual Planning Model

The processes, including the prework, are as set out in Exhibit 5.6. The budget and forecasting team in finance will complete much of the prework, including:

- Amendments to the existing model to incorporate the changes in this paper.
- Ensuring that the sales forecast appears reasonable, as already discussed.
- Updating the personnel section in the model from the payroll.
- Calculating all categories that are to be based on historic trends.

PERSONNEL COSTS   Accurate forecasting of personnel costs requires analysis of all current staff (their end date if known, their salary, the likely salary review, and/or bonus) and all new staff (their starting salary, their likely start date). See Exhibit 5.2 as an example of the payroll worksheet budget holders need.

Too many errors occur when budget holders are simply given last month's payroll total to use as a basis for annual planning. By using this number, you have multiplied the long service leave paid to employee A last month by 12. At the same time, you have not recognized that two staff positions were not included. Many of us have made this error.

AUTOMATE CALCULATION CATEGORIES WHERE TREND DATA IS THE BEST PREDICTOR   A number of categories can be prepopulated, as the budget holder will look only at past data and may even misinterpret this data. Face it, you are best equipped to do this. The obvious categories to populate are:

- Communication costs
- Accommodation costs
- Consumables
- Fleet costs

EXHIBIT 5.6 Two-Week Annual Planning Process

Process =>	Prior work			Week 1	2	3	4	5	End	6	7	8	9	10
	Budget prework	Meeting with Divisional Heads (DHs)	Present budget workshop	Budget holders prepare and load their forecast			First look at numbers	Rework some budgets		Submissions by BHs to Budget Committee			Present final annual plan	Final alterations and finishing off documentation
Activities by team =>														
Strategic Planning			Attend				Reviewing to ensure linkage to Plan, and advising of any discrepancies						Attend	
SMT	Set assumptions	One-to-one with the Finance team					First look at numbers			Review submissions, all day long			Hear presentation and give instructions for final changes	
Finance Team	Prepare system, the presentation, calculate known costs overheads, personnel costs etc	One-to-one with DHs	Give presentation to BHs	Help BHs with budget plans (extended team)			QA	Help BHs		Further QA			Complete preparation and deliver annual plan presentation	Complete documentation
Budget Holders BHs			Attend	Prepare budget			Alter numbers after feedback	Attend		Present plan to SMT when called			Document and file all calculations	

85

- Depreciation
- Miscellaneous costs

PROVIDE AUTOMATED CALCULATIONS FOR TRAVEL A key area of wasted time is the budget holder calculating the travel and expense costs. Set a simple calculator with standard costs. For example, a budget holder enters that four people are going to Sydney for three nights. The model then calculates the airfares, accommodation, transfers, and overnight allowances using standard estimates.

PREPARE A SIMPLE REPORTING TEMPLATE FOR THE ANNUAL PLAN Annual plans often end up in elaborate reports. The feeling is "Since we spent so much time on it, we better make a great job of the write-up." In reality, nobody reads these documents. It is far better to have the documentation left mostly in presentation format along with a key summary page for each business and one for the consolidation.

We do not need to report the annual plan to the board in monthly splits. A quarterly analysis of the annual plan will suffice. See Exhibit 5.7 for a suggested one-page summary format.

HAVE TREND GRAPHS FOR EVERY CATEGORY FORECASTED Better quality can be achieved through analysis of the trends. There is no place to hide surplus funding when a budget holder has to explain why the forecast trend is so different from the past trend. The graph shown in Exhibit 5.8, if made available for all the categories budget holders are required to forecast, will increase forecast accuracy. Budget holders will want to ensure their forecasts make sense against the historic trend.

IF USING EXCEL, SIMPLIFY THE MODEL TO MAKE IT ROBUST Forecasting requires a good robust tool, not a spreadsheet built by some innovative accountant that no one can understand now. However, you may not have the time to replace the existing Excel model. A new planning tool will take at least six months for researching, acquiring, and implementing for organizations with over, say, 500 full-time staff. In this case, you can:

- Improve the revenue predictions by focusing in on some major customers.
- Budget at category rather than account code level.
- Forecast the annual plan using quarterly figures rather than monthly (hiding two of the monthly columns for each quarter).
- Consolidate via the G/L instead of the spreadsheet (if you can add the category headings easily into the G/L).

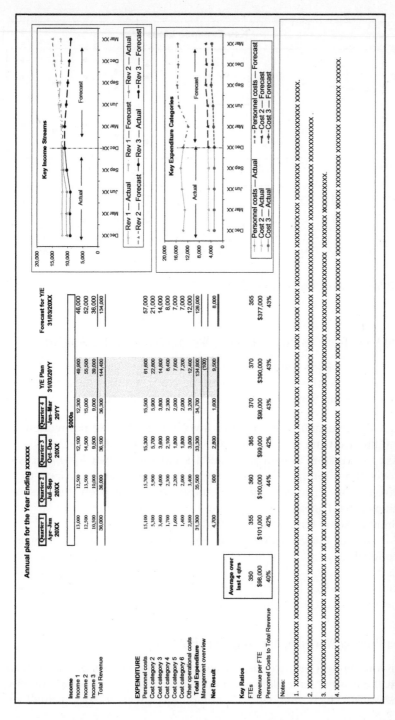

EXHIBIT 5.7 One-Page Summary of the Annual Plan

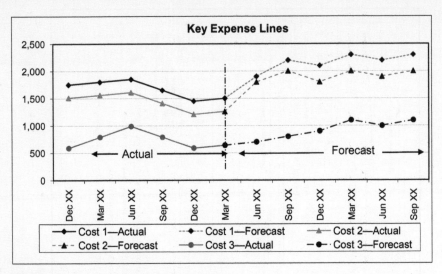

EXHIBIT 5.8 Forecast Expenditure Graph

Expand Your Team, as Budget Holders Will Need One-to-One Support

Many budget holders will need one-to-one support. Yet, as seen in Exhibit 5.6, we are to do this all in three working days. We thus need to expand the support team. Some suggestions to expand your team are:

- Get all the qualified accountants involved, even those not working in the finance team (e.g., get the CFO involved as well).
- Ask the auditors to loan some audit seniors from their local offices to cover those remote locations—the audit seniors will be happy to be involved in an interesting task (those who have been auditors will know what I mean).
- Bring in some temp staff with budget experience.
- For smaller budget holders, the senior accounts payable staff would be ideal.

Thus all budget holders, wherever they are located, who need help can be supported during the three-day window for data entry.

Hold a Briefing Workshop for all Budget Holders

Never issue budget instructions, for you already know they are never read. Follow the lesson of a leading accounting team that always holds a briefing workshop at which attendance is compulsory. With today's technology,

EXHIBIT 5.9 Annual Plan Briefing Workshop Agenda

Location: xxxxxxxxxxxxx

Date and Time: xxxxxx

Suggested attendees: All budget committee, all business unit heads, all management accountants, and all budget holders

Requirements: event secretary, desktop for every seven attendees, data show, two whiteboards

8:30 A.M.	Welcome by CEO and why this is a nonnegotiable event.
8:40	**Setting the scene**—topics covered include:
	▪ Why we cannot afford the current annual planning process
	▪ Better practice stories and research we have done
	▪ Some of the major flaws with the annual planning process
	▪ The new rules, which have been vetted by the focus group
	▪ The proposed two-week annual planning process
	▪ The setting of monthly targets, a quarter ahead, instead of annually
	The senior management team may wish to leave after this session.
9:30	**Present the new budget package.** Those who are attending via webcast leave the presentation here.
10:00	**Workshop 1: Looking at the Package.** In small groups (no more than seven), each attendee gets a chance to play with the package. Each group has a member from finance facilitating this process.
10:30	Morning break.
10:50	**Feedback on the package from the work groups.**
11:20	Wrap-up of workshop by CFO reminding about deadlines, help available, and to keep to the bigger picture.

---

you also can hold the workshop simultaneously as a webcast so budget holders in remote locations can attend, albeit electronically. (Attend a webcast to see what I mean.)

Hold a "budget preparation" workshop (see Exhibit 5.9 for an agenda example) covering how to complete the input form and explaining why budget holders do not need to forecast monthly numbers, only quarterly; the three-day window; the daily update to the CEO; and the fact that late returns will be career limiting. Stress that the bigger items should have much more detail, explain why you have automated some of the categories and the help they will receive, and so forth.

Make sure that at the workshop, the CEO makes it clear that everybody has to cooperate to achieve a quick time frame. It would be most useful if the CEO states that the organization will be monitoring compliance in the critical days and makes it clear that late forecasting will be a career-limiting activity.

The key messages we want to get across include:

- Forecasting by the categories, and why some categories are now automated.
- Stress on the fact that the more material categories should have much more detail.
- Only a three-day window to enter data.
- Help will be provided on a one-to-one basis.
- How to use the planning tool (attendees will already have some training on this).
- What they should prepare for the budget committee.
- No monthly breakdown in annual plan—monthly numbers are set just before each quarter starts.
- CEO involvement in monitoring compliance—late returns will be career limiting.

See Appendix I for a checklist on how to streamline an annual planning process.

Note

1. David Parmenter, "Timely Annual Planning Process in Two Weeks or Less," www.davidparmenter.com, 2010.

CHAPTER 6

Managing the Accounting Team

In this chapter I have extracted some of key lessons chief financial officers (CFOs) need to learn about managing staff from my recent book, *The Leading-Edge Manager's Guide to Success*.[1] At some point it would be worth reading the other issues that I have had to omit due to space constraints.

There are many ways for you to better manage your accounting staff. Some of the major ones are discussed in this chapter.

Hold an Off-Site Meeting for the Accounting Team at Least Twice a Year

Some teams hold a half-day, off-site meeting every month after they have completed their quick month-end. Exhibit 6.1 shows the agenda items of a typical off-site meeting. One of the meetings will set the annual goals of the team. The CFO will prepare the first cut of the goals for the accounting team, which support the organization's operating plan. During discussion these are broken down, developed, and taken on by individuals on the team. The benefits of this approach are that the team members are fully aware of one another's goals and there is a greater degree of ownership to make it happen.

With cost-cutting exercises over the past 10 to 15 years, organized in-house courses are a rarity, and individuals often are left to their own devices in selecting what they would consider to be a useful way to spend the training budget.

The off-site meetings, if run frequently enough, are an ideal time to have the training session. One high-performance team has a training

EXHIBIT 6.1 Agenda of a Team Off-Site Meeting

Agenda of the Accounting Team Meeting

Date and Time: xxxxxx

Location: xxxxxx

Suggested Attendees: All the accounting team with special guests xxxxxxxx, xxxxxxxx, xxxxxxxx

Requirements: Session secretary (Pat Carruthers), laptops × 2, data show, whiteboards × 2

8:30 A.M.	Welcome by CFO, a summary of progress to date, outline of the issues, feedback from the in-house customer survey, and establishing the outcome for the workshop.
8:40 A.M.	**Setting the scene**—a talk by a member of the senior management team (SMT). Topics covered include: ■ Importance of the finance team ■ Future direction of xxxxxx ■ Areas where the SMT are keen to see improvements ■ Where the accounting team can score more goals for the SMT
9:00 A.M.	**Presentation by external party on a new methodology or tool.** Topics covered could include: ■ Improving the use of the general ledger (revisiting the time-saving features) ■ Demonstration of a planning tool ■ Action meetings—a new approach to productive meetings ■ Accounts payable better practices ■ Team-building exercises (Hermann's thinking preferences, Myers-Briggs team wheel, etc.) ■ Other better practices taken from this book, etc.
10:15 A.M.	Morning break
10:30 A.M.	**Workshop 1.** How to implement changes to increase added value to the SMT and in-house customers (utilizing findings from survey and talk given by the SMT member).
11:00 A.M.	**Workshop 2.** How to implement xxxxxxxx better practice.
12:15 P.M.	Lunch at venue
1:00 P.M.	Wrap-up of workshop

session in every three monthly off-site team meeting. They invest considerable time planning the training workshop, which may include: helping staff to revisit policies and procedures; looking at how to handle likely scenarios; what makes a supervisor excellent; client management; increasing knowledge about special processes; and so forth. We can certainly learn from this high-performance team's commitment to training and the positive team spirit that these in-house workshops generate. Many accounting functions suffer from inadequate training. We are all too busy fire-fighting to have time to acquire 21st-century fire-fighting equipment.

Set Up Monthly One-on-One Progress Meetings with Your Direct Reports

Set up monthly progress meetings with your direct reports in the first week of the month and on the same day (e.g., Ted 2 P.M. first Tuesday of month; Sarah 3 P.M. first Tuesday of month; etc.) and give them performance feedback, which in most cases will be just verbal. In this meeting ask them to prepare a few PowerPoint slides rather than a written report and suggest a maximum of 30 minutes' preparation time.

These meetings also will replace the need for project progress meetings. The content for the PowerPoint would include:

- What I have done well last month
- What I have not done so well
- What I am planning to do this month
- The lessons I have learned
- The training I am going to organize

Become Known for Giving Recognition Freely

I have for a long time been aware of the significance of recognition, but only recently have I become aware that it is a fundamental foundation stone to all our relationships. The ability to appreciate and recognize all those we come in contact with defines us as a person and defines how successful, in the broadest terms, we can be. Giving recognition freely makes us a person whom people like to work for and with, and one we naturally gravitate toward. Many of us will need to count the recognitions we give, until doing so becomes a natural part of our makeup. The checklist in Exhibit 6.2 will help you achieve this behavioral change.

EXHIBIT 6.2 Recognition Checklist

	Suggested Frequency	4 Weeks Ago	3 Weeks Ago	2 Weeks Ago	1 Week Ago	Date if Not in Last 4 Weeks
Staff	weekly					
Colleagues	weekly					
Boss	weekly					
Mentor	quarterly					
Key suppliers	quarterly					
Key customers	quarterly					

Note: I would recommend extending this list to include partner, children, friends and relatives, and so on.

For some of us, the simple task of recognizing all the types of support we receive will be unnatural. If you are having difficulty trying to recognize contributions, think of GAS:

G: Guidance that has been helpful
A: Actions done by others that make your life easier
S: Unwavering support and commitment by others

Some participants have found some clever ways that work, such as handing out film tickets, vouchers for two at a good restaurant, and so on, to reward accounting staff who have gone the extra mile. Do not underestimate the power of the signed memo or letter recognizing superior performance. I have included a couple of thank-you templates in Appendix J for your convenience.

Attract the Best Staff to the Team

Making the accounting team a preferred team to join will attract high-potential accounting staff. You can do this by:

- Establishing a relationship with your local universities offering prizes to the best accounting graduates, delivering guest lectures, and offering holiday jobs—this will increase the profile of the team and enable you to try before you buy.

- Writing articles in accounting journals and delivering presentations for your local accounting branch.
- Being active in the local accounting body.

Adopt Better Recruitment Practices

Far too often managers, when looking at their calendar, throw their hands up when they realize that they have another recruitment interview to do. It is the last thing they need at this point in time. Yet recruitment should be seen as the most important thing a manager does, for these reasons:

- Recruiting well is like putting a fence on the top of a cliff—it prevents casualties. As Jim Collins, of *Good to Great* fame, says, "You need to get the right people on the bus."
- You can recruit for technical skills and through training improve skill levels, but you cannot change people's values. If their values are different from those of the organization, you will always have conflict.
- Better recruits will lead to more internal promotion, saving costs and maintaining institutional knowledge.

To have a good team, it is a good idea to start with the best resources available. There are still too many staff selections made by an antiquated interview process, accompanied by some cursory reference checking. The result is a high failure rate among new staff. A greater effort needs to be put into the selection process through the adoption of recruiting techniques that include those set out next.

- Use simulation exercises and psychometric testing on the short-listed candidates.
- Have staff members on the team somehow involved in the final selection from the short-listed candidates. This need not be too complex. A meeting over an afternoon cup of coffee can give the staff a chance to subtly quiz the candidate on his or her expert knowledge.
- Use report-writing and presentation exercises for more senior roles, such as the management accountant position.

One high-performance team asks its members if they know someone who would fit in the team before they advertise a position. Often this has proved successful, saving hours of sifting through the great unknown.

The management guru Peter Drucker, on observing great leaders, noted that there were five steps to a sound recruitment:

Step 1. Understand the job so you have a better chance of getting a good fit.

Step 2. Consider three to five people to maximize your chance to get the best fit.

Step 3. Study candidates' performance records to find their strengths so that you can ascertain whether these strengths are right for the job.

Step 4. Talk to the candidates' previous bosses and colleagues about them.

Step 5. Once the employment decision has been made, make sure the appointee understands the assignment.

Recognize Staff Performance

We all appreciate recognition, especially when we do not have to wait for it. Some participants have found some clever ways that work, such as handing out film tickets or vouchers for two at a good restaurant, to reward accounting staff who have gone the extra mile.

Team Balanced Scorecards

Organizations that have adopted balanced scorecard reporting have introduced team scorecards. These help the team score goals in a balanced way and increase the alignment of the individual members' work with their team's and organization's goals.

Even if the organization has not adopted the balanced scorecard, the accounting team can add value by leading change in reporting team performance in a balanced way by introducing the concept for their team. Exhibit 6.3 shows a team scorecard designed in Excel. Excel is an excellent tool for designing a template and testing it over a couple of months, after which it should be installed in a proper balanced scorecard system.

Better Practice Training

Some ways your peers have improved the effectiveness of training include:

- Providing in-house tailored courses so staff can easily achieve five days of training a year, some of which can be held as part of the off-site meetings mentioned earlier.
- Supporting tertiary education, especially MBA programs.

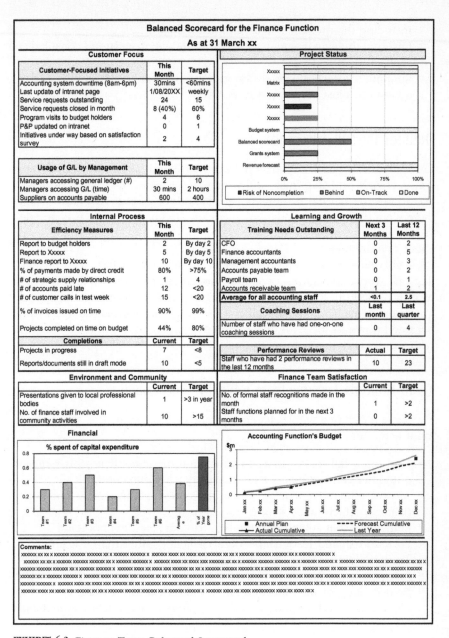

Balanced Scorecard for the Finance Function

As at 31 March xx

Customer Focus

Customer-Focused Initiatives	This Month	Target
Accounting system downtime (8am-6pm)	30mins	<60mins
Last update of intranet page	1/08/20XX	weekly
Service requests outstanding	24	15
Service requests closed in month	8 (40%)	60%
Program visits to budget holders	4	6
P&P updated on intranet	0	1
Initiatives under way based on satisfaction survey	2	4

Usage of G/L by Management	This Month	Target
Managers accessing general ledger (#)	2	10
Managers accessing G/L (time)	30 mins	2 hours
Suppliers on accounts payable	600	400

Project Status

Xxxxx · Matrix · Xxxxx · Xxxxx · Xxxxx · Budget system · Balanced scorecard · Grants system · Revenue forecast

0% 25% 50% 75% 100%

■ Risk of Noncompletion ▨ Behind ▨ On-Track ▢ Done

Internal Process

Efficiency Measures	This Month	Target
Report to budget holders	2	By day 2
Report to Xxxxx	5	By day 5
Finance report to Xxxxx	10	By day 10
% of payments made by direct credit	80%	>75%
# of strategic supply relationships	1	4
# of accounts paid late	12	<20
# of customer calls in test week	15	<20
% of invoices issued on time	90%	99%
Projects completed on time on budget	44%	80%

Completions	Current	Target
Projects in progress	7	<8
Reports/documents still in draft mode	10	<5

Environment and Community

	Current	Target
Presentations given to local professional bodies	1	>3 in year
No. of finance staff involved in community activities	10	>15

Learning and Growth

Training Needs Outstanding	Next 3 Months	Last 12 Months
CFO	0	2
Finance accountants	0	5
Management accountants	0	3
Accounts payable team	0	2
Payroll team	0	1
Accounts receivable team	1	2
Average for all accounting staff	**<0.1**	**2.5**

Coaching Sessions	Last month	Last quarter
Number of staff who have had one-on-one coaching sessions	0	4

Performance Reviews	Actual	Target
Staff who have had 2 performance reviews in the last 12 months	10	23

Finance Team Satisfaction

	Current	Target
No. of formal staff recognitions made in the month	1	>2
Staff functions planned for in the next 3 months	0	>2

Financial

% spent of capital expenditure

0.8 0.6 0.4 0.2 0

Team #1 · Team #2 · Team #3 · Team #4 · Team #5 · Team #6 · Aver'ng · % of Year gone

Accounting Function's Budget

$m

3 2 1 0

Jan xx · Feb xx · Mar xx · Apr xx · May xx · Jun xx · Jul xx · Aug xx · Sep xx · Oct xx · Nov xx · Dec xx

■ Annual Plan ---- Forecast Cumulative —▲— Actual Cumulative —— Last Year

Comments:
xxxxxx xx xx x xxxxxx xxxxxx xxxxxx xx x xxxxxx xxxxxx x xxxxxx xxxx xx xxxx xxx xxxxxx xx xx x xxxxxx xxxxxx xxxxxx xx x xxxxxx xxxxxx x
xxxxxx xxx xx xxxxxx xxxxxx xxxxxx xx x xxxxxx xxxxxx x xxxxxx xxxx xx xxxx xxx xxxxxx xx xx x xxxxxx xxxxxx xxxxxx xx x xxxxxx xxxxxx x xxxxxx xxxx xx xxxx xxx xxxxxx xx xx x
xxxxxx xxxxxx xxxxxx xx x xxxxxx xxxxxx x xxxxxx xxxx xx xxxx xxx xxxxxx xx xx x xxxxxx xxxxxx xxxxxx xx x xxxxxx xxxxxx x xxxxxx xxxx xx xxxx xxx xxxxxx xx xx x xxxxxx xxxxxx
xxxxxx xxx x xxxxxx xxxxxx x xxxxxx xxxx xx xxxx xxx xxxxxx xx xx x xxxxxx xxxxxx xxxxxx xx x xxxxxx xxxxxx x xxxxxx xxxx xx xxxx xxx xxxxxx xx xx x xxxxxx xxxxxx xxxxxx xx x
xxxxxx xxxxxx x xxxxxx xxxx xx xxxx xxx xxxxxx xx xx x xxxxxx xxxxxx xxxxxx xx x xxxxxx xxxxxx x xxxxxx xxxx xx xxxx xxx xxxxxx xx xx x xxxxxx xxxxxx xxxxxx xx x xxxxxx xxxxxx x
xxxxxx xxxx xx xxxx xxx xxxxxx xx xx x xxxxxx xxxxxx xxxxxx xx x xxxxxx xxxxxx x xxxxxx xxxx xx xxxx xxxxxxxxxx xxxx xx xxxx xxx x

EXHIBIT 6.3 Finance Team Balanced Scorecard

- Including interpersonal skills in-house courses.
- Ensuring the management accountants and advisors attend consultancy skills courses.
- Running satisfaction surveys on in-house customers and implementing training to close any noted gaps.

Outdoor Pursuit Adventure

I recently met a coach of a national team who had taken his team to three consecutive World Cup finals and won. One of his team-building exercises was to ensure that the team went on an outdoor pursuit adventure where there were basic accommodation amenities. He ensured there was no television, as he wanted the team to always be with together learning more about one another.

I also have met a senior partner in an accounting firm who recalled that one weekend a group of staff got together and went on an overnight hike. It turned out to be more of an adventure than most had anticipated. The team dynamics after the hike were truly amazing. Those who went became known as the "A framers," and to this day they still have reunions with members flying in from abroad.

Team-Building Lessons from a World-Class Coach

The same coach of a world-champion team gave me some tips about building a team, and they included:

- Find out what makes each of your team members tick—this requires a number of meetings outside the work environment.
- Always remember that an emotional outburst may create emotional damage, which takes a long time to heal.
- Remember that selling the message to your team is important.
- Focus on shared leadership—be a facilitator rather than a leader.
- Team building is vital—take your team away to outdoor pursuit centers.
- Ask your team members individually, "What do you want from me?"
- Be accepting of mistakes and analyze the decision making that led to the mistake; both the coach and the team player will learn something.

CFOs and All Direct Reports Must Find a Mentor Immediately

In this day and age, only the foolish venture forward without having a mentor supporting them from behind the scenes. A mentor is normally someone older than you, wiser, with more gray hair, who knows something about what you are doing. In other words, it could be a retired CEO of the business, a retired board member who has known you for a while, a professional mentor, or someone in the sector where this is no conflict of interest.

A good mentor will save your career a number of times. With the advent of email, a career-limiting event is only a click on the send button away. The mentor is someone whom you ask, "Please look at this. I am thinking of copying in the CEO." To which the mentor replies, "Let's have a coffee first before it is sent," after which, when asked about the email, you reply, "What email!"

Mentors are also well connected and often will further your career during discussions on the 19th hole. They often receive as payment only a good meal once a quarter, while others will do it for a living.

When looking for a mentor, start at the top and work down. Even the most successful people are happy to mentor up-and-coming younger guns. Asking someone to become your mentor is one of the largest compliments you can give.

Become a Serving Leader

Not intending to offend the reader, I mention this observation: Among many of the finance managers, financial controllers, and CFOs I have met, the one quality that seems to be missing is leadership. I believe this is mainly due to a lack of focus in the area rather than an innate inability.

I recently have developed a serving leadership model based around some great leaders of the past and present. One of the most influential leaders has been Sir Ernest Shackleton, the Antarctic explorer. I feature his story in this chapter.

Should you wish to access more about servant leadership after reading this section, read Chapter 32 of my recent book, The *Leading-Edge Manager's Guide to Success.*[2]

Where does one start to describe the feats of Sir Ernest Shackleton, the famous Antarctic explorer who saved the lives of the whole Endurance party, which was stuck from January 1915 to August 1916 in the Antarctic?

The Endurance party lived for 19 months in the harshest environment in the world, with early 20th-century equipment and no support from outside agencies. Shackleton inspired his men to make a home on a floating ice shelf and sail to an uninhabited island (Elephant Island) in three life-boats. He navigated a small lifeboat across 800 miles in the roughest water in the world—many call it the "greatest journey ever"—and then, on landing, crossed unclimbed mountains and glaciers in an epic 30-hour traverse to get to an inhabited whaling station in South Georgia.

This section attempts to pull together much that has been written about Shackleton, in a way that it can be digested and embedded in daily routines. The full leadership story is best told in a must-read book called *Shackleton's Way* by Morrell and Capparell.[3]

Five Foundation Stones of a Serving-Leader

In order to succeed as a leader, you need five foundation stones in place. These have been derived from my observations of some famous leaders, in particular Sir Ernst Shackleton.

Foundation Stone #1: Minimize Personal Baggage

Minimizing personal baggage has been addressed in the introduction of this book. Ernest Shackleton developed his character and qualities from being the favorite brother of doting sisters to becoming the Antarctic explorer men would follow regardless of risk and reward. CFOs need to ensure they have lightened their load (personal baggage) before they attempt to loftier climbs.

Foundation Stone #2: "Love Thy Neighbor as Thyself"

This foundation stone requires us to have some greater driving force than simply worshiping the dollar. Many great leaders exhibit some spiritual element that has assisted them on their journey. Love for the common man, hostmanship, humility, and integrity all form the building materials for this foundation stone.

Shackleton was a religious man. He took the Bible with him from his first trip on the sea as a cabin boy. He knew many of the scriptures and had a profound love of the common man. While an atheist can be a great leader, he or she must have a love for the common man.

Many in the corporate world do not "love thy neighbor as thyself," and that is why we quite happily create conflict in our work environment. Corporate life is littered with examples of unnecessary litigation, which has led to the decline in health of those individuals who are caught up in this self-inflicted process.

It might be appropriate for CFOs to bring into their daily activities some spiritual elements that would help reinforce good and sound business ethics.

What I am talking about is:

- Respecting your colleagues and your team members' time (in other words, allowing them quality time to process initiatives rather than interrupting them with another meaningless task).
- Investing time to actively listen (even when you are on the verge of exploding with frustration).
- Conducting your working relationships effectively with all colleagues (even those whom you would not choose to invite to your weekend barbecue).
- Not setting demanding goals when they are unnecessary (e.g., avoid asking for a report by 9 A.M. tomorrow when you will get around to reading it three days later).
- Offering appropriate assistance to poor performers.
- Better handling of stress—your own, your staff's, and your colleagues'.
- Taking control of your stimulant intake (do not underestimate the impact it has on your colleagues).
- Treating your suppliers better.

Humility is not an easy trait to master when you have climbed up the corporate tree to become the CFO. Humility does not mean that you do not lay claim to what are rightly your achievements. It simply means that when dealing with individuals, you treat them as equals.

While Shackleton loved the limelight and enjoyed the public adoration, he was very humble when communicating with his team, whether in a recruitment confirmation letter or in day-to-day leadership issues. Time and again he gave up comforts for his men. During the Antarctic trip, he gave up his fur-lined sleeping bag—his bed—for a sick member, and his gloves at a point when he risked severe frostbite. He always shared the provisions with all no matter what the team member's contribution. In other words, through humility greatness can be achieved.

Foundation Stone #3: Master of Communication and Public Relations

You cannot lead unless others understand your vision and are sold the flight tickets for the journey. Mastering communication means understanding the importance of one-to-one communications, being seen by your staff, working the public relations machine, and mastering the written and spoken word.

Shackleton had little time for Captain Scott but had only positive words for him when expressing an opinion in public. He knew it is a small world and he might need Scott's support one day.

"The Boss," as Shackleton was known, loved the press and they loved him back. This is true of many great CEOs. One who comes to mind is Richard Branson. There is no one better at working the public relations machine than Branson.

Shackleton always personalized communication. If a major change was about to be made, he would mention it in passing individually so that when he announced the change publicly, it came as no surprise. The bad news was never unexpected. He always canvassed the men when the likely options were unpleasant. In other words, when he said, "We will need to risk the trip to Elephant Island," the men knew that this was the only likely option.

Every night, no matter how many degrees below freezing it was, Shackleton would visit each tent for a pep talk. He would wake in the early hours of the morning to keep the man on watch company (his need for a basic four hours' sleep would no doubt was a considerable advantage). He always found time to cheer up team members who were feeling depressed about their prospects.

Foundation Stone #4: Have a Mentor and a Safe Haven

In business, many costly failures could have been averted if advice had been sought from a trusted and wise mentor. The key is the selection (and use) of your mentor/adviser and realizing that just because you have asked once, this does not preclude a second or third request for help. When I talk to CFOs, about 1 in every 10 has a mentor. It is little wonder why CFOs dig themselves into holes from time to time.

Shackleton realized the importance of mentorship, and he thanks Tripp in his book, *South: The Endurance Expedition*, saying:[4]

> *Leonard Tripp, who has been my mentor, counsellor, and friend for many years, and who, when the Expedition was in precarious and difficult circumstances, devoted his energy, thought, and gave his whole time and advice to the best interests of our cause.*

All CFOs will have many soul-searching moments during their journey. Their magnitude can be quite severe if the CFO is taking the finance team and organization on a significant journey of change. In order to cope with these downs, you need to have built a safe haven for yourself, a place where you can retreat and recover. CFOs need to nurture close family relationships and hobbies that offer relaxation and enjoyment. Without a safe haven, CFOs are vulnerable to the downside. They will succumb to feeling a failure if all they have in their life is their career and it is going off the rails.

Foundation Stone #5: Be Clear on Your Legacy

I firmly believe that the meaning of life for the human race can be summed up in one word—*legacy*. We all have a driving force to leave something behind to say we were here. It can be through our family, through industry, or through our devotion to others. This legacy says "I was here; I added up to something; I had something to say; I changed people's lives for the better." Understanding one's legacy is important; it is a directional beacon that will guide you through life in a more purposeful way.

Shackleton knew from an early age that he would be an explorer. He wanted to be first to the Pole, first to cross the Antarctic and bring his men back safely.

As a CFO, you need to dream of your eventual goal—to see, feel, and hear what it would be like to succeed—using the neurolinguistic programming techniques discussed in the introduction in this book.

As shown in Exhibit 6.4, the foundation stones are the basis on which your leadership is built. It is important where possible to ensure that each one is developed and maintained. Once you have the foundation stones in place, you can use them as a platform from which to juggle your time

EXHIBIT 6.4 Serving-Leader Model

among the 12 areas of focus that characterize the servant leader. Some foundation stones and focus areas impact on the organization's culture, and this influence is marked by a C in a box.

Areas of Focus for a Serving-Leader

The concept of the serving-leader will be explained as you read on. Shackleton managed to juggle the 12 serving-leadership balls (areas) with great aplomb.

Crisis Management

CFOs will forever be hit by a crisis during their career. As CFOs we will always be asked to be the first to go in and put the fire out. How we handle this type of adversity defines us. As Tom Peters says about bad times, "I can say with conviction and confidence that this is when it gets fun for talented and imaginative leaders."[5]

Shackleton respected the old dogs (the older, more experienced employees). On all his perilous journeys where life and death were in the balance, he always had the old dogs in the advance party. He made an interesting observation one day: The old dogs ate less, complained less, slept less, and were injured less!

In today's world where recruitment often is run by young human resources officers and equally young managers, the old dogs find it hard to change jobs when they are over 50. CFOs need to ensure they have some old dogs in their accounting team.

The Boss was always thinking ahead. However, some decisions would have to be reversed on a daily basis as conditions changed. Changing circumstances constantly meant changes in what could be taken on the next leg of the return journey.

When they knew it was time to leave the breaking ice floe, the Boss had to assess what was the safest option, bearing in mind the various attributes of three potential destinations. The conditions of the men, the sea, and the fact that one lifeboat was marginally seaworthy had to be weighed. Over the course of just three days, the destination for their escape changed: Clarence Island or Elephant Island; King George Island; Hope Bay (on the Antarctic mainland); and finally, Elephant Island, where they landed safely.

The vagaries of business and an expedition are the same. You will never be able to predict the future accurately. CFOs need to provision and prepare for worst-case scenarios and accurately assess what the best options are in the given circumstances.

The Boss's sense of humor was always to the fore. He was in fact the life and soul of the group. He was constantly looking for ways to maintain morale. As Tom Peters says about bad times, "I can say with conviction and confidence that 'this is when it gets fun' for talented and imaginative leaders." CFOs need to always maintain a sense of humor when all looks lost.

Abandonment

Peter Drucker frequently used the word "abandonment." He said that "the first step in a growth policy is not to decide where and how to grow. It is to decide what to abandon. In order to grow, a business must have a systematic policy to get rid of the outgrown, the obsolete, the unproductive." He also put it another way: "Don't tell me what you're doing, tell me what you've stopped doing."

Great CFOs know when to cut their losses, admit they made an error of judgment, and move on. The act of abandonment gives a tremendous sense of relief to the CFO, and it stops the past from haunting the future. It takes courage and conviction and is a skill that one needs to nourish. I believe CFOs need to be the flag bearer of abandonment.

Knowing when to abandon and having the courage to do so are the two attributes every CFO needs. To help you know what to abandon, you need to seek advice from sages and of course your mentor. These people have been there before you and can recognize the difference between projects that you should persevere with and those that you should give up.

Recruiting Your Team

Recruiting your finance team, and particularly your direct reports, is the most important activity a CFO can ever undertake, yet so many times it is carried out in a cursory and casual manner.

The Boss chose his people carefully; he was always looking for character, competence, and multiple skills. The Boss's interview questions penetrated the individual to see if he had a positive attitude and a light-hearted, even whimsical nature. His recruitment strategy was as follows:

- "Loyalty comes easier to a cheerful person than one with a heavy countenance," in the Boss's words.
- His inner core members had to be loyal and strong leaders. The Boss knew the importance of not just leading by oneself, but ensuring leadership by others within the team.
- He set difficult tasks for the interviewees to see how keen they were to join.

■ He used trials to test whether some applicants were able to undertake the menial chores that such an expedition entailed, such as cleaning decks, sorting out tack, assisting at mealtimes, and so on.

The Boss's second in command was Frank Wild. An old dog, as the Boss would say. He was totally dedicated to acting on behalf of the Boss in his absence. He was in many respects a Shackleton clone. Wild followed the Boss on all his adventures. He started off as a seaman and became a great explorer.

The Boss and Wild were the perfect fit. Wild left the planning to the Boss and focused on maintaining a happy and friendly nature no matter what prevailed.

Abundance of Positive Energy

As Jack Welch says, it is important that a leader "has positive energy, the capacity to go-go-go with healthy vigor and an upbeat attitude through good times and bad." Based on observation, CFOs have plenty of energy; unfortunately, I cannot say that it is positive energy. For many CFOs, acquiring positive energy will require gleaning a new technique, the use of the neurolinguistic programming techniques discussed in the introduction.

Shackleton had an abundance of positive energy. He worked the hardest, slept the least, and led from the front. He was fitter than all others on the team, possibly with the exception of Wild.

The Boss never gave up: He was a believer in the principle that "there's always another move, you just have to find it." Having arrived at the whaling town in South Georgia, the Boss made four attempts to rescue the men from Elephant Island; it took another seven months to rescue his men stuck on the other side of Antarctica.

The Boss was always a purveyor of hope and optimism. When setbacks occurred, he had to remain outwardly optimistic, despite his own feelings, to prevent growing despair among his men. He knew that such despair could, in the face of adversity, lead to dissension, mutiny, or simply giving up.

The Boss loved a party. Every Saturday night the group would celebrate and toast their loved ones. Birthdays were always celebrated. Shackleton even went to the trouble of taking a Christmas pudding on the arduous walk to the then "furthest south" with Captain Robert Scott. On Christmas Day, out came the small pudding with a piece of holly. Though near starvation, he had kept this to share with Scott and his other companion.

"The Boss was so young at heart that he appeared to be younger than any of us," McIlroy (the expedition's surgeon) was quoted as saying.

Shackleton was always looking for ways to amuse his team—plays, sing-alongs, cards, football matches under moonlight.

Develop and Maintain Relationships

We are talking here about relationships with stakeholders, the SMT, fellow peers within the organization, and the many and varied contacts we have made during our career. This is an area that many CFOs are weak. Due to a heavy workload and a lack of focus, they often find themselves isolated, with an undernourished support network.

Shackleton knew that his dream of being the first to the South Pole could be achieved only through the support of the Royal Geographical Society and wealthy sponsors who needed to be inspired by the epic proportions of the enterprise. Shackleton not only was close friends with these decision makers, he was a favorite with many of their wives—his charm, good looks, and attentiveness assured a constant stream of support.

Let Psychology Be Your Friend

For a CFO to be a great leader, he or she has to really understand the staff; in fact; the CFO must be an amateur psychologist. To get to this stage requires an understanding of what makes the human being tick; see the introduction for some suggested courses that will help with this.

Shackleton was ahead of his time. He read widely in psychology and wanted on his return to England to write his thoughts on the psychology of leadership. Generations have lost much by his failure to complete this task.

His understanding of psychology played a big part in saving the lives of his team. He appreciated the importance of understanding the team's physical needs and their psychological needs.

- On the hike over the mountains of South Georgia, two team members wanted a short break. The Boss knew that would be the end of them and the crew members stuck on Elephant Island. He let the men sleep for 5 minutes and then woke them up, saying they had slept for 30 minutes.
- On the famous boat trip he took two members who would be of no use but could not be left behind. These two were the negative soothsayers who would have poisoned the minds of those left on the godforsaken Elephant Island.

- His selection of crews on the escape from the sinking ice floe took into account the dynamics of the friendships, the men's seamanship, and finally the state of the boats. One team had to handle a constantly sinking boat.

The Boss was the master of conflict resolution: He avoided emotional outbursts. He would gently point out the reason why it should be done a different way. He would tell staff off only in private, and when he did, it was normally in a careful manner.

The Boss was able to manage his anger and frustration. He had seen many times leaders letting go at their subordinates and had promised himself he never to be like that. He had the ability to choose whether he wished to get angry. When you possess this ability, you soon realize that anger does not help; the emotional damage caused by the outburst cannot be healed quickly and in some cases the damage done can never be repaired.

The Boss engaged the dissidents and avoided needless power struggles. At critical times he ensured that they shared their experiences with him rather than pollute the minds of the younger members.

Seeing the Future

The CFO as a leader is expected to spend blue-ocean time thinking about what the future may bring and prepare for expected outcomes.

Shackleton could visualize things ahead and plan accordingly. The extent of the Boss's detail in planning included:

- Different gear to avoid the problems he had experienced in past expeditions.
- Provisioning food and equipment that saved the lives of the members of the expedition many times.
- The standardization of packing cases made of a new material (plywood) that could be reused to build huts.

Shackleton's original plans were to be away for just over a year, but he had wisely provisioned for two years based on 4,000 calories a day.

Only the best was good enough for the *Endurance* expedition. New equipment never tried before was designed; backup equipment was the best that money could buy. Last but not least, the food on board was fit for a king. Unusual treats that could be stored for years were taken. In the bleakest moments, the Boss used a treat to say to his men "There is more of this when we get home."

Lack of provisioning for team members is a common failing of many managers. They expect their teams to work flat out without the correct equipment. CFOs need to put the equipment that the finance staff use high up on their agenda.

Focus on Learning and Innovation

CFOs need to be constantly focused on learning. This is made difficult by the fact many CFOs stopped regularly attending training courses when their professional body ceased to keep adequate records on members' continuing professional education. Combined with a lack of suitable courses and literature (many professional journals lack articles of interest to CFOs), often are isolated from cutting-edge developments.

Shackleton always learned from prior experiences. His experience with the expedition with Captain Scott showed him the type of leader he did *not* want to be.

Shackleton designed special clothing, the equivalent of GORE-TEX® today. He also designed a tent that could be quickly erected in a blizzard. These two innovations no doubt saved the lives of his men.

The *James Caird* lifeboat that made the crossing to South Georgia was modified, and these modifications saved the team as a 40-foot-plus rogue wave swamped the boat during the journey. The wave was so large that Shackleton at first mistook it for a cloud.

It is important for a CFO to attend a leadership course. While truly great leaders are probably born, not made, many good qualities can be embedded in one's makeup. Shackleton trained himself from being an ordinary man to becoming an exceptional leader. He learned from prior mistakes, he was a student of other explorers' experiences, and his hero was the Norwegian explorer Roald Amundsen.

It is thus for CFOs to be carefully prepared for their role. Too often today a young, bright-eyed accountant is thrust into the CFO role totally unprepared, as the board mistakenly confuses technical competence with leadership and management acumen.

Finishing What You Start

Many finance-based initiatives fail because the CFO does not get behind them enough. Many CFOs, like other members of the senior management team, have an attention deficit disorder that rivals any teenager's. An additional problem is that some projects are started that, with proper counsel, never would have left the drawing board.

Some ways you can make a difference in this area include:

- Monitor all late projects each week and make it career-limiting for project managers to be on the late project list on a regular basis.

- Have a projects-in-progress summary and review it at least twice a month, thus ensuring the projects are finished as fast as new ones are started.
- Set up a focus group workshop to assess the feasibility of all new major projects—these focus groups typically are comprised of experienced individuals across the organization. During the day they discuss the main problems, discuss the technology that is being proposed, see a presentation of the proposed new systems, and brainstorm the main hurdles the project team will need to clear. If at the end of the workshop the focus group gives the green light, you then have 20 or so sales agents for the new system around the organization.

Develop, Engage, and Trust (Your Staff)

This is a huge area of people management that is best learned attending a management/leadership training course. If you are a CFO and have not attended a weeklong course, I would recommend that this is rectified immediately.

Shackleton freely gave recognition to his staff. To him gratitude was all part of the day's work for a leader. He understood that recognition is more important than most of us understand. He knew that some members needed it more than others, and he did not worry about the potential inequality of this.

As already mentioned in this chapter, I believe that recognition is one of the most important driving forces in performance. Yet so many companies, managers, and leaders believe it has to be given sparingly, as if too much recognition would water it down. There appears to be a tax on recognition. McDonald's and other companies have taken this tax on recognition to the ultimate by having an employee of the month, indicating that only one staff member can achieve this. What does it say to the rest of the staff? Surely if four staff members succeeded, then four staff members should be given the award.

The Boss removed the barriers of rank to build cohesion. He would have loved the changes of open plan offices, rotational teams, and so on. Tasks were assigned based on an individual's skills. All members, including the Boss, did the dishes, cleaned the floor, and other tasks.

The Boss always minimized status differences and insisted on courtesy and mutual respect between all members of the team.

Shackleton had the knack of energizing others. The team members were prepared to take on any task the Boss wanted, as they knew he would be in the line with them, whether it was the fruitless one of spending weeks trying to break the ship free from the ice, hauling the lifeboats over the ice floe, or the seemingly impossible transverse of South Georgia.

Great leaders care about their staff. The Boss devised many activities on the ice floe to keep the team in good health. Health, fitness, and general well-being of accounting team is a core value some CFOs pursue vigorously and other CFOs merely pay lip service to.

Shackleton spent time with each member of his team to find out what made them tick, how he could best lead them, and how he could serve them. He went to great lengths to suit tasks to individual capabilities and personalities. While stuck on the ice, the Boss ensured that all team members were occupied in relevant activities. "He never expects one to do more than one is capable of."

This model is very different from a common approach used by CFOs of throwing staff in the deep end and seeing who can swim. These same CFOs, not surprisingly, then complain about the high staff turnover.

Valuing Results and People

Many senior managers, CFOs, and CEOs have presided over organizations where staff have been killed or staff have had to take unnecessary risks. Some examples are: making staff drive long distances after working 12 hours, demanding that a chartered flight go when the pilot has warned that it is too risky, or sending staff to war-torn countries with inadequate support or training or without a functional escape plan.

The Boss valued life. No goal or target was worth the loss of life. History proves that Shackleton would never attempt a goal if the return journey was not guaranteed. He could have been the first to the Pole, but he knew that he and his men would have died reaching it.

Gather and Learn From Experiences

To be a CFO, you will have acquired a variety of experiences. The important thing is to learn from these experiences and to seek help when confronted with new circumstances. A discussion with a wise CFO (a mentor), who has been there before, will ensure you can benefit from their experience and lessons learned, thus avoiding the same mistakes yourself.

From an early age, Shackleton looked for experience. At the age of 14, he was a cabin boy on his first sea voyage. He learned from working with both great and not-so-great captains. He sought to go on as many polar adventures as he could, to prepare himself to get to the South Pole.

A Viking with a Mother's Heart

The Boss looked after the comforts of the team. He was a mother hen. He genuinely cared for his team members as if they were his own flesh and blood. He saw a leader as one who served rather than one who was served.

EXHIBIT 6.5 Checklist for Locking in Good Leadership Habits

	1	2	3	4	5	6	7	8	9	10	11	12	13
1. Have you done a few walks around the office this week? (target daily when in the company of staff)													
2. Have you found out about a staff member's life, needs, ambitions this week? (target one staff member a week)													
3. Have you looked at one team member this week to see how you can suit tasks to his or her capabilities and personality?													
4. Have you demonstrated, by an action/deed, your concern over the welfare of your staff this week?													
5. Have you demonstrated "*bostmanship*" this week??													
6. Have you thanked someone this week?													
7. Have you shown your humorous side to staff this week?													
8. Have you read a management article, a chapter in a development book this week?													
9. Have you met your mentor this week? (target at least every two weeks during change process)													
10. Have you approved an innovation to be implemented this week? (target is ten a year per every staff member)													
11. Have you set realistic and acheivable goals for your staff this week?													
12. Have you performed tasks this week to improve public perception? (speaking engagement, press release, acted on a professional body or charity, etc.) (target at least two actions a month)													
13. Have you had a one-to-one with all of your direct reports this week?													

14. Have your supported your second-in-command this week?																
15. Have you been conveying positive energy and optimism this week?																
16. Have you personally orchestrated a celebration this week?																
17. Have you been involved in some future-gazing this week to ensure you have thought of options if circumstances change?																
18. Have you ensured that difficult and complex assignments have a few "old dogs" in the team?																
19. Have you promoted any health initiative? (target at least one per month)																
20. Have you invested time developing your staff? (target one person a week whose training will be influenced positively by what you have actioned)																
21. Have you taken measures to reduce risk of injury in your organization by observing and thinking about safer alternatives?																
22. Have you practiced this week any new understanding of psychology? (e.g., in the way you act with your staff)																
23. Have you been active in recruitment process of staff? (weekly involvement)																
24. Have you "energized" any of the team this week, using a Shackleton approach?																
25. Have you coached any young leaders this week? (target two a month)																

(Continued)

113

EXHIBIT 6.5 (*Continued*)

26. Have you introduced the book *Shackleton Way* to your direct reports? (quarterly reminder)																	
27. Have you spent time this week thinking about the future?																	
28. Have you undertaken actions this week that clearly demonstrate the values the organization has?																	
29. Have you met an adversary this week to develop a better understanding?																	
30. Have you consulted with your *sandpaper* mentors this week?																	
31. Have you spent some time developing your safe heaven this week?																	
32. Have you managed any crisis well this week?																	
33. Have you abandoned something in the last fortnight/month?																	
34. Have you been "*young at heart*" this week?																	
35. Have you avoided emotional outbursts this week?																	
36. Have you been bold in planning but careful in execution this week?																	
37. Have you practices a leadership trait this week?																	
38. Have you ensured the activities for next week/next fortnight are aligned with the organization's mission, vision, values and strategy?																	
39. Have you linked into the critical success factors of the organization this week?																	
40. Have you thought more about what is your "*legacy*" this week?																	

Source: Used with permission. David Parmenter, *Leading Edge Managers Guide to Success* (Hoboken NJ: John Wiley & Sons, 2011)

He dutifully took his turn performing the most menial of chores and expected his leadership team to do the same. A member of the *Endurance* expedition described him as "a Viking with a mother's heart." This sums up beautifully what a serving-leader is.

Ken Blanchard and Mark Miller's book *The Secret*[6] neatly records that a leader exists to serve others rather than to be served. The Boss would be the first to nurse an ailing member or to make a cup of tea if he knew his staff were at the end of their tether.

CFOs need to perceive this kind of voluntary servitude as an *asset*, not a weakness.

Three-Month Planner

Set out in Exhibit 6.5 is a planner that will get you started on a journey to become a servant-leader.

Notes

1. David Parmenter, *Leading Edge Managers Guide to Success* (Hoboken, NJ: John Wiley & Sons, 2011).
2. Ibid.
3. Margot Morrell and Stephanie Capparell, *Shackleton's Way—Leadership Lessons from the Great Antarctic Explorer* (New York: Penguin, 2002).
4. Ernest Shackleton, *South: The Endurance Expedition* (New York: Penguin Classics, 2004).
5. Tom Peters, "Thriving on Chaos: Bold Leaders Gain Advantage," *Leadership Excellence* (February 2010).
6. Ken Blanchard and Mark R. Miller, *The Secret: What Great Leaders Know—And Do*, 2nd ed. (San Francisco: Berrett-Koehler, 2009).

CHAPTER 7

Quick Annual Reporting: Within 15 Working Days Post Year-End

The annual reporting activity is part of the trifecta of lost opportunities. While annual reporting is an important legal requirement, it does not create any value within your organization, and thus seldom is it a task where your team has received any form of gratitude. Accounting functions therefore need to find ways to extract value from the process while at the same time bringing it down into a tight time frame.

Before you can have a quick year-end, you need to speed up month-end reporting monthly so staff are disciplined to a tight month-end. Your goal should be reporting monthly numbers and comments by day 3 (see Chapter 2 on quick month-end reporting).

This chapter is an extract from a white paper[1] I deliver around the world that has revolutionized many finance team's year-end processes.

Costs of a Slow Year-End

The costs of a slow year-end include:

- Months where the accounting team is simply doing annual and monthly reporting—thus little added value is created by the finance team in that time.
- Too much time going into the annual report as we lose sight of Pareto's 80/20 principle.
- Little or no client management during this time, and thus bad habits are picked up by budget holders.

Accounting teams are often hijacked "by the annual reporting process."
CFO with blue chip international experience

Given the amount of time this activity takes, the 80/20 rule still applies.
Most organizations look at the annual report financials as being
"special" numbers that they have reworked many times. There is abso-
lutely no reason in 99 percent of the cases why the "first cut" of year-end
for internal reporting should not be the same as the last cut for external
reporting. Most adjustments are trivial and result in printing delays. The
annual report comes out so late virtually nobody reads it anyway!"
CFO with blue chip international experience

There are many ways in which we can improve the way we do year-
end, and they can all be grouped around three words:

1. **Organization.** Establish an audit coordinator, the working paper files,
   the deadlines, and so on.
2. **Communication.** Communicate with both the auditors and staff.
3. **Pre–year-end work.** Bring forward many year-end routines earlier,
   such as cutting off at month 10 or 11 and rolling forward. This also
   includes preparing a comprehensive auditors' file, saving the audit team
   considerable time.

Cost the Annual Accounts Process

In order to create a change in the way the senior management team (SMT),
board, and management address the annual accounts, you need to establish
what is the full cost of the annual accounts process, including all board,
management, and staff time, and all external costs (audit fees, printing
costs, public relations, and legal fees, etc.).

Exhibit 7.1 shows how to calculate the costs of an annual accounts
process. The times are estimates and show what a 300- to 500-member
full-time employee public company may be investing in its annual report
preparation. It does not include investor relations and so forth. The SMT
has lower productive weeks in a year because you have to take out, in
addition to holidays, training, and sick leave, the time they spend traveling
and in general meetings.

A Quick Year-End Is a Good Year-End

Exhibit 7.2 shows a rating scale for the time frames to have an audited and
signed annual report (time from year-end date).

	Accounting Team	Budget Holders	SMT
Liaison with auditors throughout audit	3–5		1–2
Planning audit	1–3		
Interim audit assistance	4–6	20–40	
Preparing annual accounts	2–5		
Preparing audit schedules	2–5		
Extra work finalizing year-end numbers	20–30		
Final audit visit assistance	10–20	20–40	
Finalizing annual report	10–20		5–8
Total weeks of effort	52–94	40–80	6–10
Average salary cost	$80,000	$55,000	$200,000
Average productive weeks	42	42	32

	Low	High
Average personnel cost	$190,000	$350,000
Printing costs	45,000	75,000
Audit fees	45,000	65,000
Estimated cost	$280,000	$490,000

EXHIBIT 7.1 Cost of the Annual Accounts Process

EXHIBIT 7.2 Year-End Reporting Time Frames (from the Year-End to Signed Annual Report)

Exceptional	Outstanding	Above Average	Average
Less than 10 working days	10–15 working days	16–20 working days	21–30 working days

Many top U.S. companies report very quickly to the stock exchange. In my days as an auditor, IBM was well known for its speed of reporting.

If your organization reports very quickly at year-end, ignore this section; otherwise, read and implement, as you and your organization are wasting too much time in this area. There are a number of benefits, including:

- Better value from the interim and final audit visits
- Improved data quality through improved processing
- Reduced costs, both audit and staff time
- More time for finance staff for critical activities, such as analysis, decision making, and forecasting
- Improved investor relations

Help Get the Auditors Organized

An audit can very easily get disorganized. The audit firm will more than likely have a change in either the audit senior or audit staff, and first-year staff members will know little about what they are trying to audit, no matter what training they have had.

So, help the audit team (it is in your interests) by:

- Allocating appropriate facilities for the audit room (desks, phones, security).
- Providing an induction session for new audit staff, as up to 40 percent of junior audit time is wasted in an unknown environment.
- Preparing a financial statement file and handing it over on day 1 of the final visit. (This file will contain papers supporting all numbers in the financial statements, including completed audit lead schedules ready for the auditors' papers, 12 months of monthly reports, etc.)
- Advising staff to assist the auditors and having a specific person in every section who should be contacted first should the auditors need assistance.
- Holding meetings at key times with the auditors (e.g., the planning meeting, the interim meeting, and the meetings to discuss the final results). The steps in each of these stages are set out and analyzed in detail in the annual accounts checklist in Appendix D.

Appoint an Audit Coordinator

The first step to improving communication between staff and the audit team is to have a full-time audit coordinator. This person should be a staff member, not necessarily in finance, who knows most people in the company and knows where everything is, in other words, "an oracle."

You may find the ideal person is someone in accounts payable or someone who has recently retired. The important point is that the individual should have no other duties during the audit visits (both interim and final) than helping the audit team. Give the individual a nice room and say, "When not helping the audit team, you can simply put your feet up." Do not get tempted to give the person additional duties. The audit coordinator's tasks include:

- Providing an induction session for new audit staff
- Gathering any vouchers, and so forth, that the auditors need
- Responding to information requests the auditors have made that are still outstanding

- Setting up designated contact points in every function (e.g., whom to speak to in the marketing department)
- Organizing meetings with the designated person in the section they need to visit
- Arranging meetings at key times between the CFO and the auditors

Complete the Drafting of the Annual Report before Year-End

It is desirable to complete the annual report, other than the final year's result, by the middle of month 12. This will require coordination with the public relations consultant who drafts the written commentary in the annual accounts and discussions with the chairman of the board and the CEO. Your last month's numbers will not greatly impact the commentary.

Also remember that nobody reads the annual report. If you are a publicly listed company, stockbroker analysts rely on the more in-depth briefing you give them, shareholders in the main do not understand the report, and the accounting profession just skims it.

Limit when Changes Can Be Made

It is important to be disciplined about cut-offs and when journal vouchers can be processed. One company I know allows only three opportunities to adjust the year-end numbers, and one of them is for the final tax numbers. The stages are:

Stage 1: Close of the second working day
Stage 2: Sixth working day
Stage 3: Tax entries only

The best advice is to make your month 12 numbers your final-year numbers. Run an "overs and unders" schedule as shown in Exhibit 7.3. This works particularly well when you have shortened the period the auditors have post year-end.

Negotiate and Plan for a Sign-off by the Auditors within 15 Working Days

Most auditors have already signed a set of audited accounts quickly. Sometimes it is because the companies wish to seek additional finance or

EXHIBIT 7.3 "Overs and Unders" Schedule

Source	Raised by	JV #	Adjustment		Profit/ Loss Impact		Balance Sheet Impact	
					Dr	Cr	Dr	Cr
xxxxx	Pat	1	Dr	xxxxxxxxx xxxxx xxxx	45			
			Cr	xxxx xxxxx xxxxx		45		
xxxxx	John	2	Dr	xxxx xxxx	10			
			Cr	xx x x xxxxxxxxx		10		
xxxxx	Jean	3	Dr	xxxx xxxx	25			
			Cr	xx x x xxxxxxxxx				25
xxxxx	Dave	4	Dr	xxxx xxxx	15			
			Cr	xx x x xxxxxxxxx		15		
		etc.						
					80	70		
					−70			
				Net impact on P/L	10			

want to be seen as a leading organization. The auditors have standard processes in these events. The benefits include:

- A level playing field—you have closed the numbers quickly and they also have to report back quickly.
- Any dirty washing is not hanging on the line for very long—the auditors do not have the benefit of three to six months of hindsight to say "Why did you not find this, and so forth?"
- It encourages good practices, such as using the Pareto 80/20 rule, Post-it reengineering of year-end processes, a hard close at month 11, and so on.

Have a Month 10 or 11 Hard Close

The larger and more complex the organization is, the greater the need for a hard close at month 10 results. All other organizations should go for a hard close at month 11. Effectively, month 11 becomes the year-end, with all major assets, such as debtors, stock, and fixed assets, being verified. If a debtors' circularization is to be performed, this will need to be performed on month 9 or 10 balances, thus allowing enough time for responses. Once the auditors have confirmed that the stock, fixed assets, and debtors' balances are a true and fair view, the auditors need only to confirm the movements of these balances in the remaining month or two.

Effective Stock Takes

Stock takes should never be conducted at any month-end, let alone at year-end. There is no need to do this, as your stock records should be able to be verified at any point in time. It is a better practice to conduct rolling stock counts rather than one major count that closes all production. A well-organized stock take includes:

- Trained stock takers working in pairs, each from a different department, to enhance independence and thoroughness.
- Highlighting obsolescent stocks, which can be targeted in the preceding months to reduce the write-down at year-end.
- Rolling stock inventory (counts) throughout the year (e.g., a jewelry company with a chain of stores counts watches one month), in rings the next month, in the quiet times during the month.
- Ensuring the stock area is clean and organized before the counting, to ensure a more accurate count (e.g., same stock items are together).
- Adding visible tags to counted items.
- Having a good celebration once the count has been done (this will ensure willing helpers next time).

Estimating Added Value in Work in Progress and Finished Goods

Auditors can get lost very easily in auditing the added value in work in progress (WIP) and finished goods. On one audit it took me a couple of weeks of elapsed time to trace the WIP through its stages, using random samples.

In the second year it was suggested that I look at how many weeks of production there were in WIP, which was easy to confirm, then at how much direct and indirect overhead could and should be absorbed. The audit of WIP took two days.

Thus, help your auditors see the forest for the trees and provide working papers to support complex valuations such as WIP.

Effective Fixed Asset Verification

The key to better use of the fixed asset register (FAR) is change in attitude. Many finance teams see the FAR as a necessary evil, and thus little focus is given to really driving it properly. The rare few grab the opportunity and turn the FAR into a valuable system by:

- Using bar codes on all assets so asset verification is a paperless exercise with a scanner.
- Setting higher capitalization levels than those stated by the tax authorities, radically reducing the volume in the FAR—it being recognized that a tax adjustment can be performed easily, if necessary.
- Logging maintenance for key plant as well as the up-to-date expected life, so useful graphics of expected lives of key assets can be shown to the board.
- Reducing the number of fixed asset categories, as every extra coding serves only to create more chances for miscoding (remember that we are to apply Pareto's 80/20 rule).
- Performing rolling fixed asset counts rather than doing it all at one time (e.g., verify equipment in the factory this month, computer equipment next month, etc.).

Importance of the Internal Auditors

The internal auditors can significantly reduce the external auditors' work. Many organizations contract out this function to an independent firm. I believe an in-house internal audit team will pay for themselves many times over by:

- Increasing the use of efficient and effective procedures.
- Providing a great training ground for new graduate staff.
- Focusing on reengineering exercises and other revenue-generating or cost-saving activities (e.g., in a one-week exercise, most internal auditors would be able to save 5 percent off the future telecommunication costs).
- Providing the external auditors with all their main working papers filled out—the internal auditors will know how to do this if they have attended the external auditors' staff training courses.

Extract More Value from the Management Letter

It is important that you insist that the auditors put a bit more care and attention into the management letters and that they are delivered within two weeks of the interim and final visits. Prompt management letters mean that management can rectify a problem immediately.

A minor comment about a procedural failure can easily be taken out of context by the board. All errors that management wants to comment on should be stated in context (e.g., We found 20 invoices with the wrong prices, we understand this was because. . . . Management has rectified the situation and we tested a further sample of xxxx and found no further errors. We note that of all the other price tests we performed, there were no other errors. We do not believe this has led to a loss of profits greater than $xxxx.).

Also we want the auditors to comment on our strengths (e.g., We would like to comment that the new monthly report formats are the best we have seen; they are clear, concise, and cost effective in terms of production time).

> *During the audit we commented to the auditors that we had found a better way of carrying out a process. They turned around this knowledge and noted the current process as a weakness in the management letter when in fact it had not created a problem. I blew up the audit partner and they apologized and removed comment.*
>
> *CFO with blue chip international experience*

Derive More Value from the Interim Audit

In conjunction with the external auditors, look at making more use out of the interim audit. You may have implemented a new expense system, so ask the auditors to spend some time testing compliance. Ask them to cover more branches, ensuring nearly all branches are covered every two years. This will cost more but will be worthwhile. Always remember that it is perception that rules the roost; staff members in remote branches will begin to conform to company policies if they know that auditors are to arrive and that they always test the compliance of the key systems along with all the new systems.

It is a good practice to have (before year-end) the first interim visit in the first half of the year assuring the organization's staff maintain a vigilance on compliance.

Run a Workshop to Post-it Reengineer Year-End Reporting

The Post-it reengineering exercise is very similar to the month-end process reengineering. To assist you, I have drafted a set of workshop instructions in Exhibit 7.4. You will need to refer the section "Some Tips on Running a Post-it Reengineering Session" in Chapter 2. The only difference is:

- The time scale is week −2, week −1 (last week before year-end), week +1 (first week after year-end), week +2 instead of day −2, day −1, etc., see Exhibit 7.5.
- There will be different attendees at the workshop.

EXHIBIT 7.4 Outline of Workshop on Implementing Quick Annual Reporting within Existing System Constraints

Agenda and Outline of the Quick Year-End Workshop

Date and Time: xxxxxx

Location: xxxxxx

Suggested Attendees: All those involved in year-end reporting including accounts payable, accounts receivable, fixed assets, financial and management accountants, representatives from team's interface with year-end routines (e.g., someone from information technology, payroll, public relations, auditors (audit partner/manager) etc.

Learning Outcomes:
Attendees after this workshop will be able to:
- Discuss and explain to management why their organization should have quicker year-end reporting.
- Use better practices to streamline their current bottlenecks.
- Use a step-by-step implementation framework.
- Describe better practice year-end routines.
- Recall all agreements made at the workshop (these will be documented).

9:00 A.M.	Welcome by CFO/Financial Controller
9:10 A.M.	**Setting the scene**—a review of better practices among accounting teams that are delivering swift annual reporting; topics covered include:

- What is quick year-end reporting?
- Benefits of quick annual reporting to management and the finance team
- Better practice year-end procedures—stories
- Current performance gap between xxxxxxxxx and better practice
- Precision versus timeliness

Senior management, PR expert involved in annual report, representative from the legal team, and a selection of budget holders (who are locally based) will be invited to attend this session

9:50 A.M.   Agreement on the current key bottlenecks of year-end reporting presented by CFO/Financial Controller
- Current cost estimate of year-end reporting
- Human cost of the annual accounts process (weekends and late nights worked)
- What we are doing well
- We need to work within existing systems
- Goal is "signed annual accounts by 15 working days"

EXHIBIT 7.4 *(Continued)*

10:05 A.M.	**Workshop 1 to analyze the year-end procedures using Post-its** (yellow—accounts payable, green—accounts receivable, red—production, purple—annual report, blue—finance accounting team, CAPEX—pink, management accounting team—light yellow, etc.)
10:30 A.M.	Morning break
10:45 A.M.	**Workshop 1 continues**
11:20 A.M.	Feedback and pulling it together. Participants will document agreed changes and individuals will be encouraged to take responsibility for implementing the steps.
12:00 P.M.	**Workshop 2 to set out the appropriate implementation steps to implement quick annual reporting.** Each team prepares a short presentation of the key steps they are committed to making (teams will use PowerPoint on laptops).
12:30 P.M.	Lunch
1:15 P.M.	**Workshop 2 continues**
2:00 P.M.	Each team presents reports to the group what changes it is going to implement and when. Each can also raise any issues it still has.
	The members of the senior management team and budget holders who attended the first session will be invited to attend this session
2:30 P.M.	Wrap-up of workshop by Financial Controller
2:45 P.M.	Finish

EXHIBIT 7.5 Demonstration of Post-it Notes

- The auditor partner is invited to attend along with a member of the board.
- You are aiming to be done by week 3 instead of day 3.

Restrict Access to Confidential Information to the Audit Partner

It is important to inform the staff and audit team about what is subject to restricted access (e.g., it may be that only the audit partner is able to see the SMT's payroll). I remember the days when the audit team would fight over who was to look at payroll; just remember, it is human nature to be nosy. Make it clear to the audit manager that only they are to review the senior management team's payroll etc.

Speeding Up the Reporting Supply Chain

In order to achieve a fast year-end, Excel has to be replaced by 21st-century systems. There are several potential areas to consider if an organization is to achieve substantial time savings in the reporting supply chain.

The main areas to tackle here include:

- Data capture from reporting entities (including minimizing their returns).
- Mapping to group systems and control.
- "Last-mile" information handling.

Data Capture from Reporting Entities

Those of us who have reported to a finance department in an international conglomerate will know that the reporting pack was designed by a rocket scientist without any regard to materiality. Endless pages of data are gathered and sent, most of it meaningless. "It could be useful to have this," "Better ask for that in case I might get a question." The result is hours upon hours spent around the world gathering this data, which, by the way, is never used by the subsidiaries to manage their business.

How did this happen? First, the CFO delegated the task and then took little or no interest in the eventual monster. The CFO may have observed, "The reporting pack looks a bit large. Are you sure you need all of this information?" Second, nobody ever calculated the data-gathering process and compared it against the benefit/usage. If this task was done, common sense would have won out. Third, there are seldom effective forums for management accountants in the subsidiaries to challenge those in the head office by saying "Why do you need this?" or "Tell me what you do with all of this."

The chart of accounts also creates problems. In his recent book,[2] Jeremy Hope of *Beyond Budgeting* fame talks about leading companies having fewer than 50 buckets for the profit and loss expenditure. These companies recognize that it is far more efficient to delve into these buckets when you need to than to have a myriad of codes that increase mispostings exponentially.

> *Collecting data from subsidiaries has always been fraught with diffi- culty. The heterogeneous nature of the many global businesses, reflected in their diverse operational systems and chart of accounts, has acted as a significant drag on the reporting supply chain (RSC) as group finance grapple with a multitude of different systems interfaces.*
>
> Gary Simon, *author of* Fast Close to the Max

Mapping to Group Systems and Control

Often the mapping of data from reporting entities involves extensive manual procedures, spreadsheets, and the batch transfer of files, all of which introduce the potential for serious error every step of the way. It is often very difficult to spot these errors, which have a nasty habit of rearing their ugly heads during the final audit.

In addition, the scope for mistakes increases by the number of entities involved and the frequency of changes in the group's reporting pack, brought about by management accountants having brain waves and the need to meet regulatory changes.

"Last-Mile" Information Handling

The efficient marshaling of information postconsolidation is vital and is known as the last mile in annual reporting. In the last mile, there are PDF files, spreadsheets, PowerPoint slides, Word documents, and email communications, all of which provide input for the notes to the annual accounts. It is important that they are accessible to all those on the annual accounts team rather than residing in individuals' email in-boxes and C drives.

Moving Forward

There are a variety of actions that need to take place in order to move forward. They include:

- Establish tight rules on permitting an account code in the chart of accounts by applying the 1 percent rule for expenditure and the 3 percent rule for revenue, explained in Chapter 13.
- Have a forum where all senior management accountants from around the world meet to discuss the adoption of better practices from winning finance teams.
- Acquire intercompany software where one party does the accounting for both parties regardless of the general ledgers they are both running.
- Acquire a consolidation package.
- Acquire or set up an in-house a system to trap, centrally, all information flows in the last mile.

A fast-close project at Henkel took a giant step forward when managers at the $13 billion maker of toiletries, home-care products, and industrial goods began using web-based software for intercompany reconciliations. "Having web-enabled software for intercompany reconciliations is a great way to let managers anywhere in the company see their receivables against the liabilities of their partners within Henkel. The software—combined with tougher guidelines in terms of what the 280 reporting units are allowed to book and when—has really reduced the obstacles that were slowing down our closing process."

Matthias Schmidt, vice president of financial planning and control

Some Case Studies

- AT&T has its financial results available by the fourth working day. The organization has a month 10 close, with full stock inventory taken at the end of month 10. The auditors audit the 10 months and then the remaining 2 months. They ensure that comprehensive coordination and communication exist between the company and the auditors.
- One government agency had its annual accounts completed by working day 15, signed by directors on working day 18, and signed off by the auditors on the 20th working day. This pace was required because of a major refinancing deal.
- One finance company completed its annual accounts in 24 working days; it had only three opportunities or stages for adjustment:
  Stage 1: at the close of the second working day
  Stage 2: on the sixth working day
  Stage 3: for tax entries only
  Within these deadlines, it completed three reporting packs for its overseas parent.

- One public sector hospital ensures a smooth year-end by providing the external auditors with comprehensive end-of-year files. The finance staff completes lead schedules, provides copies of key documentation, and provides analytical review comments and copies of every month's accounts. The audit is completed within two weeks by an audit team of three people. The finance team raised 20 key accounting issues prior to year-end and sought the audit team's judgment. The finance team also ensures the management letter is more constructive, including both positive comments as well as areas for improvement.

Notes

1. David Parmenter, "*Quick Annual Reporting: Within 15 Working Days Post Year-End*," www.davidparmenter.com, 2010.
2. Jeremy Hope, *Reinventing the CFO: How Financial Managers Can Transform Their Roles and Add Greater Value* (Boston: Harvard Business Press, 2006).

CHAPTER 8

Managing Your Accounts Receivable

M any books have been written on debt management and collection practices. This chapter assumes that your accounts receivable staff have read some of them or attended a workshop on the subject.

Operational Improvements to Accounts Receivable

Some better practices you may wish to adopt are:

- Have the right mental attitude about credit control (e.g., do not feel guilty asking for money—it is yours and you are entitled to it; and when asking for your money, be hard on the issue but soft on the person).
- Provide immediate notice of overdue debt to the sales team.
- Establish clear credit practices and communicate these credit practices to staff and customers.
- Be professional when accepting new accounts, especially larger ones (e.g., perform the credit checks that a bank would when lending the same amount).
- Continuously review credit limits, especially for major customers, if tough times are coming or if operating in a volatile sector.
- Monitor sales invoicing promptness and accuracy.
- Charge penalties on overdue accounts.
- Consider accepting credit cards for smaller high-risk customers.

  People will take as much credit as you give—and that doesn't mean what your credit policy allows, it means what you let them take.

A lot of bad practice has grown around the giving and taking of credit. Conventional wisdom says that the less credit you give and the more you take, the better off you are. However, this ignores the real overhead cost created by tracking and reconciling "overdues" and outstandings. It also makes your suppliers dislike you. They won't support you when you need them if you constantly pay late. Credit is best minimized on both sides. Demand quick payment and provide incentives. Pay your bills right away. Your administration costs will fall!!

CFO with blue chip international experience

Reporting on Your Accounts Receivable

The graph shown in Exhibit 8.1 will reduce much of the need for a larger debtor report. This exhibit focuses on debtors' aging trend. You need to go back at least 12 months, preferably 15 to 18 months' to catch the impact of last year's seasonal fluctuations.

Avoiding Accounts Receivable Month-End Processing Bottlenecks

Once again, electronic interfaces with key customers and electronic cash receipting are the keys to moving out of the processing battle at month-end within accounts receivable. Some better practices are:

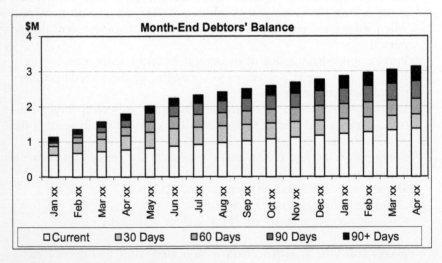

EXHIBIT 8.1 Aged Debtors over Time

- Cut off accounts receivable at noon on the last working day, with the afternoon sales being dated as the first day of the new month—you will need to ensure that customers still pay invoices according to your terms.
- Change the sales invoice cycle for all "monthly sales invoices" to customers (e.g., May 26 to June 25).
- Consider invoicing all transactions to the 25th of the month, with a second invoice for the remaining period of the month.
- Send electronic invoices to your major customers, including their general ledger codes—the easier you make it for them, the better for both parties.
- If you need details from subcontractors in order to invoice, look to streamline processes in a meeting between your customers and your main subcontractors to ensure a prompt and accurate billing process.
- If you have a lot of subcontractors, consider offering them a free accounting system that has an automatic link to yours for all invoices relevant to you.

Increasing the Use of Direct Debiting of Customers' Accounts

My father walks into town to pay many of his bills by check. It is good exercise and an excuse to get out of the house. However, this activity is very costly to the receipting supplier, typically some utility. Many companies have tried in vain to get customers to allow them access to customer bank accounts. There are many hurdles to cross, including customers' perception that their bank accounts are now at the mercy of another company. Some of the better practices to sell this change are:

- Offer a cash draw each month financed by the cash flow savings from receiving prompt payment. One telecommunications company offers three $10,000 prizes each month. My father would sign up for this.
- Offer to waive your next price increase for all those who sign up for direct debiting.
- Offer a direct debiting discount each month on the total invoice, splitting the benefit you gain between you and the customer. You can make this appear more attractive by offering a large discount on a small fixed-price component of the transaction (e.g., one energy retailer gave a 20 percent discount on the fixed charges, which was only $4 per customer, for every month where a direct debiting authorization was present).

Debtors' Collection before Year-End

While debtors should be a focus all year round, and in some cases involve the CFO and CEO in direct contact with their counterparts, there needs to be an added drive from month 9 onward to clean up everything over 60 days old. A phone call from your CEO to the other CEO could save thousands of legal fees and possibly the whole debt, if you collect it before the company has gone into receivership.

Remember, if it takes 10 hours of CFO time to collect $50,000 from a high-risk account, that is a very good return on time—$5,000 per hour.

CHAPTER 9

Marketing the Accounting Team

A ccounting teams can never do enough marketing. Lack of marketing is the main reason why accounting teams are not appreciated fully by management and why many accounting team implementations take longer and are less successful than anticipated. If accountants were good marketers, many may well have chosen a different career path. It is important to recognize these shortcomings and to fill the gap with expert advice. Find yourself a marketing mentor, touch base with your in-house public relations (PR) expert, or acquire some PR external advice—you will not regret it.

Some ways you can improve your marketing of your team are:

- Have informative intranet pages, including success stories and the photos and short-form CVs of all of the accounting team members (see Exhibit 9.1 for an example of a team's intranet page).
- Walk about more—encourage the management and financial accountants, accounts payable staff, and so forth to spend more time on proactive visits.
- Ensure someone from the finance team is attending corporate functions.
- Contribute to your organization's newsletter.
- Spend time adding value to the senior management team by increasing their understanding of the business.
- Run "coffee for a cause" events where the finance team organizes a coffee break to raise funds for a local charity, and budget holders donate a dollar or so and enjoy some hospitality at the finance team's office.

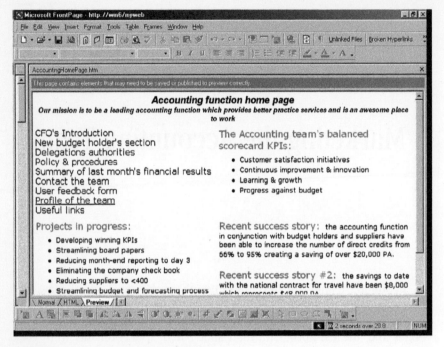

EXHIBIT 9.1 Team's Intranet Site Example

- Use morning or afternoon break times for networking with budget holders and other stakeholders.
- Make the revenue forecasting process a good way to learn about what your major customers need from your organization.
- Invite new staff from major subsidiaries or departments to call in when they are next in the head office.

Fitting into the Wider Team

Why is it that many hardworking corporate accountants who are dedicated to the organization are at best ignored or at worst ostracized by their colleagues? Some of the reasons are:

- They are workaholics who make all others feel inferior.
- They undertake tasks in such detail that they make work for their team members and colleagues.
- They are always complaining about being overworked, albeit most of their excess workload is self-inflicted.

- They seldom take time out to network.
- They treat every activity as if their life depended on it.
- They are too intense, often boring others with unnecessary detail.

If you are one of these people, there is time to change before it is too late. I suggest taking these actions:

- Limit your working hours to no more than 50 hours a week to ensure that you have to change your habits.
- Ensure that you network with your peers and in-house clients, over a coffee in an outside location, at least twice a week for the next 12 weeks.
- Before embarking on a major project, speak to your mentor, as you may well be on the wrong track.
- Have a makeover so you look and feel like a million dollars.
- Ensure that you talk positively to others. (Popular people are seldom the fountains of negative thoughts—learn to keep these to yourself.)
- Avoid writing long reports, as nothing was ever changed by a report; it was the follow-up action that made the change.
- No matter how much pressure you are under, learn to smile every time someone comes to your desk. (This needs plenty of practice.)
- Remember to always try to see the bigger picture—nobody, to my knowledge, ever died because a corporate accountant's work was late; fortunately or unfortunately, our work is not that important.
- Learn to give recognitions more freely.

CHAPTER 10

Client Management: Improving Relationships with Budget Holders

The accounting teams need to focus much more on client management. Too much time is spent sitting behind a desk instead of scoring goals in front of managers and the senior management team (SMT). Accountants need to be business advisors first.

Here are some ways you can improve your relationships with budget holders:

- Give them new insights into their operations.
- Include trend information (rolling 15- or 24-month graphs) and key performance indicators in the reporting.
- Talk through the monthly results with them—they might not understand the reports.
- Provide training sessions for budget holders' staff.
- Introduce a new cost-saving initiative each month.
- Help budget holders with their new reforecast—you can expand your team temporarily for this purpose.
- Help budget holders with bringing forward projects.
- Run a satisfaction survey on your in-house customers and implement the recommendations.
- Give a bottle of wine to the first budget holder to submit a correct monthly return.

Perform an In-House Customer Satisfaction Survey

Initially once a year and then twice a year, run a statistically based sample survey on your in-house customers. Send the survey set out in Appendix K. The key features are:

EXHIBIT 10.1 Extract from a Commentary Section Showing Identification of
Comments

Judgment on Comment	Comment
Customer focus	Staff prepared to go the extra mile
	Helpful (trying to be)
	Good PA
	Good ability to respond to circumstances and needs that change rapidly
	Fairness and courtesy to all
	Staff willingness and very positive attitude
	Supportive well-trained support staff
	Client focus and we give all parties more than reasonable time and attention
	If there are upsets, there is usually immediate attention by senior staff
	Pleasant and efficient staff
Communication	Initiatives to improve communication within the xxxxxxxx have been positively received and changes (for the better) have been made
	Good communications
	Good liaison with the xxxxx and xxxxx
	My staff were not told that they were not needed for the meeting in xxxxxxx when it was cancelled. Much time was wasted!
Database	Improvements of the database are overdue
	Computer database inadequacies are causing major problems for us

- Ask two open-ended questions that will generate most of the benefit of the survey: "What are the three things we do well?" and "What are the three things we can improve on?" Never ask about the problems, as half of them will not be fixable.
- Categorize all responses to these questions in a database and sort by positive comments and suggestions for improvement (see Exhibit 10.1).
- Use a five-point scale (5 = very satisfied, 4 = satisfied, 3 = neither satisfied nor dissatisfied, 2 = dissatisfied, 1 = very dissatisfied, X = not applicable/cannot rate).
- Separate accounting system dramas from the services your team provides by asking a series of system-related questions.
- Send the survey by email or use a web-based survey package.

■ Never ask questions whose answers you will not act on; in other words, make the questionnaire simple and able to be completed in ten minutes.

One CFO who has experience with running satisfaction surveys wanted to improve results. So he went around to every budget holder and member of the senior management team and asked, "What would the finance team need to do to get at least a very good rating from you on services our team provides?" Surprise, surprise, the team listened, actioned the suggestions, and in the next survey they got the best result out of all teams.

CFO from the electricity sector

CHAPTER 11

More Emphasis on Daily and Weekly Reporting

Why is the monthly reporting so important? For leading organizations, decision-based information is based around daily/weekly information on progress within the important areas of the business. In these organizations, the month-end has become less important, and consequently the management papers have been reduced to 15 pages or less.

In one company the senior management team (SMT) has a 9 o'clock news report every morning followed by further weekly information. At the monthly management meeting to discuss the results, even the human resources manager is able to enter the sweepstakes guessing the month-end result. Talking about the monthly numbers is a small part of the meeting, which happens in the first week of the following month.

I believe as a corporate accountant, you have arrived when members of your management team intuitively know during the month whether it is a good or bad month, which enables them to do something about it if it is a bad month.

Corporate accountants should look at providing this daily and weekly reporting:

- Yesterday's sales reported by 9 A.M. the following day
- Transactions with key customers reported on a weekly basis
- Weekly reporting on late projects and late reports
- Reporting some weekly information of key direct costs
- The key performance indicators, which are reported daily/weekly (see Chapter 19)

Daily Sales Report

	$000s		

	Yesterday's Sales	Daily Average Last 90 Days	Variance	>$100k & 10%
Sales by Key Product				
Product 1	450	400	50	
Product 2	440	560	−120	×
Product 3	375	425	−50	
Other products	185	175	10	
Total Sales	1,450	1,560		×
Sale by Branch				
Branch 1	580	700	−120	×
Branch 2	440	420	20	
Branch 3	220	210	10	
Branch 4	180	160	20	
Other branches	30	70	−40	
Total Sales	1,450	1,560		×
Sale by Customer Type				
Platinum customers	710	600	110	✓
Gold customers	480	440	40	
Silver customers	380	410	−30	
Bronze customers	280	510	−230	×
Total Sales	1,450	1,560	−110	×

- - - Total Sales   ——— Monthly target (average daily amount)

EXHIBIT 11.1 Yesterday's Sales Report

Yesterday's Sales Report

If the CEO and SMT receive a report on the daily sales, they will better understand how the organization is performing. Exhibit 11.1 shows the sort of detail they will be interested in.

Weekly Key Customers' Sales

In a similar vein, it is important for the SMT to monitor how products are being purchased by the key customers. This is especially important after a

Weekly Sales to Key Customers

	Last Week's Sales	$000s Weekly average for Last 180 Days	Variance	
Customer #1				
Product 1	450	400	50	
Product 2	400	460	−60	
Product 3	340	310	30	
Product 4	375	425	−50	
Other products	185	105	80	✓
Total Revenue	1,750	1,700	50	
			0	
Customer #2			0	
Product 1	340	480	−140	✗
Product 2	380	450	−70	
Product 3	120	190	−70	
Product 4	180	190	−10	
Other products	180	220	−40	
Total Revenue	1,200	1,500	−300	✗
Customer #3				
Product 1	220	160	60	
Product 2	190	140	50	
Product 3	160	120	40	
Product 4	190	150	40	
Other products	1,140	1,130	10	
Total Revenue	1,500	1,300	200	✓

Sales of Product xx to Customer xxxx

■ Sales of product xx to Customer xxxxx

--- Weekly average (based on last 6 months, weekly average)

Areas to note:
1. Xxxxxxxxxxxxxxxxxxxxxxxxxxxxxxxxxxxxxxxxxxx
xxxxxxxxxxxxxxxxxxxxxxxxxxxxxxxxxxxxxxxxxxxxxxxxxxxxxxxxxxxxxxxxxxxxxxxx
xxxxxxxxxxxxxxxx xxxxxxxxx xxxxxxx xxxxxxxxxxxx xxxxxxxxxxxxxxxxxxxxxxxxxxxxxxxx
2. Xxxxxxxxxxxxxxxxxxxxxxxxxxxxxxxxxxxxxxxxxxx
xxxxxxxxxxxxxxxxxxxxxxxxxxxxxxxxxxxxxxxxxxxxxxxxxxxxxxxxxxxxxxxxxxxxxxxx
xxxxxxxxxxxxxxxx xxxxxxxxx xxxxxxx xxxxxxxxxxxx xxxxxxxxxxxxxxxxxxxxxxxxxxxxxxxx
3. Xxxxxxxxxxxxxxxxxxxxxxxxxxxxxxxxxxxxxxxxxxx
xxxxxxxxxxxxxxxxxxxxxxxxxxxxxxxxxxxxxxxxxxxxxxxxxxxxxxxxxxxxxxxxxxxxxxxx
xxxxxxxxxxxxxxxx xxxxxxxxx xxxxxxx xxxxxxxxxxxx xxxxxxxxxxxxxxxxxxxxxxxxxxxxxxxx
4. Xxxxxxxxxxxxxxxxxxxxxxxxxxxxxxxxxxxxxxxxxxx
xxxxxxxxxxxxxxxxxxxxxxxxxxxxxxxxxxxxxxxxxxxxxxxxxxxxxxxxxxxxxxxxxxxxxxxx

EXHIBIT 11.2 Weekly Sales to Key Customers

EXHIBIT 11.3 Overdue Projects Report

Manager	Number of Projects Currently Outstanding	Number of Projects Outstanding Last Month	Total Projects Currently Being Managed
Kim Bush	7	0	8
Pat Carruthers	5	3	10
Robin Smith	3	3	12
XXXXXXX	3	2	5

List of Major Projects Past Their Deadline	Original Deadline	Project Manager (Sponsor)	Risk of Noncompletion
Xxxxxxxxxxxx	1/06/1X	AB (YZ)	(neutral face)
Annual report	1/07/1X	DE (RS)	(smiling face)
Strategic plan publication	1/08/1X	AB (RS)	(frowning face)
Balanced scorecard report	1/09/1X	DE (YZ)	(smiling face)
Outcomes 20XX	1/12/1X	AB (YZ)	(frowning face)

Risk of Nondelivery at Year-End

Will be completed within five working days	Will be completed this month	Will be completed this quarter	Risk of noncompletion at year-end
(smiling face)	(neutral face)	(neutral/frown face)	(frowning face)

launch of a new product, or after your competitors launch a new competing product. Exhibit 11.2 shows the sort of detail they will be interested in.

Weekly Reporting on Late Projects and Late Reports

Many managers are innovative people who love to get on with a project but often fail to tie up the loose ends or finish it. I am always encountering

EXHIBIT 11.4 Weekly List of Overdue Reports

Past Deadline Reports
Week Beginning xx/20/xx

Report Title	Date: First Draft	Manager's In-Tray	Original Deadline
Annual Report	2/1/xx	DP	9/15/xx
20xx/20x1 annual budget	9/15/xx	DP	3/15/xx
xxxxxxxxxxxxxxxxxx	9/1/xx	DP	7/30/xx
xxxxxxxxxxxxxxxxxx	8/30/xx	DP	4/15/xx
xxxxxxxxxxxxxxxxxxxxxxxxxxx	2/15/xx	DP	1/30/xx
xxxxxxxxxxxxxxxxxx	3/30/xx	PC	2/1/xx
xxxxxxxxxxxxxxxxxxxxxxxxxx	8/1/xx	PC	5/15/xx
xxxxxxxxxxxxxxxxxxxxx	2/15/xx	PC	1/30/xx
xxxxxxxxxxxxxxx	9/1/xx	PC	2/1/xx
xxxxxxxxxxxxxxx	3/15/xx	PC	3/1/xx
xxxxxxxxxxxxxxxxxxxx	9/1/xx	MM	7/30/xx
xxxxxxxxxxxxxxxxxx	3/15/xx	MM	1/15/xx

Actions to be taken:

Xxxxxxxxxxxxxxxxxxxx xxxxxxxxxxxxxxxxxxxxx
  xxxxxxxxxxxxxxxxxxxxx xxxxxxxxxxxxxxxxxx
Xxxxxxxxxx xxxxxxxxxx xxxxxxxxx xxxxxxxxxx xxxxxxxxxxxx
  xxxxxxxx xxxxxxxxx xxxxxxxx
Xxxxxxxxxxxxxxxxxxxx xxxxxxxxxxxxxxxxxxxxx
  xxxxxxxxxxxxxxxxxxxxx xxxxxxxxxxxxxxxxxx
Xxxxxxxxxx xxxxxxxxxx xxxxxxxxx xxxxxxxxxx xxxxxxxxxxxx
  xxxxxxxx xxxxxxxxx xxxxxxxx
Xxxxxxxxxxxxxxxxxxxx xxxxxxxxxxxxxxxxxxxxx
  xxxxxxxxxxxxxxxxxxxxx xxxxxxxxxxxxxxxxxx
Xxxxxxxxxx xxxxxxxxxx xxxxxxxxx xxxxxxxxxx xxxxxxxxxxxx
  xxxxxxxx xxxxxxxxx xxxxxxxx
Xxxxxxxxxxxxxxxxxxxx xxxxxxxxxxxxxxxxxxxxx
  xxxxxxxxxxxxxxxxxxxxx xxxxxxxxxxxxxxxxxx
Xxxxxxxxxx xxxxxxxxxx xxxxxxxxx xxxxxxxxxx xxxxxxxxxxxx
  xxxxxxxx xxxxxxxxx xxxxxxxx

projects who are stuck in limbo. They will be of value to the organization only when someone refocuses them. Exhibits 11.3 and 11.4 present two report formats that I believe should be presented weekly to senior and middle management to enable them to focus on completion. Exhibit 11.3 has a dual focus, on the project manager and the project. Exhibit 11.4 is a shame and name list. It focuses management on those reports that are well past their deadline. The version number helps management realize the cost of revisions. The manager's in-tray column focuses on the guilty manager and helps encourage action.

Daily and Weekly Reporting of Performance Measures

For a performance measure to be important, it needs to be reported *during* the month as opposed to at the end of the month. Visit Chapters 18 and 19 to understand how to develop, implement, and use winning key performance indicators.

CHAPTER 12

Working Smarter, Not Harder

In this chapter I have extracted some of key lessons CFOs need to learn from *The Leading-Edge Manager's Guide to Success*.[1] At some point it would be worth reading the other issues that I have had to omit due to space constraints.

I have been fortunate to have witnessed a number of amazing teams. Set out in this chapter are some of their practices, along with some of my thoughts on working smarter, not harder.

Staff Debriefing at the End of the Day

Staff debriefings are rare these days, and if they are scheduled, they are often the first meeting to be deferred or canceled. This is often because the debriefings are not handled in the appropriate way, and thus staff members may consider them a waste of time. The situation can be different. One high-performance team has an open-ended debriefing daily in the last 15 minutes of the working day. Normally it takes only the allotted 15 minutes, but it can extend should the team require it. In their debriefing sessions, team members cover these issues:

- How best to help a particular in-house client who is having difficulties
- Ways to improve operations
- Plans for the next day and next week
- Finishing off communication that due to the pressures of the day was not completed
- Popping the balloon on those difficult issues that may have grown out of proportion during the day

Another point worth noting is that this high-performance team could not operate if it chose to have meetings during its key service delivery time. Yet that is the very thing we all tend to do.

Banning Morning Meetings for the Finance Team

A good start is to avoid having meetings during your productive time (e.g., mornings). I fail to see why CEOs feel the need to have meetings with their direct reports at 9 A.M. on Monday mornings. Such meetings often are followed with more meetings as the debriefing is passed down the chain in the finance team. Why not have this meeting at 4:30 P.M. on a Friday? It certainly would be a quick meeting.

Ask anybody about their productivity, and you will find frustration about how time has been taken away with nonproductive activities. Would it not be better to schedule meetings toward the tail end of the day and leave the morning for service delivery? Exhibit 12.1 shows how a manager's calendar often looks and how it could look.

The main change is bigger chunks of service delivery time, delaying email duties, and meeting time rescheduled to the afternoons, allowing us

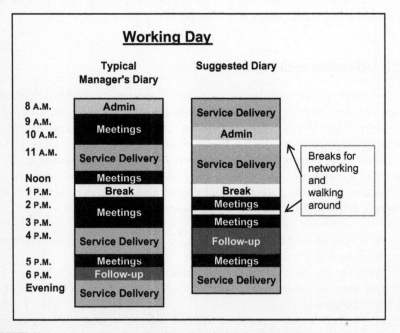

EXHIBIT 12.1 Before and After Working Day Calendar Example

to be more relaxed because we have scored some early goals. Once we have rescheduled meetings, we need to make them more productive.

Implementing "Action Meetings" Methods

A majority of meetings are totally flawed. They are held because they were held last week, two weeks ago, last month. The fundamental purpose of the meeting has long ago been forgotten.

Most managers at some time have received training in managing meetings, yet the level of frustration with meetings remains the same. The problem has been that the training has not looked at all the core reasons for failure. Even the legendary John Cleese's training video, *Meetings Bloody Meetings*, serves to entertain rather than tackle these issues.

Two management consultants, Mike Osborne and David McIntosh, have developed a methodology that is breathtaking in its simplicity yet profound in its impact.

Action Meetings (see www.actionmeetings.com) has attacked the core of dysfunctional meetings and their common features: unclear agendas, lack of engagement, rambling discussions, a total lack of understanding of "the space" fellow attendees are in, and, worst of all, poorly defined action points and follow-through.

There are a number of key features. Some of them are:

- **Getting people properly into and out of the meeting.** This is done through the introduction of a first word and last word, where attendees briefly say what state they are in. The first words could range from "I am very time challenged and this meeting is last thing I need," to "Eager to make progress with this assignment and to hear Bill's view on the XYZ development." The last words could range from "This meeting once again promised little and delivered nothing," to "I look forward to receiving Pat's report and working with the project team." The key to the first and last word is that attendees can say anything about how they feel at that point in time. Their comment is just that and is to remain unanswered.
- **An effective agenda constructed as outcomes.** This involves the use of precise wordings about meeting outcomes (see Exhibit 12.2). Outcomes provide focus and the ability to easily check whether an item has in fact been completed. One major benefit of establishing "meeting outcomes" worded in this way is that requested attendees can and should not attend if they do not think they can add value or assist in achieving the outcomes.

EXHIBIT 12.2 What Meeting Outcomes Could Include Example

- Project XYZ progress examined and **understood**
- Monthly results **understood**
- Next steps for project XYZ **agreed** and **assigned**
- This month's key initiatives **agreed**
- Responsibilities on the acquisition of ABC Limited **assigned**

- **Meetings are participant-owned, not chairperson-owned.** All attendees are trained in the new methodology. Thus meetings are owned and policed by all participants and are less reliant on the capability of the chairperson.
- **Once an outcome is closed, it remains closed.** During the meeting, remind anyone who is opening a closed item that the item has been closed.
- **Nonrelated issues are tabled.** Any issues raised that are not related to the outcome under discussion are tabled for another, future discussion.
- **Action steps.** Action steps are written carefully on a special pad and then entered into a web-based application so all can see the progress.

Golden Rules with Emails

If you are receiving over 30 emails a day, here are some golden rules to save you time.

Rule 1: Never Open Emails before 10:30 A.M.

In the good old days, we would handle mail at 10:30 A.M. when the mail finally arrived from the mailroom. We thus started the day with scoring a goal—undertaking a service delivery activity. Now the first thing we do is open up the email, and suddenly one hour has evaporated. Some of us even get interrupted every time a new email arrives.

As a therapy, I suggest not opening your email until after your morning coffee and then looking at emails only once or twice more during the day. If something is very important, you will get a phone call. This technique will help you get more 1.5-hour blocks of concentrated time in your day. (See Exhibit 12.1).

If you do receive the odd urgent email, you could, as a friend of mine does, scan for these at 8:30 A.M. My friend, however, has the control only to handle these urgent emails and then moves on with the day, leaving the replies to the bulk of the emails to late in the day. For me, even looking at the in-box before 10:30 A.M. is too risky as curiosity wins every time.

Rule 2: You are not Barack Obama so Do Not Live and Sleep with Your Blackberry!

Most of us (fortunately or unfortunately) are not heart or brain surgeons. Our work is not critical to life. Many emails we handle have little or no relevance to where we or our organizations want to go. The silliest thing is surely to handle an email twice, once on the Blackberry "Will get back to you when in the office" and once in our office.

Rule 3: The Five-Sentence Rule

Treat all email responses like text messages and limit them to something you can count easily: five sentences. A campaign has been started (see http://five.sentenc.es/) to promote this brevity. With only five sentences, the writer is forced to ensure that all terms, conditions, and papers are attached to the email. This has the added benefit of ensuring the saving of possibly important documents in the document management system.

Rule 4: Have an Attention-Grabbing Header

Make the header the main message of the email. If you cannot think of a good email header, maybe you should not send the email.

Rule 5: Actively Terminate Email Exchanges

Manage your email exchanges. If you needed feedback in order to get to closure, often a phone call is better. Ping-pong emails on the same topic are screaming out for "Let's speak tomorrow!" Think about you desired outcome and promote a course of action to avoid the table tennis. If necessary use the sentence "No more emails on this one, thank you."

Rule 6: Promote Yourself by Your Endeavors, Not by Your Use of Broadcast Emails, Reply All, or Copy Correspondence (cc)

Avoid sending broadcast emails unless you are prepared to call up each person to advise them that there is a key document that they need to read. Ensure that you do not add to the spam in your organization. Forwarding business material may be well meaning but it is creating havoc in many organizations, where managers often are receiving up to 240 emails a day. Ask yourself: Is it necessary to copy the CEO—just for visibility?

Rule 7: If You Would Not Put Your Words in a Letter, Do Not Put Them in an Email

Far too often the content of emails, while amusing, is not appropriate. Be careful about being the bearer of silly jokes. Today many people seem to want to be remembered by their joke telling. Now, don't get me wrong, I love a joke, but when you are sent a couple a week by the same person, you do wonder what they do all day. Remember, perception rules everything. You do not want to be perceived as a person whose prime focus is to entertain. You want to be thought of in more positive terms.

Rule 8: Master Email Application's Tools Section

The experts have been busy improving the ways we can handle emails. The applications you use for emails will have many features you have never opened. Many readers have mastered word and spreadsheet applications, yet they know least about the one application they use the most. Master the new features; it will take a 30 minute session with a tech. You need to know and master:

- How to turn off auto-notifiers.
- How to use filters to sort and prioritize.
- How to get newsletters to automatically straight to a folder that you access twice weekly.
- How to set up auto-responders to acknowledge and advise response time.
- How to use filters, flags, colors, and sorting tools.

Rule 9: Your Inbox Is Not a Storage Area

The inbox should be for collection only, just like your in-box. Messages should be deleted, actioned, or filed. Do you keep all your texts and phone messages? NO! Be ruthless with deletions. You have gone far enough only when you start having to ask people to resend their email.

Rule 10: Have a Night's Sleep before You Send a Complaint/Rebuff Email

For complex responses, complaints, rebuffs, and the like, draft the email and file in the draft section of your email application overnight, as you may well have second thoughts. It is a good idea to send these draft emails to your mentor. Many a career has been dented by a poorly thought out email written in anger.

Rule 11: Monkey-on-the-Back Emails

Many people are using the email system to pass their workload on to others. In many cases people contact known experts and ask for their help without having done any research themselves. In other words, they are passing the monkey on their back to the expert.

My friend, an internationally recognized expert, advises me that the best way is to politely thank the sender for the email and then say, "Please call when convenient to discuss." Based on his experience, this gets rid of 95 percent of the requests.

Continuous Innovation in the Finance Team

For one high-performance team, innovation is discussed every day during the end-of-day debrief. In many organizations that I have worked in and visited, this is not the case. Innovation needs to be on every agenda, and it needs to be pushed so that staff members know what is expected; otherwise teams do not progress forward. I get the impression that in many organizations, staff members have the perception that innovation is not required, because the person who is building his yacht in his backyard after work is performing the same unproductive tasks day after day like a laboratory rat hunting for its cheese. How is it that organizations can take an individual who is innovative at home and turn him or her into an automaton? There are many aspects of the culture that need to change— more delegation, more risk taking, less witch-hunting, and more celebration of success—before you truly can have continuous innovation.

Getting the Induction Process Right

All good finance teams put a lot of time and effort into a good induction process, which is committed to not only by the CFO but by all other finance staff as well. Far too often the induction process gets relegated to an item on the agenda. The new staff person arrives and is given the feeling that he or she is a burden.

An induction should include:

- Detailed handover with the person leaving or, failing that, with someone familiar with routines.

- Morning or afternoon coffee with some of the general or middle managers depending on seniority of new recruit.
- Specified meeting times with the manager (e.g., 3:00 P.M. Wednesday, 3:00 P.M. Friday) to pick up any loose ends, give feedback, revise training program, and plan the week ahead.
- A selection of simple tasks where goals can be scored easily.
- Vetting of meetings so the new employee gets to go to meetings that are functioning well.
- Meeting with help desk and information technology support to cover intranet, systems, email, hours of operation, remote access, security, and so on.
- Meeting with a representative from the human resources team scheduled for three months after joining date.
- Visit to any production facilities.
- Phone number and email address of previous person who did the job, if permission has been sought and granted.

Creating a Service Culture in the Finance Team

Instilling in the finance team a focus on customer satisfaction is difficult. It requires commitment, training, and good recruitment practices. I was speaking to the chief steward on a plane where the service level was exceptional. I asked, "Can you train for this level of service?" She replied, "No, you have to recruit for it."

For those finance teams that work for organizations that are legendary at service delivery, things will be easier, as they most likely have recruited for it or at least attracted recruits who are service oriented. Make being service oriented a priority, organize some training, have an in-house workshop to discuss what this means in day-to-day activities, and ensure that the CFO and all the corporate accountants lead by example.

One feature I have noted when you walk through the door at a high-performance team's workplace is that you are greeted with a smile and eye contact by all staff members whom you meet. Often finance teams' workplaces are less than welcoming places; you arrive and everybody is head down and the greeting is, at best, a reluctant one. For one high-performance team, making eye contact is part of their training and part of their job, as it should be for every finance team.

Having Fun in the Workplace

Finance teams need to be seen as teams that work hard and have fun doing this. Some initiatives you can undertake to improve the work environment are:

- Buy 10 movie tickets (a discounted 10-pack) and give two tickets to finance team members who have gone beyond the call of duty. Besides the initial shock from the recipients, you will find it will create a small shift in the right direction.
- Hold a staff meeting in a coffee shop once a month, and treat the team to coffee and muffins. If you cannot find a budget for this bona fide expenditure, nobody can.
- Set up a routine where birthdays are acknowledged and celebrated. The staff person is actively encouraged to take that day off (out of their vacation allowance) and then celebrate it the next day in the office. The birthday staff member would be expected to bring in the cake and would receive a small gift from the team. (To save time, don't bother with a collection; pay for it out of the finance budget.)
- Occasionally treat the team to a matinee visit to the movies, with the organization investing one hour and the staff investing their lunch hour. This is great for staff with young children, where going to movie may be a distant memory.
- For the end-of-the-year finance team function, give your staff options; for example, my staff elected to go to the movies once a week, at lunchtime, for the five weeks rather than have a year-end function.
- During team meetings, ensure that you find at least three team members to thank and recognize their achievements, some of which may have occurred outside work.

Note

1. David Parmenter, *The Leading-Edge Manager's Guide to Success* (Hoboken, NJ: John Wiley & Sons, 2011).

CHAPTER 13

Limit the P&L to 50 Account Codes

Show me a company with fewer than 100 account codes for its profit and loss statement (P&L) and I will show you a management accountant who has seen the light. However, I have seen many charts of accounts with more than 300 expense account codes in the general ledger (G/L), with up to 30 accounts for repairs and maintenance.

A poorly constructed chart of accounts leads to many problems:

- It encourages detailed reporting, with budget holders getting a 60- to 70-line P&L
- Budgeting at account code level instead of at category level
- Excessive codes, which increase the number of coding errors and time wasted
- A finance team wedded to detail
- A project accounting nightmare
- Subsidiaries slowly suffocating under the weight of their holding company's process and procedures

Far too often the job of setting up the chart of accounts is given to management accountants who look skyward like a child yearning to become a rocket scientist. They live out this dream when they have an Excel spreadsheet or the chart of accounts in their hands. Common sense goes out the window, the CFO's eyes glaze over at the chart of accounts progress meetings, the objective to reduce the account codes by over 40 percent gets lost, and, slowly but surely, just like the budget instructions, the chart of accounts takes on a life of its own.

Some rules to stop this from happening are:

- Allocate an account code when the relevant annual expenditure represents represent 1 percent or more of total annual expenses. This will limit your expense items to less than 50 account codes.
- Allocate an account code when the annual revenue stream represents three percent or more of total annual revenue. This will limit your revenue account codes to less than 20.
- The CFO should ensure he or she has a strong coffee before the chart of accounts meeting and keeps the strategic vision in the forefront.

Stand back and ask yourself why you should be spending time analyzing minor levels of transactions. Jeremy Hope, in his book *Reinventing the CFO*,[1] makes this point well.

Project Accounting

One of the common reasons for a chart of accounts nightmare is setting up myriad projects and then duplicating the account codes within them. Such nightmares end up with 30 to 50 pages of codes. Pareto's logic needs to be applied to project accounting. Work out at what level you need to manage projects (e.g., all projects where expenditures are over $50,000 or $500,000). Small projects should be reported together as "XXX's other projects." We do not need the detail.

Subsidiary Chart of Accounts

With a 21st-century consolidating tool, all subsidiaries can have a chart of accounts that is relevant to them. All the holding company accountants have to do is map the chart of accounts in the consolidation tool, which is a simple one-off exercise. All new codes established by the subsidiary must be communicated to the parent company in advance to avoid consolidation issues at the eleventh hour.

Note

1. Jeremy Hope, *Reinventing the CFO: How Financial Managers Can Transform Their Roles and Add Greater Value* (Boston: Harvard Business School Press, 2006).

PART II

Areas to Focus on Once Core Gains Have Been Achieved

The better practices in Part One, if implemented, will free up time so Part Two initiatives can be attempted successfully.

The main goals worth achieving in this part are:

Goal	Reason
1. Commence the selling process to throw out your annual planning and associated monthly budget cycle.	This is an important sale—ensure you use public relations advice to maximize the sale. Remember, you need to use emotional drivers rather than logic and reason.
2. Commence the process to purchase a planning and forecasting tool and begin quarterly rolling forecasting.	This project has a six-month time frame and thus you need to start now.
3. Plan to cease using monthly budgets from the annual planning cycle; instead use the forecast from the most recent quarterly rolling forecast.	This assumes goal 1 has been scored and goal 2 is on its way.
4. Commence the investigation into your organization's critical success factors (CSFs).	Again, this is a big sale; once the senior management team is on board, this project will have a profound impact on the organization.

(Continued)

Goal	Reason
5. Implement winning key performance indicators (KPIs) throughout the organization.	KPIs are the only thing that links day-to-day activities to the organization's strategic objectives. Enough said!
6. Place a ban on Excel spreadsheets in all daily, weekly, and monthly routines within the finance function.	This will improve the reliability of these routines.
7. Maximize the use of the general ledger (G/L).	Many G/Ls are replaced without their full potential being exploited. Far better to invest in auxiliary applications.
8. Make better use of the organization's intranet.	The finance team can lead the way in maximizing the intranet's potential.

A checklist has been developed covering the major steps. This is set out in Appendix E.

CHAPTER 14

Throw Out Annual Planning and the Associated Monthly Budget Cycle

L et us get one thing straight: The standard annual planning process takes too long, is not focused on performance drivers, is not linked to strategic outcomes or critical success factors, leads to dysfunctional behavior, builds silos, and is a major barrier to success. Organizations around the world are questioning the value of the traditional annual budgeting process.

Jeremy Hope is the world's foremost thought leader on corporate accounting issues. Hope has an uncanny ability to always be at least five years ahead of what better corporate accounting practices should be. Hope has stated that not only is the budget process a time-consuming, costly exercise generating little value, but it also, and more important, is a major limiting factor on how your organization can perform. He has many examples of how companies following the philosophies he has expounded have broken free and achieved success well beyond their expectations. Here are three quotes that challenge the very concept of budgeting.

> *So long as the budget dominates business planning a self-motivated workforce is a fantasy, however many cutting-edge techniques a company embraces.*

> *Modern companies reject centralization, inflexible planning, and command and control. So why do they cling to a process that reinforces those things?*

The same companies that vow to respond quickly to market shifts cling to budgeting—a process that slows the response to market developments until it's too late.

Jeremy Hope and Robin Fraser, Beyond Budgeting[1]

Let us now look at why the budget process, as it currently stands, is a no-brainer. A survey performed in 1998 found:

- The average time for a budget process was four months.
- 66 percent of CFOs stated their budget was influenced more by politics than strategy.
- Nearly 90 percent of CFOs were dissatisfied with their budget process.
- 60 percent of CFOs acknowledged that there was no link from the budgets to strategy.

This level of dissatisfaction is similar among boards, CEOs, general managers, and budget holders. As a CFO said to me, "The incessant game playing extended the budget round and limited the need for us to stretch or seek breakthrough solutions." Does this sound familiar?

There is an answer: Throw the annual budgeting cycle out; it takes too long and is not linked to strategy, strategic outcomes, or critical success factors.

By 2020, very few progressive organizations will be doing annual planning as we know it today.

Beyond Budgeting in New Zealand: A Major Road Contracting Company

I was presenting Beyond Budgeting and key performance indicators (KPIs) in New Zealand and was introducing myself to the managing director of a large road contracting company. He politely informed me that he was mainly interested in hearing the KPI part of my presentation, as the beyond budgeting session was of little interest as they were already doing it. In fact, the group had never had an annual planning process. He said if the group could predict when it was going to sunny and when it was going to rain, annual planning would be useful.

The business encompasses concrete, transport (local and rural), fuel distribution, and roading. The group has around 1,000 staff members and a consistent profit growth, the envy of many larger organizations.

The growth path has been either to grow from scratch or buy existing family companies. As the CEO says, expansion is often driven by opportunity. It has 23 companies as well as a number of joint ventures.

The business has different performance tables depending on the size of operations, so the companies can compare with one another. Each table shows the ranking of the operations within that table with reference to some key ratios. The ratios they monitor include:

- Return per km—revenue and cost per km
- Margin per liter
- Delivery cost per liter
- Concrete cost per cubic meter
- Cubic meter delivered by pay hour

Monthly reports are short and based on major cost categories (not at detail account code level). They do not waste time showing a consolidated result each month; this is done at year-end only.

There is much delegation to the other offices, which manage staff levels within given limits, set staff salaries, and choose which suppliers to use (providing there is not a national contract in place).

Reporting without a Budget

A major mistake in all annual planning cycles has been the monthly apportionment of the plan. If you still need to perform an annual planning process, at least you can remove the need for 12 monthly targets. You instead should report against more recent targets derived from the quarterly rolling forecasting process (see Exhibit 14.1). This change has a major impact on reporting. You no longer will be reporting against a monthly budget that was set, in some cases, over 15 months before the period being reviewed.

Organizations that are using quarterly rolling forecasting are no longer comparing actual against a flawed monthly budget.

This report compares last month's actual against the most recent forecast. The year to date (YTD) actual is no longer compared against a YTD budget. Instead, YTD progress is evaluated alongside progress against the year-end forecast and the accompanying trend graphs. Trend analysis now becomes much more the focus. The forecast year-end numbers are now more prominent and moved to where the YTD numbers traditionally are

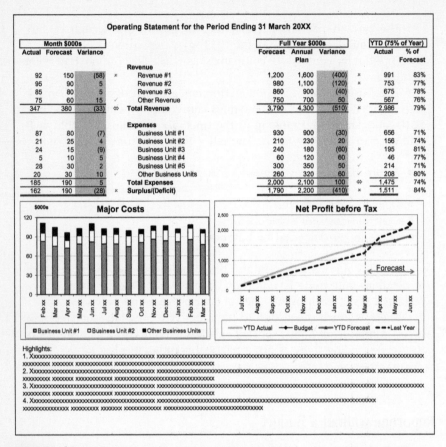

EXHIBIT 14.1 Business Unit Reporting against Latest Forecast instead of a Budget Example

placed. Commentary is much more targeted, as there is no place for the explain-it-all-away timing difference comment as the forecast is updated quarterly.

Note

1. Jeremy Hope and Robin Fraser, *Beyond Budgeting: How Managers Can Break Free from the Annual Performance Trap* (Boston: Harvard Business Press, 2003).

CHAPTER 15

Quarterly Rolling Planning: An Evolvement from Quarterly Rolling Forecasting

Q uarterly rolling planning is a process that will revolutionize any organization, whether public or private sector. It removes the four main barriers to success that an annual planning process erects: an annual funding regime where budget holders are encouraged to be dysfunctional, a reporting regime based around monthly targets that have no relevance, a three-month period where management is not particularly productive, and a remuneration system based on an annual target. The only thing certain about an annual target is that it is certainly wrong; it is either too soft or too hard for the operating conditions.

This chapter is an extract from a white paper[1] I deliver around the world that has revolutionized the way organizations perform rolling forecasting. At some point it would be worth reading the other issues that I have had to omit due to space constraints.

Quarterly Rolling Forecasting Is the Most Important Management Tool of This Decade

This chapter explains why quarterly rolling forecasting (QRF) is the most important management tool of this decade and why the rolling forecasts of the past are different from the 21st-century QRF.

- QRFs, normally going out six quarters, are a bottom-up process, with the forecast of the next quarter being the reporting benchmarks.

▪ Quarterly rolling planning (QRP) takes QRF a step further—budget holders are now funded quarterly in advance from the approved forecast.

The quarterly forecasting process is where management sets out the required revenue and expenditure for the next 18 months. Each quarter, before approving these estimates, management sees the bigger picture six quarters out. All subsequent forecasts, while firming up the short-term numbers for the next three months, also update the annual forecast. Budget holders are encouraged to spend half the time on getting the details of the next three months right, as these will become targets, on agreement, and the rest of the time on the next five quarters. Each quarterly forecast is never a cold start, as budget holders have reviewed the forthcoming quarter a number of times. With the appropriate forecasting software, management can do the forecasts very quickly; one airline even does this in three days. The overall time spent in the four quarterly forecasts should be no more than five weeks.

Most organizations can use the cycle set out in Exhibit 15.1 if their year-end falls on a calendar quarter-end. Some organizations may wish to stagger the cycle, say, May, August, November, and February. An explanation of how each forecast works, using a June year-end organization, follows.

December. We forecast out to the June year-end, with monthly numbers, and the remaining period in quarterly breaks. Budget holders obtain approval to spend January-to-March numbers subject to their forecast, still going through the annual plan goalposts. The budget holders at the same time forecast next year's numbers for the first time. Budget holders are aware of the expected numbers, and the first cut is reasonably close. This is a precursor to the annual plan. This forecast is stored in the forecasting and reporting tool. This update process should take only one elapsed week.

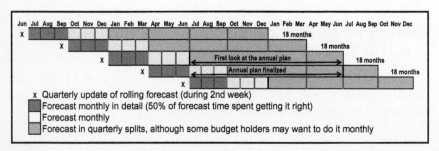

EXHIBIT 15.1 How the Rolling Forecast Works for an Organization (June Year-End)

March. We reforecast to year-end and the first quarter of next year with monthly numbers, and the remaining period in quarterly breaks. Budget holders obtain approval to spend April-to-June numbers. The budget holders at the same time revisit the December forecast (the previous forecast) of next year's numbers and fine-tune them for the annual plan. Budget holders know that they will not be getting an annual lump-sum funding for their annual plan. The number they supply for the annual plan is guidance only.

For the annual plan, budget holders will be forecasting their expense codes using an annual number and in quarterly lots for the significant accounts, such as personnel costs. Management reviews the annual plan for next year and ensures all numbers are broken down into quarterly lots. This is stored in a new field in the forecasting and reporting tool called "March XX forecast." This is the second look at the next year, so the managers have a better understanding. On an ongoing basis, they would need only a two-week period to complete this process.

June. We can reforecast the end of June numbers, and we should be able to eliminate the frantic activity that is normally associated with the spend-it-or-lose-it mentality. Budget holders also are now required to forecast the first six months of next year monthly and then on to December in the following year in quarterly numbers. Budget holders obtain approval to spend July-to-September numbers, provided their forecast once again passes through the annual goalposts. This is stored in a new field in the forecasting and reporting tool called "June XX forecast." This update process should take only one elapsed week.

September. We reforecast the next six months in monthly numbers and quarterly to March, 18 months forward. Budget holders obtain approval to spend October-to-December numbers. This is stored in a new field in the forecasting and reporting tool called "September XX forecast." This update process should take only one elapsed week.

You will find that the four cycles take about five weeks, once management is fully conversant with the new forecasting system and processes.

Ten Foundation Stones of a Rolling Forecasting Process

A number of QRF foundation stones need to be laid down and never undermined. You need to ensure the entire construction of the QRF model is undertaken on these 10 foundation stones:

1. Separation of targets from forecasts (telling management the truth rather than what the managers want to hear).

2. A bottom-up process performed quarterly.
3. Forecast past year-end (e.g., six quarters ahead).
4. The monthly targets are set, a quarter ahead, from the QRF.
5. A quarter-by-quarter funding mechanism.
6. The annual plan becomes a by-product of the QRF.
7. Forecasting at a detailed level does not lead to a better prediction of the future. (We do not need to forecast at account code level.)
8. The QRF should be based around the main events/key drivers.
9. A fast light touch (an elapsed week).
10. Based on a planning application—not Excel.

Separation of Targets from Forecasts

It is so important to tell management the truth rather than what the managers want to hear. Boards and the senior management team often have been confused between setting stretch targets and a planning process. Planning should always be related to reality. The board may want a 20 percent growth in net profit, yet management may see that only 10 percent is achievable with existing capacity constraints. The performance gap should be reported to the board so it can direct its attention to strategic decisions to manage the shortfall. The board has every right to say the stretch target is the basis for the bonus.

In these turbulent times, the separation of targets and realistic forecasts is fundamental and a survival necessity. It is vital that the forecasting process generate realistic forecasts rather than forecasts that the board or senior management want to achieve. Exhibit 15.2 shows where management has forced the plan prepared in March 2009 to meet the target set by the board. Each subsequent reforecast continues the charade until, in the final-quarter reforecast, performed in March 2010, the truth is revealed.

Even with foundation stones 2–10 working like clockwork, the end result doesn't benefit from all this good work because all or some of the following factors are in operation:

- *Senior management is running the organization through fear.*
- *There is no clarity between what can be reasonably achieved and an unreasonable arbitrary target.*
- *The accountants doing the forecasting do not have the ability to articulate and sell bad news stories as the most likely future outcomes.*

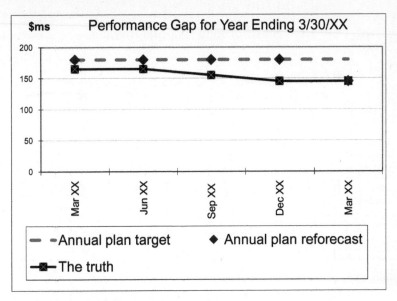

EXHIBIT 15.2 Reporting What the Board Wants to Hear

Therefore, by getting foundation stone 1 right, you then get the maximum benefit on foundation stones 2–10.

John Poppe, a respected planning expert

A Bottom-Up Process Performed Quarterly

Many forecasts have little input and no buy-in from the budget holders. We do not have the time, process, or tools to get the budget holders involved. I call these forecasts top-top forecasts, where the finance team members talk among themselves and with senior management.

Typically management reforecasts the year-end numbers on a monthly basis. Why should one bad month, or one good month, translate into a change of the year-end position? We gain and lose major customers, key products rise and wane; this is the life cycle we have witnessed many times. Besides, if you change your forecast each month, management and the board know whatever number you have told them is wrong—you will change it next month. As shown in Exhibit 15.3, we now have only 4 reforecasts a year, instead of the 12 updates.

Only businesses that are in a volatile sector would need to forecast monthly (e.g., the airline industry). Even for these organizations, you do not need to get all budget holders to participate in a monthly reforecast.

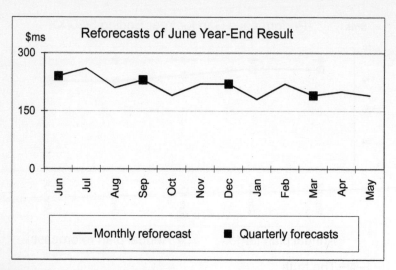

EXHIBIT 15.3 Quarterly Reforecasting

You may be able to limit this extra work to sales and production, with the major all-embracing cycle still being quarterly.

Forecast Past Year-End (e.g., Six Quarters Ahead)

Typically corporate accountants reforecast only to year-end. Two months before year-end, management appears to ignore the oncoming year. A foundation stone of a QRF process is forecasting for a rolling period that passes through the year-end barrier. There are various options as to how far forward you go, including:

- Always forecast two years ahead—this is particularly relevant where the business is very seasonal and much activity happens in the last quarter.
- Forecast six quarters ahead.
- Use variations such as four or five quarters ahead.

I advocate the six-quarter-ahead (18-month) rolling forecast regime, as it has some substantial benefits, which include:

- You see the full next year halfway through the current year (e.g., the third-quarter forecast can set the goalposts for next year's annual plan).
- The QRF is consistent each time it is performed, as opposed to organizations that always look ahead for two financial years (the QRFs will vary between 15 to 24 months).

- Your annual plan is never set from a cold start, as you have seen the whole financial year in the previous quarter's reforecast.

Monthly Targets Are Set, a Quarter Ahead, from the QRF

As accountants, we never needed to break the annual plan down into 12 monthly breaks before the year had started. We could have been more flexible. Instead we created a reporting yardstick that undermined our value to the organization. Every month managers throughout the organization writes variance analyses, which I could do just as well from my office.

A sporting game analogy can be used to explain the folly of the monthly budget, as shown in Exhibit 15.4. Imagine a game where you have to get a ball from your end of the field to the other end and place it between two goalposts. The annual plan is the establishment of goalposts at the end of the field, and the budget process is where we set 12 × 10 yard lines to report against. The problem is that the 10-yard lines (the monthly budgets) are wrong as soon as the year has started. When there is stoppage, the trainer comes on the field and asks, "Why are you here? You should have been over there." The reply from the team is "The ball is over here." This progress reporting is as useful as our monthly variance commentary.

We instead should report against more recent targets derived from the quarterly rolling forecasting process. This process will give us the monthly targets for the next quarter. It is important to realize that monthly targets are not set any farther out than the quarter ahead. In fact, information for quarters 3, 4, 5, and 6 are set only quarterly. In other words, we patiently wait until the relevant quarter is upon us before putting the budget holders' estimates in the reporting tool.

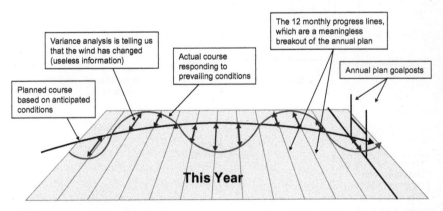

EXHIBIT 15.4 Annual Plan Analogy

This change has a major impact on reporting. We no longer will be reporting against a monthly budget that was set, in some cases, 17 months before the period being reviewed.

A Quarter-by-Quarter Funding Mechanism

The key to a better allocation of resources is to fund budget holders on a rolling quarter-by-quarter basis. In this process management asks, "Yes, we know you need $1 million and we can fund it, but how much do you need in the next three months?" At first the budget holder will reply, "I need $250,000 this quarter," The management team replies, "How is this? Your last five quarterly expenditures have ranged between $180,000 and $225,000. Pat, you are two team members short and your recruiting is not yet under way; realistically you will need only $225,000 tops."

It will come as no surprise that when a budget holder is funded only three months ahead, the funding estimates are much more precise and there is little room or nowhere to hide those slush funds.

Using the sporting game analogy once more, the ground staff then draws these lines on the field and management becomes very accountable about progress (see Exhibit 15.5). This means that the approval process through the senior management team (SMT) will be quicker as the SMT

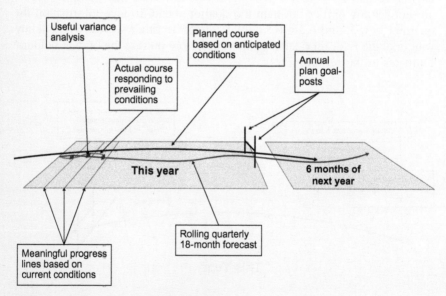

EXHIBIT 15.5 Quarterly Rolling Plan Analogy

are approving only the annual number and can adjust the quarter-by-quarter allocations as the conditions and environment dictate.

Some organizations are recognizing the folly of giving a budget holder the right to spend an annual sum and at the same time are saying "If you get it wrong there will be no more money." By forcing budget holders to second-guess their needs in this inflexible regime, you enforce a defensive behavior, a stockpiling mentality. In other words, you guarantee dysfunctional behavior from day 1. The quarterly rolling planning process thus highlights "free funds," that can be reallocated for new projects earlier in the financial year.

The released funds can provide for new initiatives that the budget holder could not have anticipated at the time of the budget round. This will get around the common budget holder dilemma, "We cannot undertake that initiative, although we should, as I did not include it in my budget." In the new regime the budget holder would say, "I will put it in my next update and if funds are available, I am sure I will get the go-ahead."

This more flexible environment, as long as it is communicated clearly and frequently to budget holders, will have good buy-in. The logic of quarterly rolling funding can be shown in an analogy.

> The quarterly rolling funding process has a lot in common with the cutting of a nine-year-old's birthday cake. A clever parent says to Johnny, "Here is the first slice. If you finish that slice and want more, I will give you a second slice." Instead, what we do in the annual planning process is divide the cake up and apportion all of it to the budget holders. Like nine-year-olds, budget holders lick the edges of their cake so that even if they do not need all of it, no one else can have it. Why not, like the clever parent, give the managers what they need for the first three months and then say, "What do you need for the next three months?" and so on. Each time we can apportion the amount that is appropriate for the conditions at that time.

THE ANNUAL PLAN BECOMES A BY-PRODUCT OF THE QRF With quarterly rolling forecasting, one of the quarters also generates the annual plan. The QRF process will allow you to have a quick annual planning process, as:

- Budget holders will become more experienced at forecasting (they are doing it four times a year), and they have already looked at the next year a number of times.

- Politics is taken out of the annual planning cycle, as budget holders realize that they no longer obtain an annual entitlement. There is no use demanding more than you need, as the real funding is sorted out on a quarter-by-quarter basis, where slush funds cannot be hidden.
- The third-quarter forecast firms up both the fourth quarter's funding and the annual plan numbers.
- The CEO supports the guillotined process.
- There is no point spending too much time, as the next quarter's forecast is a more up-to-date view of the future.

Organizations that have truly adopted the Beyond Budgeting principles also will throw out the annual plan target. Why should one view of year-end be any better than a subsequent, more current view? The March quarter forecast is no longer called the annual plan; it simply is the March quarter forecast. The board will want to monitor the extent of forecast creep, and this can be easily shown in a graph.

Forecasting at a Detailed Level Does Not Lead to a Better Prediction of the Future

A forecast is a view of the future. It will never, can never, be right. As Harry Mills, a business writer, says, "It is better to be nearly right than precisely wrong." Looking at detail does not help you see the future better; in fact, I would argue it screens you from the obvious.

While precision is paramount when building a bridge, when every small detail needs to be right, a forecast should concentrate on the key drivers and large numbers.

Following this logic, it is now clear that as accountants, we never needed to set budgets at account code level. We simply have done it because we did it last year, without thinking. Do you need a target or budget at account code level if you have good trend analysis captured in the reporting tool? I think not. We therefore apply Pareto's 80/20 principle and establish a category heading that includes a number of general ledger (G/L) codes, as shown on Exhibit 5.1 in Chapter 5.

Rules that can be used include:

- Limit the categories that budget holders need to forecast to no more than 12.
- Select the categories that can be automated, and provide these numbers.
- Separate out a forecasting line if the category is over 10 percent of total (e.g., show revenue line if revenue category is over 10 percent of total revenue). Remember that a category will have a number of

EXHIBIT 15.6 Categories Used in One Case Study

Budget Holders Forecast Only These Categories	Categories that Can Be Automated
Revenue (three to four categories)	Operational equipment repair and maintenance
Salaries and wages ordinary time	Office equipment, computers, and consumables
Other personnel expenditure	Communications costs
Health and welfare	Fleet costs
Training and conferences, including travel	Building maintenance
Operational equipment—that is not capitalized	Miscellaneous costs
Property costs	Depreciation
Promotional activities	

account codes within it. This rule applies at budget holder and consolidated forecasting levels.

- Allow the budget holders to have some flexibility in the categories to best reflect their operation. Planning tools can easily cope with this complexity by the mapping of G/L codes to categories—try doing this in an Excel spreadsheet.
- Accurate forecasting of personnel costs requires analysis of all current staff (their end date if known, their salary, the likely salary review, and/or bonus) and all new staff (their starting salary, their likely start date).

In one workshop I ran for a service sector organization, the group came up with the decision that there would be a maximum of 15 categories, 7 of which would be automated, as shown on Exhibit 15.6.

The QRF Should Be Based around the Main Events/Key Drivers

A forecasting tool needs to be based on the main events/key drivers and thus be able to quickly inform management should there be a major change with any of these drivers. In-depth interviews with the SMT, coupled with some brainstorming, will quickly identify the main drivers, which may include:

- What if we contract (e.g., stop production of one line, sell a business)?
- What if we grow through acquisition?
- What if we lose a major customer?

- What if there is a major change to key economic indicators (e.g., interest rates, inflation)?
- What if a major overseas competitor sets up in our region?
- What are the plant capacity ramifications from gaining a large increase in business (e.g., collapse of a major local competitor)?

If you have second-guessed the likely SMT requests and have designed the model around them, you will have a planning tool that can quickly model the implications of such changes robustly.

American Express found that its forecast is based principally around two drivers, customer numbers and average customer expenditure.

A Fast Light Touch (an Elapsed Week)

QRFs should be performed within five working days (see Exhibit 15.7). The one exception is the fourth-quarter forecast, which creates the annual plan (see Exhibit 15.8), will have one extra week for additional negotiations and quality assurance. QRFs can be quick because:

- Consolidation is instantaneous with a planning tool.
- Since you have run a workshop on budget preparation with budget holders, they know what to do.
- The model is based on Pareto's 80/20 principle.
- Training has been given to budget holders so they can enter into the planning tool directly.
- The quarterly repetition aids efficiency.
- Forecasting is at a high level, at the category, not account code, level (e.g., only 12 to 15 categories per budget holder).
- Repeat costs can be standardized for the whole year (e.g., New York–to–London return flight: US$2,500, overnight in London US$250)
- As much pre-work is done as possible by the forecasting team.
- The annual planning dates are set away from school holidays.
- One-to-one support is offered by expanding the budget team.
- Only monthly data is requested for the first two quarters.
- New funding requests or error-prone forecasts require an audience with the forecasting committee.
- The forecast approval committee sits in a lock-up.

Make sure you have the CEO's support for a quick time frame and encourage the CEO to get involved in making late forecasting career limiting.

Every quarter you will need to prepare the best view using this fast light touch process. See Appendix H for a checklist on performing a quarterly rolling forecast. This will help with the quality assurance process.

Process =>	Prior Work		7 Working Days							
	Forecast pre-work	Present forecast workshop	1	2	3	4	5	Weekend	6	7
			Budget holders (BHs) prepare and load their forecast		First look at numbers	Submissions by BHs to management board (for more funding or to justify unrealistic forecast)			Rerun of forecast and give presentation to CEO	Final alterations and finishing off documentation
Activities by team =>										
Strategic Planning		Attend				Review to ensure linkage to strategic plan; advise if any discrepancies			Attend	
SMT	Set assumptions				First look at numbers	Review submissions, etc., full time			Hear presentation and give instructions for final changes	
Finance Team	Prepare system, presentation, calculate known costs, overheads, personnel costs, etc.	Give presentation to BHs	Help BHs with forecast (extended team)		Quality checks (QC)	Further QC and prepare presentation			Present forecast presentation	Finish off documentation
Budget Holders		Attend		Prepare forecast		Present forecast and business plan where there is a major change			Present to SMT if required	Document and file all calculations

EXHIBIT 15.7 Timeline for the First Three Quarterly Forecasts in a Financial Year

181

10 Working Days

Process =>	Prior Work			1	2	3	4	5	Weekend 6	7	8	9	10
	Budget prework	Meeting with divisional heads (DHs)	Present budget workshop				First look at numbers	Rework some budgets	Submissions by BHs to budget committee			Present final annual plan	Final alterations and finishing off documentation
Activities by team =>				BHs prepare and load their forecast									
Strategic Planning			Attend					Reviewing to ensure linkage to plan and advising of any discrepancies				Attend	
SMT	Set assumptions	One-to-one with the finance team					First look at numbers		Review submissions, all day long			Hear presentation and give instructions for final changes	
Finance Team	Prepare system, presentation, calculate known costs, overheads, personnel costs, etc.	One-to-one with DHs	Give presentation to BHs	Help BHs with budget plans (extended team)			Questions and answers	Help BHs	Further questions and answers			Complete preparation and deliver annual plan presentation	Complete documentation
Budget Holders			Attend	Prepare budget			Alter numbers after feedback	Attend	Present plan to SMT when called				Document and file all calculations

EXHIBIT 15.8 Timeline for the Fourth-Quarter Forecast (which Generates the Annual Plan)

Based on a Planning Application—Not Excel

Forecasting requires a good robust tool, not an error-prone spreadsheet built by some innovative accountant that now no one can understand how it works. The main hurdle is the finance team's reluctance to divorce itself from Excel. It has been a long and comfortable marriage, albeit one that has limited the finance team's performance.

Acquiring a planning tool is the first main step forward, and one that needs to be pursued not only for the organization but also for the future careers of the finance team members. It will soon be a prerequisite to have planning tool experience, and, conversely, it will be career limiting to be an Excel guru.

See Appendix F for how a QRF can be laid out in a planning tool.

New planning tools are being built all the time, and Exhibit 15.9 is certainly out of date at the time of you reading it. The exhibit is not intended to be a comprehensive list, as that would be a white paper in itself. The next search strings will help unearth many applications:

- "Planning tools" + "name of your country" (e.g., USA)
- "Quarterly rolling forecasting" + "applications" + "name of your country"
- "Forecasting tools" + "rolling" + "name of your country" + "planning tools"

EXHIBIT 15.9 Some Planning Tool Providers and Their Applications

Company	Package Name	Web Address
Bi Predict	Proclarity Analytics	www.bipredict.co.nz
Adaptive Planning	Adaptive Planning Software	www.adaptiveplanning.com
PROPHIX Software Inc.	Prophix	www.prophix.com
Business Forecast Systems, Inc.	Forecastpro	www.forecastpro.com
Alight	Continuous Planning & Scenario Analysis	www.alightplanning.com
Hyperion	Hyperion Planning	www.hyperion.com
IBM	IBM® Cognos® TM1™	www.ibm.com
Corvu Corp	CorStrategy	www.corvu.com
Beacon Group	GEAC Performance Mngt Suite	www.beaconit.com.au
Forecast Vision	Forecast Vision	www.forecastvision.com.au
Sage	Winforecast	www.sage.com

Better Practices in a QRF

There are a number of better practices in QRF, and these are set out next.

Linkage to Chapter 5 (Timely Annual Planning Process)

If you have implemented the practices set out in Chapter 5, you are already part of the way to implementing the better practices for QRP. The following practices need to be adopted and have been covered in Chapter 5:

- Accurate revenue forecasting
- Bolting down your strategy beforehand
- The forecasting team doing as much prework as possible
- Holding a briefing workshop instead of issuing instructions
- Expanding your forecasting help team
- Forecasting categories only in monthly splits for the first two quarters
- Establishing a forecasting committee
- Including trend graphs for every category forecasted
- Accurately forecasting personnel costs
- Providing automated calculator for travel and accommodation costs

Selling Quarterly Rolling Planning through the "Emotional Drivers"

As mentioned in the Introduction, nothing was ever sold by logic. You sell through emotional drivers. This project needs a public relations (PR) machine behind it. No presentation, email, memo, or paper should go out unless it has been vetted by your PR expert. All your presentations should be road tested in front of the PR expert. Your PR strategy should include selling to staff, budget holders, SMT, and the board.

These are some of the emotional drivers around the annual planning process that you would use if selling the acquisition of a planning tool:

- The meaningless month-end reports (e.g., "It is a timing difference").
- The lost evenings/weekends producing meaningless variances comments.
- The lost months and the lost weekends with family producing the annual plan.
- The huge costs (estimate on the high side, because costs motivate boards).
- The time spent by the board and SMT second-guessing the next year—it is more efficient on a rolling quarterly basis.
- It is better practice to implement quarterly rolling forecasting and planning (e.g., 80 percent of major U.S. companies expect to be doing QRFs, etc.).

The project team needs to focus on the marketing of a new concept as much as it does on the training. Budget holders will need to understand how this process is going to help them manage their business. Providing success stories throughout the implementation is therefore a must.

Recognize that Quarterly Rolling Forecasts Involve All Budget Holders

Most forecasting models built in Excel tend to have restricted consultation with budget holders and are carried out by staff members at headquarters who are remote from the workforce. This is done for practical reasons; it would be a disaster to unleash the Excel model once a quarter, as it takes weeks to get completed even once a year. These forecasts do not have any buy-in from budget holders, cannot be used to create meaningful targets for the months in the next quarter, and are often a skewed view of the future business operations, simply reiterating the misconceptions that head office management wishes to believe.

Having all budget holders involved requires an investment in training and good coordination. The benefits include buy-in to the numbers, a forecast that more closely resembles reality, and a positive learning curve, as budget holders get better at a repetitive task.

Beware of the Dangers of Scenario Planning

When I worked for BP Oil, we would spend a lot of time trying to pigeon-hole a series of events into what we called a high-case, medium-case, and low-case scenario. Each scenario had many different variables. The chance of a high case coming off in the way we had forecast it was nil. The permutations would make a statistician dizzy.

I believe it is better to focus on the key drivers and bring to management's attention the impact of:

- Losing a major customer (e.g., ABC Limited)
- Exchange rate (e.g., for every cent the US$ appreciates against the euro it means this to the bottom line)
- Having to halt production in a product that may be subjected to an intense price war, and so forth

Quarterly Rolling Forecast Is a Quarterly Process

Only businesses that are in a very dynamic environment would need to forecast monthly. One has to remember that for every event that goes your way, there will be another event in the future negating the positive impact (e.g., it is not worthwhile to change your year-end forecast due to the loss or gain of a large customer). These changes are better picked up on a quarterly basis; this will help ensure less oscillation of your year-end numbers.

For those organizations that are in a dynamic environment, you do not need to get all budget holders to participate in a monthly reforecast; you may be able to limit this monthly reforecast work to sales and production, with the major reforecast still being quarterly.

Implementing a Quarterly Rolling Forecasting and Planning Process

The foundations stones already mentioned and the processes that you need to adopt, set out next need to be understood, developed, and implemented. Due to space constraints I have briefly outlined the key processes. For further information, see the white paper 'How to Implement Quarterly Rolling Forecasting and Quarterly Rolling Planning—and Get It Right First Time" on www.davidparmenter.com.

Overcoming the Barriers

Before you can make much progress, you need to understand the likely barriers and surmount them all. Set out in Exhibit 15.10 are the ways to overcome the common barriers accountants face in implementing QRF.

Hold a Focus Group Workshop

A focus group needs to be formed; see Exhibit 15.11 for a workshop agenda. The workshop is important for a number of reasons:

- There are many pitfalls in such a project, and many projects have failed to deliver.
- A wide ownership is required, and a focus group can have a huge impact on the selling process.
- The foundation stones need to be understood and put in place early on in the project.
- We need to reengineer the annual plan process using Post it Notes as discussed in Chapter 2.
- The focus group will give valuable input into how the implementation should best be done to maximize its impact.

Post-it Reengineering Forecasting Procedures

Each quarterly forecasting update will be a bottom-up process with each budget holder submitting an update for the next six quarters. The process is thus like updating the annual plan. If you have not already Post-it reengineered the annual planning process, set out in Chapter 5, you will

EXHIBIT 15.10 Ways to Surmount the Main Issues

Common Barriers	Suggested Actions
Lack of budget holder skills	▪ Find those staff who thrive with new technology and train them first.
	▪ Set up a new forecasting regime in one unit, a quarter ahead, to iron out the bugs and to promote the efficiencies.
	▪ Train all significant budget holders, including one-to-one training.
	▪ Set up from the outset a quarterly follow-up course (as you should be using the model for forecasting).
Stop-and-start annual planning syndrome	▪ Big sell to management (historic evidence, including costs, better practices, benefits to them).
	▪ Get commitment for quick bottom-up forecasts.
	▪ Work closely with the executive assistants regarding calendar bookings so SMT and budget holders are all present during the forecasting weeks.
	▪ Maintain momentum with daily progress reports flagging budget holders who are behind with their forecasts (show on an intranet page).
Inaccurate and late data	▪ Provide more one-to-one support.
	▪ Workshop the forecast process with all major budget holders (with laptop and projector).
	▪ Provide incentives for prompt forecast returns (e.g., movie vouchers).
	▪ Provide daily progress report to CEO of the late names.
	▪ If still using Excel, have all returns go to the CEO's office first.
Lack of management ownership	▪ Take SMT to some better practice forecasting sites.
	▪ Deliver more interesting information from forecast process (e.g., trend graphs, key performance indicators).
	▪ Market better practice stories constantly.
	▪ Ensure budget holders are directly involved in the forecasting process (i.e., not delegating tasks).
Lack of faith in the reliability of the forecast	▪ Establish in-depth quality assurance procedures.
	▪ Have good working papers.
	▪ Provide reasonableness checks.
	▪ Audit the forecast application prior to use.
	▪ Migrate away from Excel to a planning tool.

(Continued)

EXHIBIT 15.10 *(Continued)*

Common Barriers	Suggested Actions
Lack of under-standing of application	■ Have forecasting/budget models reviewed and audited prior to use. ■ More than one person involved in design of the QRF. ■ Full documentation of logic. ■ Keep to Pareto's 80/20 principle (e.g., personnel costs should have much more detail). ■ Key drivers should be easily identifiable.
Lack of linkage to strategic decisions	■ Brainstorm with SMT members regarding their likely scenarios. ■ Ensure you can accommodate the key drivers of the business in the model design.
Competency of forecasting team	■ Select for: self-starter, innovator, good communicator, finisher, big-picture thinker, team player, prepared to work overtime. ■ Broad experience of organization. ■ Experience with problem solving, interviewing, process reengineering, forecasting. ■ Train to cover shortfalls. ■ External facilitator can help here.

need to do it now; otherwise the four quarterly rolling forecast updates will take you all year.

To understand what is required, you will need to refer to the Post-it reengineering section in Chapter 2; see Exhibit 15.12 as a reminder. The only difference is:

■ The time scale is week −2, week −1 (last week before annual planning), week +1 (first week after year-end), week +2 instead of day −2, day −1, and so on.
■ There will be different attendees to the workshop (e.g., forecasting team; budget holders, marketing team, SMT etc).
■ The invitation to attend comes from the CEO with a career-limiting nonattendance warning. See Appendix J for a suggested draft.

Implementation Road Map

The implementation plan shown in Exhibit 15.13 should help those about to start an implementation. One key feature is the time frame. A rolling

EXHIBIT 15.11 Agenda and Instructions for a One-Day Focus Group Workshop

---

Date and Time: xxxxxx

Location: xxxxxx

Suggested Attendees: Budget committee, selection of business unit heads, all management accountants, and a selection of budget holders involved in forecasting.

Learning Outcomes:
After this workshop attendees will be able to:
- Discuss and explain to management why Xxxxxxx should adopt QRP
- Use better practices to streamline current forecasting bottlenecks
- Describe better practice month-end routines
- Recall all agreements made at the workshop (these will be documented)

Prework: Teams to document forecasting procedures on Post it Notes. One procedure per Post-it. Each team should have a different color Post-it.

Requirements: Event secretary, two laptops, data show, two whiteboards

8:30 A.M.   Welcome by CFO, a summary of progress to date at Xxxxxxx, an outline of the issues, and establishing the outcome for the workshop.

8:40 A.M.   **Setting the scene**—why clever organizations are not involved in the annual planning cycle—a review of better practices among public and private sector organizations. Topics covered include:
- Why annual planning is flawed and the rise of the Beyond Budgeting movement
- Why quarterly rolling planning can and should work at Xxxxxxx
- Benefits of QRP to the board, SMT, finance team, and budget holders
- Better practice stories
- Current performance gap between Xxxxxxx and better practice
- Some of the building blocks are already in place at Xxxxxxx
- Some better practice features within Xxxxxxx's forecasting process
- How the annual plan drops out of the bottom-up quarterly rolling forecasting regime
- Impact of assigning funds on a quarter-by-quarter basis
- Impact on monthly reporting
- How each subsequent forecast works
- Involvement of SMT in a forecasting process

This session would be attended by a wider audience. After the questions and answers, these people would leave.

(Continued)

EXHIBIT 15.11 (*Continued*)

9:40 A.M.	**Workshop 1: Analyzing the Current Pitfalls of Xxxxxxx's Forecasting.** Separate teams look at the key pitfalls and how they can be overcome.
10:15 A.M.	Morning break.
10:30 A.M.	**Workshop 2: Mechanics of Rolling Forecasting.** Workshop where separate teams look at the key components:

- Who should be involved in a bottom-up forecasting process
- Potential pitfalls
- Reporting needs
- When can it be implemented
- Training requirements
- What cost categories should be forecast (higher than general ledger account code)
- Project structure

11:00 A.M.	**Workshop 3: Workshop on Post-it Reengineering of Xxxxxxx's Forecasting Process.** During the workshop we analyze the bottlenecks of the forecasting process. In this workshop we use Post-its Notes to schedule the steps (e.g., yellow—budget holder activities; red—forecasting team activities; blue—SMT activities during the forecast).
12:15 P.M.	Lunch at venue.
12:45 P.M.	Feedback from work groups on both workshops and action plan agreed (date and responsibility). Individuals will be encouraged to take responsibility for implementing the steps.
1:15 P.M.	The team prepares a short presentation of the key steps it is committed to making.
2.00 P.M.	The team presents reports to an invited audience on what changes it would like to implement and when. It can also raise any issues it still has. Suggested audience consists of all those who attended the setting the scene morning session.
2.30 P.M.	Wrap-up of workshop.

EXHIBIT 15.12 Demonstration of Post-it Note Reengineering

> October 15
> First cut from
> Budget holders

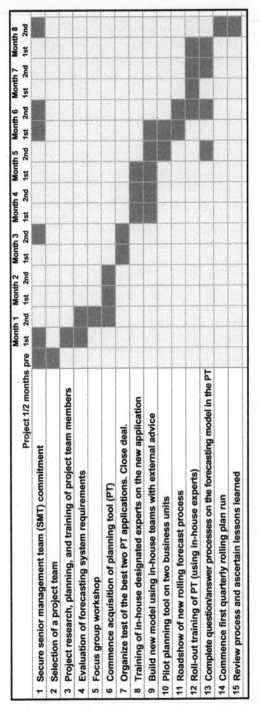

EXHIBIT 15.13 Timeline for Implementing a QRF Process Example

forecast implementation is a five- to six-month process, including the acquisition of an appropriate planning tool.

See Appendix G for a checklist on implementing a QRF. This checklist should be treated as an evolving tool and thus be tailored to better suit your needs. Using a checklist will help ensure that while you are juggling the balls, you do not drop the ones that matter.

Note

1. David Parmenter, "How to Implement Quarterly Rolling Forecasting and Quarterly Rolling Planning—and Get It Right First Time," 2010, www.davidparmenter.com.

CHAPTER 16

Cost Apportionment:
Do Not Do It Monthly!

Traditionally we have spent much time apportioning head office costs to business units to ensure they have a net profit bottom line. However, few ask the budget holders and business unit managers whether they look at these apportioned head office costs. I have never found any business unit managers who showed much interest other to complain about the cost of information technology (IT), accounting, and other apportioned costs.

In fact, these cost apportionments, besides slowing down reporting, often lead management to complain about strategic costs, which cannot be reviewed for a few years due to locked-in agreements (e.g., the accounting system).

Pareto's principle reminds us that the hours spent processing levels upon levels of apportionments to arrive at some arbitrary full costing are not creating management information that leads to decision making. Corporate accountants often can arrive at full costing approximations through a more simplistic route.

Some better practices are:

- Keep head office costs where they are, as budget holders see them as uncontrollables in any case.
- Use product costing as periodic one-off exercises to understand a full costing situation.
- Develop a full costing model, if you really need one, in an appropriate planning application that has been designed with the big picture in mind.
- Engage in major process reengineering to simplify head office processes.

- Analyze head office costs by activities rather than account codes, for example, where the head office IT costs are spent—delivering new projects, correcting errors, providing one-to-one training, provision of equipment, and so forth, and compare these over time and against third-party benchmarks.
- Set targets in the future where you expect to see head office costs. These can be expressed as acceptable ratios to sales. Naturally you will have researched the lowest-cost operators as benchmarks (e.g., by 20XX we want finance cost to be between x percent and y percent of revenue). This sets a general direction for the head office teams and helps curb empire building.

If you have on-charged head office costs and it is creating the right environment, then continue with the process. There are a number of case studies where on-charging head office costs appears to work well. They, however, are the exception rather than the rule.

CHAPTER 17

Ban Excel from Core Monthly Routines

Excel has no place in reporting, forecasting, budgeting, and other core financial routines. Excel was never intended for the uses we put it to. In fact, many of us, if we worked for NASA, would be using Excel for the space program and, believe me when I say this, probably would make a good go of it. I, however, would not like to be the astronaut, in outer space, when I found out that there was a 90 percent chance of a logic error for every 150 rows in the workbook.

Excel is a great tool for doing one-off graphs for a report or designing and testing a reporting template. It is not and never should have been a building block for your company's forecasting and reporting systems. There are better alternatives, as shown in Exhibit 17.1.

As a forecasting tool, Excel fails on a number of counts:

- It has no proper version control; we have all burned the midnight oil pulling our hair out wondering whether all spreadsheets are the correct versions.
- For every 100 formula cells on average between one and two will contain an error (Powell, Baker, Lawson, Dartmouth College, USA, 2009).
- It lacks robustness. (Show me a CFO who can be confident of the number an Excel forecast churns out.)
- It cannot accommodate changes to assumptions quickly (e.g., respond to the CEO asking "What if we stop production of computer printers? Please tell me the impact by close of business today").
- It was designed by accounting staff who are not programmers and have not been trained in documentation, quality assurance, and so forth, which you might expect from a designer of a core company system.

EXHIBIT 17.1 Replacements for Excel

Current Use for Excel	Replacement
Reporting—downloading from the general ledger (G/L) to get better-quality reports	Reporting package
Cash flow forecasting	Planning application
Rolling accrual forecasting	Planning application
Budgeting	Planning application
Consolidations	Reporting package or your G/L
Balanced scorecards	Balanced scorecard package

Jeremy Hope of *Beyond Budgeting* fame and more recently author of the groundbreaking book *Reinventing the CFO* points out that Sarbanes-Oxley may be the sword that finally removes the spreadsheet from key financial monthly routines. "[I]n theory at least, every change to a formula or even a change to the number of rows needs to documented."[1]

Note

1. Jeremy Hope, *Reinventing the CFO: How Financial Managers Can Transform Their Roles and Add Greater Value* (Boston: Harvard Business Press, 2006).

CHAPTER 18

Identifying the Organization's Critical Success Factors

M any organizations fail to achieve their potential because they lack clarity regarding the more important things to do. This lack of clarity means that often staff members will schedule their work based around their team's priorities rather than the priorities of the organization, that performance measures are often meaningless, and that many reports are prepared that serve no purpose. As Exhibit 18.1 shows, even though an organization has a strategy, teams often are working in directions very different from the intended course.

This mayhem stems from a complete lack of understanding of their critical success factors (CSFs). While most organizations know their success factors, few organizations have:

- Worded their success factors appropriately
- Segregated out success factors from their strategic objectives
- Sifted through the success factors to find their critical ones—their critical success factors
- Communicated the CSFs to staff

If the CSFs of the organization are clarified and communicated, staff members will be able to align their daily activities closer to the strategic direction of the organization, as shown in Exhibit 18.2.

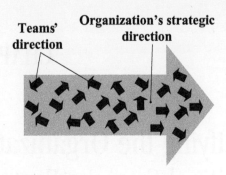

EXHIBIT 18.1 Discord with Strategy

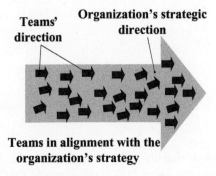

EXHIBIT 18.2 Alignment with Strategy

Benefits of Understanding Your Organization's Critical Success Factors

Knowing an organization's CSFs, communicating them to staff so they can better align their activities, and measuring teams' progress with the CSFs is the El Dorado (the gold mine) of management. There are some profound benefits of knowing your CSFs, including:

- It leads to the discovery of an organization's winning key performance indicators (KPIs).
- Measures that *do not* relate to your CSFs or impact them cannot, by definition, be important and thus often can be eliminated.
- Staff members know what should be done as a priority, and thus their daily actions now are linked to the organization's strategies.
- The number of reports that are produced throughout the organization is reduced, as many reports will be clearly exposed as not important or irrelevant.

■ Reporting the progress the organization is making within each CSFs gives the board and senior management a much clearer understanding about the current status of the organization's performance.

An Airline CSF

A good CSF story is about Lord King, who set about turning British Airways around in the 1980s reportedly by concentrating on one CSF and one KPI within it. Lord King appointed some consultants to investigate and report on the key measures he should concentrate on to turn around the ailing airline. They came back and told Lord King that he needed to focus on one CSF, the "timely arrival and departure of airplanes."

I imagine the Lord King was not impressed, as everyone in the industry knows the importance of timely planes. However, the consultants pointed out that while he knew that "timely arrival and departure of airplanes" was a success factor, it had not been separated out from all the other success factors, and thus staff members were trying to juggle too many things.

The consultants' analysis proved that "timely arrival and departure of airplanes" was different from all the other success factors; it was in fact the most important one, as shown on Exhibit 18.3. With this knowledge, it was a relatively short step to find the appropriate measure that would transform the organization. Was it timely planes or late planes? Analysis would have pointed them quickly to selecting late planes over a certain time. This late plane KPI is discussed in more detail in Chapter 19.

Relationship among CSFs, Strategy, and KPIs

The relationship between CSFs (also referred to as key result areas) and KPIs is vital, as illustrated in Exhibit 18.4. If you get the CSFs right, it is

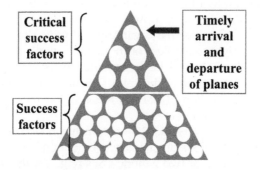

EXHIBIT 18.3 Hierarchy of Success Factors

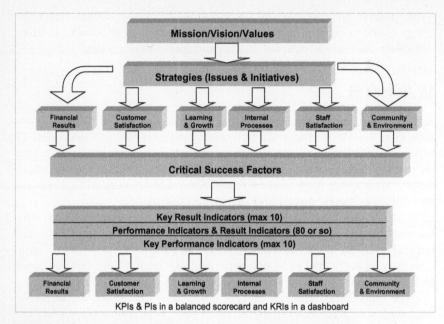

EXHIBIT 18.4 How CSFs and KPIs Fit Together and Link to Strategy

Source: David Parmenter, *Key Performance Indicators: Developing,
Implementing, and Using Winning KPIs*, 2nd Edition, Copyright © 2010 John
Wiley & Sons, Inc. Reprinted with permission of John Wiley & Sons, Inc.

very easy to find your winning KPIs (e.g., once the "timely arrival and
departure of airplanes") was identified as being the top CSF, it was relatively
easy to find the KPI—"planes currently over X hours late."

CSFs identify the issues that determine organizational health and vital-
ity. When you first investigate CSFs, you may come up with 30 or so success
factors that are important for the continued health of the organization. The
second phase of thinning them down is crucial.

Better practice suggests that organizational CSFs should be limited to
between five and eight, regardless of the organization's size. However, for
a conglomerate, the CSFs will be largely industry specific (e.g., the CSFs
for an airline are different from those for a retail record chain store). Thus,
there would be a collection of CSFs in the conglomerate greater than the
suggested five to eight.

It is important to understand the relationship between CSFs and strategy. An organization's CSFs are impacted by a number of features. Most
industries will have one or two generic CSFs (e.g., for the airline industry,
"timely arrival and departure of airplanes"). However, each organization
has some unique temporary conditions (e.g., a cash flow crisis), some CSFs

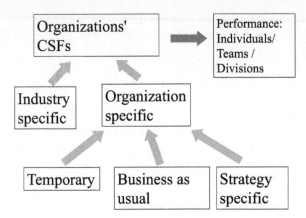

EXHIBIT 18.5 What Impacts the CSFs

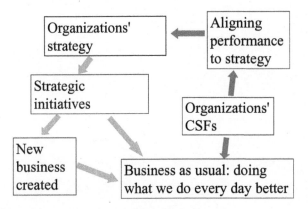

EXHIBIT 18.6 How Strategy and the CSFs Work Together

specific to strategy, and other CSFs relating to normal business conditions (see Exhibit 18.5).

The main impact of an organization's CSFs is on its business-as-usual activities. Strategic initiatives if implemented successfully will create new business ventures that then become managed through the CSFs (see Exhibit 18.6).

Finding Your Organization's CSFs

To help organizations around the world find their CSFs, I have developed a three-stage process. This process is covered in Chapter 7 of my book

Key Performance Indicators.[1] Other materials available are a webcast and a white paper on the topic,[2] which can be accessed at www .davidparmenter.com.

Notes

1. David Parmenter, *Key Performance Indicators: Developing, Implementing, and Using Winning KPIs*, 2nd ed. (Hoboken, NJ: John Wiley & Sons, 2010).
2. David Parmenter, "Finding Your Organization's Critical Success Factors," 2010, www.davidparmenter.com.

CHAPTER 19

Reporting Your Winning Key Performance Indicators

Many companies are working with the wrong measures, many of which are incorrectly termed key performance indicators (KPIs). Very few organizations really monitor their true KPIs. The reason is that very few organizations, business leaders, writers, accountants, or consultants have explored what a KPI actually is. There are four types of performance measures:

1. **Key result indicators (KRIs).** Give an overview on past performance and are ideal for the board as they communicate how management has done from a critical success factor (CSF) or balanced scorecard perspective.
2. **Performance indicators (PIs).** Tell staff and management what to do.
3. **Result indicators (RIs).** Tell staff members what they have done.
4. **Key performance indicators (KPIs).** Tell staff and management what to do to increase performance dramatically.

Many performance measures used by organizations are an inappropriate mix of these four types.

An onion analogy can be used to describe the relationship of these four measures, as shown in Exhibit 19.1. The outside skin describes the overall condition of the onion: how much sun, water, and nutrients it has received; and how it has been handled from harvest to supermarket shelf. However, as we peel the layers off the onion at home, we find out more information. The layers represent the various performance indicators and the core—the key performance indicators.

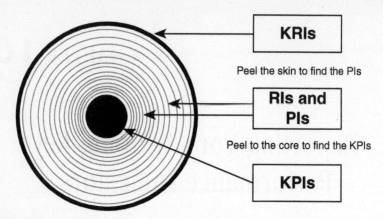

EXHIBIT 19.1 Four Types of Performance Measures

Source: David Parmenter, *Key Performance Indicators: Developing, Implementing, and Using Winning KPIs*, 2nd Edition, Copyright © 2010 John Wiley & Sons, Inc. Reprinted with permission of John Wiley & Sons, Inc.

In this chapter I have extracted some of the key points CFOs need to learn about performance measures from my book *Key Performance Indicators.*[1] At some point it would be worth reading the other issues that I have had to omit due to space constraints.

The 10/80/10 Rule

Kaplan and Norton[2] recommend no more than 20 KPIs, and Jeremy Hope[3] of *Beyond Budgeting* fame suggests fewer than 10. To aid those involved in performance measurement, I have developed the 10/80/10 rule. This means an organization should have about 10 KRIs, up to 80 performance and result indicators, and 10 KPIs. Very seldom does there need to be more measures than these numbers, and in many cases fewer can be used.

Key Result Indicators

The common characteristic of KRIs is that they are the result of many actions. They give a clear picture of whether you are traveling in the right direction and of the progress made toward achieving desired outcomes and strategies. They do not, however, tell management and staff what they need to do to achieve desired outcomes. Only PIs and KPIs can do this.

KRI measures that often have been mistaken for KPIs include:

- Customer satisfaction
- Employee satisfaction
- Return on capital employed

A car's speedometer provides a useful analogy. The board simply will want to know the speed the car (the organization) is traveling at. Still using this analogy, management needs to know more information since the car's speed is a combination of what gear the car is in and what revs the engine is doing. In fact, management might be concentrating on something completely different, such as how economically the car is being driven (e.g., a gauge telling how many miles the car is getting per gallon or how hot the engine is running). These are two completely different PIs.

Separating out KRIs from other measures has a profound impact on the way performance is reported. There is now a separation of performance measures into those impacting governance (up to 10 KRIs in a dashboard, see Chapter 4) and impacting management (PIs, RIs and KPIs).

Performance and Result Indicators

The 80 or so performance measures that lie between the KRIs and the KPIs are the performance and result indicators. The PIs, are all non-financial measures and are linked to specific teams and help the teams to align themselves with their organization's strategy. The RIs, are financial and non-financial measures that summarize a number of teams activities.

Performance indicators are all non-financial and team specific and could include:

- Late deliveries to customers
- Number of employees' suggestions implemented in last 30 days
- Sales calls organized for the next week, two weeks

Result indicators (financial and non financial, cover more than one team:

- Sales made yesterday
- Net profit on key product lines
- Customer complaints from key customers

Key Performance Indicators

KPIs represent a set of measures focusing on those aspects of organizational performance that are the most critical for the current and future success of the organization. They have certain characteristics.

FINANCIAL	CUSTOMER	ENVIRONMENT/ COMMUNITY
Utilization of assets, optimization of working capital	Increase customer satisfaction, targeting customers who generate the most profit	Supporting local businesses, linking with future employees, community leadership

INTERNAL	EMPLOYEE SATISFACTION	LEARNING AND GROWTH
Delivery in full on time, optimizing technology, effective relationships with key stakeholders	Positive company culture, retention of key staff, increased recognition	Empowerment, increasing expertise, and adaptability

EXHIBIT 19.2 A Six-Perspective Balanced Scorecard

Source: David Parmenter, *Key Performance Indicators: Developing, Implementing, and Using Winning KPIs*, 2nd Edition, Copyright © 2010 John Wiley & Sons, Inc. Reprinted with permission of John Wiley & Sons, Inc.

Late Planes KPI

Lord King set about turning British Airways (BA) around in the 1980s by reportedly concentrating on one KPI. He was notified, wherever he was in the world, if a BA plane was delayed. The senior BA official at the relevant airport knew that if a plane was delayed beyond a certain threshold, he would receive a personal call from the chairman. It was not long before BA planes had a reputation for leaving and arriving on time. This KPI affected all six of the balanced scorecard perspectives.

Staff satisfaction and environment and community should be added to the standard four perspectives of financial, customer satisfaction, internal process, and learning and growth, as shown in Exhibit 19.2.

The late planes KPI also linked to many CSFs for the airline, such as the "delivery in full and on time" CSF namely, the "timely arrival and departure of airplanes." The importance of the CSF "timely arrival and departure of airplanes" can be seen by its impact on all of the six perspectives of a modified balanced scorecard.

Late planes:

1. Increased cost in many ways, including additional airport surcharges and the cost of accommodating passengers overnight as a result of late planes being "curfewed" due to noise restrictions late at night.

2. Increased customers' dissatisfaction and alienated those people meeting passengers at their destination (possible future customers).
3. Contributed more to ozone depletion (environmental impact), as additional fuel was used as a result of the pilot using full boost to make up time.
4. Had a negative impact on staff members, particularly in their development, as they would replicate bad habits that created late planes.
5. Adversely affected supplier relationships and servicing schedules, resulting in poor service quality.
6. Increased employee dissatisfaction, as they had to deal with both frustrated customers and the extra stress each late plane created.

Underweight Trucks KPI

A CEO of a distribution company realized that a CSF for its business was trucks leaving as close to capacity as possible. A large train truck capable of carrying more than 40 tons was being sent out with small loads, as dispatch managers were focusing on "deliver in full and on time" to customers.

Each day by 9 A.M., the CEO received a report of those trailers that had been sent out underweight. The CEO called the dispatch manager and asked whether any action had taken place to see if the customer could have accepted that delivery on a different date that would have enabled better utilization of the trucks. In most cases the customer could have received it earlier or later, fitting in with a past or future truck going in that direction. The impact on profitability was significant.

Just as with the airline example, some staff members did their utmost to avoid a career-limiting phone call from their CEO.

Characteristics of a KPI

From a number of years of study, I have come up with these characteristics of a KPI:

- It is a nonfinancial measure (not expressed in dollars, yen, pounds, euros, etc.).
- It is measured frequently (e.g., daily or 24/7).
- It is acted upon by CEO and senior management team.
- All staff members understand the measure and what corrective action is required.

- Responsibility can be assigned to a team.
- It has a significant impact (e.g., it impacts most of the core CSFs and more than one balanced scorecard perspective).
- It has a positive impact (e.g., affects all other performance measures in a positive way).

When you put a dollar sign on a measure, you have already converted it into a result indicator (e.g., daily sales are a result of activities that have taken place to create the sales). The KPI lies deeper down. It may be the number of visits to/contacts with the key customers who make up most of the profitable business.

KPIs should be monitored 24/7, daily, and a few maybe weekly. A monthly, quarterly, or annual measure cannot be a KPI, as it cannot be *key* to your business if you are monitoring it well after the horse has bolted. KPIs are therefore "current" or future-oriented measures as opposed to past measures (e.g., number of key customer visits planned in next month or a list by key customer of the date of next planned visit). When you look at most organizational measures, they are very much past indicators measuring events of the last month or quarter. These indicators cannot be and never were KPIs.

All good KPIs that have made a difference had the CEO's constant attention, with daily calls to the relevant staff. Having a career-limiting discussion with the CEO is not something staff members want to repeat, and in the airline case, innovative and productive processes were put in place to prevent a recurrence.

A KPI should tell you about what action needs to take place. The BA "late planes" KPI communicated immediately to everybody that there needed to be a focus on recovering the lost time. Cleaners, caterers, ground crew, flight attendants, and liaison officers with traffic controllers would all work some magic to save a minute here, a minute there, while maintaining or improving service standards.

A KPI is deep enough in the organization that it can be assigned to a team. In other words, the CEO can call someone and ask, "Why?" Return on capital employed has never been a KPI as it cannot be tied down to a manager; it is a result of many activities under different managers.

A good KPI will affect most of the core CSFs and more than one balanced scorecard perspective. In other words, when the CEO, management, and staff focus on the KPI, the organization scores goals in all directions.

A good KPI has a positive flow-on effect. An improvement in a key measure within the CSF of customer satisfaction would have a positive impact on many other measures. Timely arrival and departure of planes give rise to improved service by ground staff, as there is less "fire fighting" firefighting to distract them from a quality and caring customer contact.

KPIs could include:

- Late projects at the end of the week (projects past their deadline, still unfinished).
- *Key customer* complaints not rectified within 4 hours
- Planes in the sky that are two or more hours late
- Trucks sent on a journey less than 75 percent full
- Orders not delivered in full or on time to *key customers*

Importance of Daily CEO Follow-up

If the KPIs you currently have are not creating change, throw them out because there is a good chance that they may be wrong. They are probably measures that were thrown together without the in-depth research and investigation KPIs truly deserve. CEOs will know intuitively that you have struck gold when six weeks of intense monitoring and a follow-up action create significant change. The CEO should follow up every shortfall with a personal phone call.

Branch managers, store supervisors, or sales reps, after their first phone call from the CEO about nonperformance, will move heaven and earth to avoid another such call. Performance will change quickly. It, however, should be balanced with publicly congratulating high-performance teams. Do not fall down the hole an airline has. As one flight attendant said to me, "Our bosses monitor performance, real time; you are contacted immediately if there is a problem, but you never hear from them when we deliver timely planes day in, day out."

Selling KPIs through the Emotional Drivers

As mentioned in the beginning of the book, nothing was ever sold by logic. You sell through emotional drivers. This project needs a public relations (PR) machine behind it. No presentation, email, memo, or paper should go out unless it has been vetted by your PR expert. All your presentations should be road-tested in front of the PR expert. Your PR strategy should include selling to staff, budget holders, the SMT, and the board.

Here are some of the emotional drivers that will help sell the KPI process. In the current situation you may have:

- A lack of linkage of daily activities to strategy
- Endless performance management meetings that are not improving the performance, yet adversely affecting job satisfaction
- Many lost weekends with family, producing performance reports that are meaningless
- A lack of linkage between the CEO and key staff in the organization
- A lack of focus in management, as the CSFs have not been identified and or communicated
- Staff not sharing the same vision as the management team due more to ignorance than to any disagreement

The project team needs to focus on the marketing of a new concept as much as it does on the training. Budget holders will need to understand how this process is going to help them manage their business. Providing success stories throughout the implementation is therefore a must.

Reporting KPIs 24/7 or Daily to Management

Reporting KPIs to management needs to be timely. As mentioned, KPIs need to be reported 24/7, daily, or at the outside weekly; other performance measures can be reported less frequently, that is, monthly and quarterly.

The main KPIs are reported 24/7 or daily via the intranet. Exhibit 19.3 shows how they should be reported, giving the SMT contact details, the problem, and some history so a meaningful phone call can be made.

Another benefit of providing senior management with daily/weekly information on the CSFs is that the month-end becomes less important. In other words, if organizations report their KPIs on a 24/7 or daily basis, management knows intuitively whether the organization is having a good or a bad month.

Reporting Weekly KPIs and PIs to Management

Some KPIs need to be reported only weekly. Set out in Exhibit 19.4 is an example of how they could be presented. Note that while all the KPIs will be graphed over at least a 15-month time frame, only the 3 KPIs showing a decline would be displayed. The other 2 KPI graphs would be maintained and used when necessary.

Reporting Monthly PIs and RIs to Management

There are endless ways results indicators and performance indicators can be shown monthly—through icons, gauges, traffic lights, and so on. You

EXHIBIT 19.3 Intranet-Based KPI Exception Report Example

Time:

Late planes over 2 hours

	Statistics of last stop					Contact details			No. of late planes over 1 hour		
Flight number	Arrival late by	Departure late by	Time added	Region manager's name	Current time at location	Work	Mobile	Home	last 30 days	30-day ave. of last 3 months	30-day ave. of last 6 months
BA1243	1:40	2:33	0:53	Pat Carruthers	18:45	xxxxx	xxxxx	xxxx	4	3	4
BA1598	1:45	2:30	0:45	xxxxxxx	19:45	xxxxx	xxxxx	xxxx	2	3	4
BA12	1:45	2:27	0:42	xxxxxxx	20:45	xxxxx	xxxxx	xxxx	4	4	5
BA146	1:45	2:24	0:39	xxxxxxx	21:45	xxxxx	xxxxx	xxxx	5	4	4
BA177	1:45	2:21	0:36	xxxxxxx	22:45	xxxxx	xxxxx	xxxx	2	4	3
BA256	1:45	2:18	0:33	xxxxxxx	23:45	xxxxx	xxxxx	xxxx	5	4	5
BA1249	1:45	2:15	0:30	xxxxxxx	0:45	xxxxx	xxxxx	xxxx	2	4	3
Total	7	planes									

Source: David Parmenter, *Key Performance Indicators: Developing, Implementing, and Using Winning KPIs*, 2nd Edition, Copyright © 2010 John Wiley & Sons, Inc. Reprinted with permission of John Wiley & Sons, Inc.

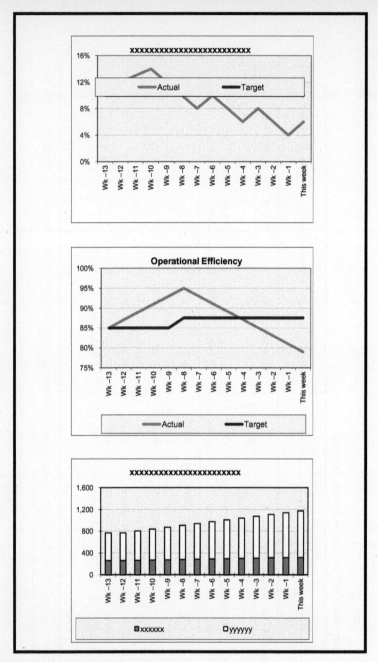

EXHIBIT 19.4 Weekly KPI Report Example

Source: David Parmenter, *Key Performance Indicators: Developing, Implementing, and Using Winning KPIs*, 2nd Edition, Copyright © 2010 John Wiley & Sons, Inc. Reprinted with permission of John Wiley & Sons, Inc.

would not be reporting KPIs monthly as this would be too late. KPIs as already mentioned are reported 24/7, daily, or weekly.

It is best to visit www.davidparmenter.com for good examples or search the web using these search strings: "balanced scorecard" + "formats" + "templates". Exhibit 19.5 shows two formats.

Too often too little thought goes into the design of these management reports. A must-visit for all report designers is Stephen Few's Web site (www.perceptualedge.com), where you can access, free of charge, many high-quality white papers on graphical displays.[4] His book on dashboard design is also highly rated.[5]

Reporting the Key Result Indicators in a Dashboard to the Board

Key result indicators are the perfect performance measure to communicate to the board/council/minister, whether on a monthly, bimonthly, or quarterly basis. They show the reader how the organization has performed in the broadest terms, how it has fared in the organization's CSFs.

I have already covered dashboard reporting in Chapter 4. It would be worth rereading the section titled "Reporting of Key Result Indicators in a Dashboard to the Board."

Reporting to Staff: The Team's Progress

Set out in Exhibit 19.6 is an example of a monthly team scorecard using Excel. This can be a holding tool until a more robust and integrated solution is found. Every week the team will need to focus on some of the more important issues as shown in Exhibit 19.7.

Reporting to Staff: The Organization's Progress

It is a good idea to have some form of monthly icon report for staff, a report that would not be damaging to the organization if it found its way to a competitor. Icon reports, as shown in Exhibit 19.8, are ideal as they tell you what is good, what is adequate, and what needs to be improved, without disclosing sensitive data.

The exhibit is a particularly good example as it shows icons and reminds staff about the strategies.

12-Step Model for Implementing Performance Measures

Many organizations that have operated with KPIs have found they made little or no difference to performance. In many cases this was due to a fundamental

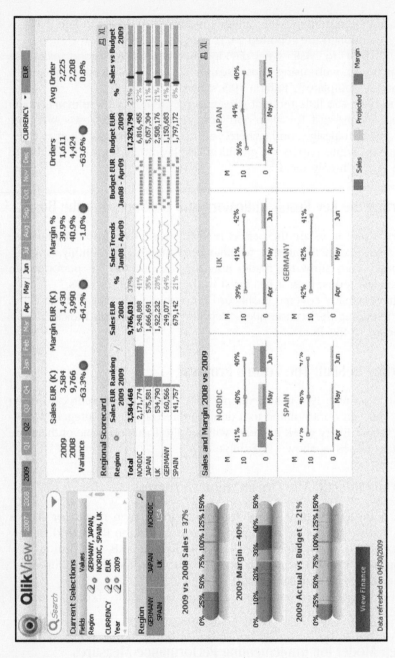

EXHIBIT 19.5 Monthly Report to Management Examples

Source: Inside Info; Visit www.insideinfo.com.au.

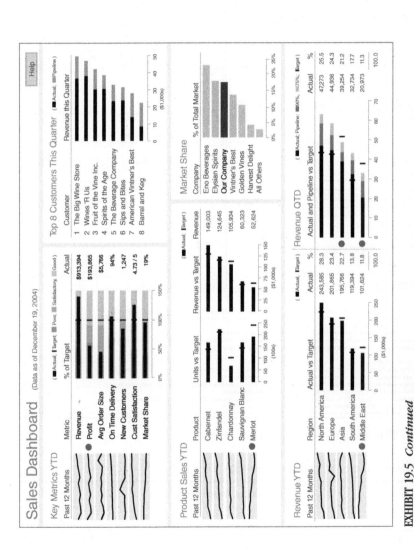

EXHIBIT 19.5 *Continued*

Source: Used with the permission of Stephen Few www.perceptualedge.com.

EXHIBIT 19.6 Team Scorecard Produced Monthly

EXHIBIT 19.7 List of Weekly Measures for a Team

	Weekly Progress Update			
		Week-2	Week-1	Target (mth)
1	Proactive visits to managers	0	1	6
2	No. of staff recognitions made	0	0	6
3	Projects in progress	7	7	<8
4	Reports/documents still in draft mode	12	15	<5
5	Initiatives underway based on satisfaction survey	0	0	5 by 30/6/xx

Progress Report to Staff - For our Operations Throughout September 20XX

Our mission	**To provide energy at the right price at the right time**
Our vision for next five years	**To be the preferred energy provider in the xxx**
Our Strategies (what we are doing to achieve our vision)	**1. Acquiring profitable customers** **2. Increase cost efficiencies** **3. Innovation through our people** **4. Using best business practices**

What we have to do well every day - our Critical Success Factors (CSFs)	Our performance measures in the CSFs		Actual	Target
Delivery in full on time to key customers (KC)	On time deliveries to key customers (KC)		98%	99%
	Goods rejected by KC due to quality defects		3%	4%
We are warriors against waste	Wastage reduction programs started in month		0	2
	Waste reduced from existing programs		9%	10%
We finish what we start	Number of late projects		5	15
	Number of project finishes in month by due date		9	10
We are a learning organisation	Staff training hours this month		150	220
	Staff with mentors		35	80
We grow leaders	Leaders appointed from within last month		4	2
	Managers in leadership programs		8	10
Attracting new profitable customers	Orders from new customers		3	10
	Positive feedback from new customers		3	2
Innovation is a daily activity	Ideas adopted last month		9	20
	Ideas for implementation within 3 months		20	50
We are respected in the communities we work in	Community participation by employees in month		30	20
	New initiatives planned for community, next 3 months		3	2
Increase in repeat business from key customers (KC)	Order book from key customers		$320,000	$400,000
	Number of product developments in progress		3	2

Amber (acceptable)
Red (poor)
Green (good)

EXHIBIT 19.8 Icon Report to Staff Example

Project Week	pre	1	2	3	4	5	6	7	8	9	10	11	12	13	14	15	16	post
1 SMT commitment	■	■											■			■		■
2 Establishing a "winning KPI" project team		■																
3 Establishing a "just do it" culture and process			■	■														
4 Setting up a holistic KPI development strategy				■	■													
5 Marketing KPI system to all employees											■							
6 Identifying organization-wide critical success factors							■	■										
7 Recording of performance measures in a database					■	■	■	■	■									■
8 Selecting team performance measures														■	■	■		
9 Selecting organizational winning KPIs										■							■	
10 Developing the reporting frameworks at all levels																	■	
11 Facilitating the use of winning KPIs																		■
12 Refining KPIs to maintain their relevance																		■

EXHIBIT 19.9 Twelve-Step Implementation 16-Week Timeline

Source: David Parmenter, *Key Performance Indicators: Developing, Implementing, and Using Winning KPIs*, 2nd Edition, Copyright © 2010 John Wiley & Sons, Inc. Reprinted with permission of John Wiley & Sons, Inc.

misunderstanding of the issues. Organizations often begin to develop a KPI system by immediately trying to select KPIs without the preparation that is indicated in the 12-step implementation plan. Like painting the outside of the house, 70 percent of a good job is in the preparation. Establishing a sound environment in which KPIs can operate and develop is crucial. Once the organization understands the process involved and appreciates the purpose of introducing KPIs, the building phase should begin.

A 12-step process has been developed to incorporate better practice and facilitate a swift introduction—in a 16-week time frame. This can be concentrated into a 6-week time frame for organizations with fewer than 200 full-time employees where there is a motivated CEO and senior management team (see Exhibits 19.9 and 19.10).

Note: The blocks indicate the elapsed time, not actual time taken.

This 12-step process can be implemented successfully if four solid foundation stones are laid during the implementation (see Exhibit 19.11). The foundation stones are:

1. Partnership (employees, stakeholders, management, the board)
2. Transfer of power to the front line (so they can fix "late planes" immediately)
3. Measuring and reporting only what matters (each measure has a reason for existing, a linkage to a CSF or a success factor)
4. Linkage of performance measures to strategy (to CSFs balanced scorecard perspectives, and then back to strategy)

How KPIs and Financial Reporting Fit Together

Exhibit 19.12 shows how the components of performance management fit together. The reporting framework has to accommodate the requirements

Phase	Steps		Project Week	pre	1	2	3	4	5	6	post
1	1,4	Selling the change and agreeing on the appropriate timing									
2	1,6,7,8	Workshop to find the organization's CSFs and start team scorecards									
3	2,3	KPI project team trained and empowered									
4	7,8	Teams complete their scorecards and record their measures									
5	9	Selecting organizational "winning KPIs"									
6	10	Developing the reporting frameworks at all levels									
7	11	Facilitating the use of winning KPIs									
8	12	Refining KPIs in 12 months to maintain their relevance									

EXHIBIT 19.10 Twelve-Step Implementation Six-Week Timeline

Source: David Parmenter, *Key Performance Indicators: Developing, Implementing, and Using Winning KPIs*, 2nd Edition, Copyright © 2010 John Wiley & Sons, Inc. Reprinted with permission of John Wiley & Sons, Inc.

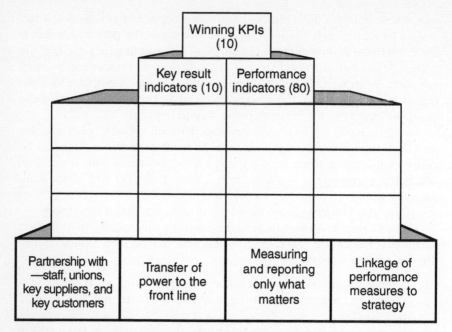

EXHIBIT 19.11 Four Foundations for KPI Development

Source: David Parmenter, *Key Performance Indicators: Developing, Implementing, and Using Winning KPIs*, 2nd Edition, Copyright © 2010 John Wiley & Sons, Inc. Reprinted with permission of John Wiley & Sons, Inc.

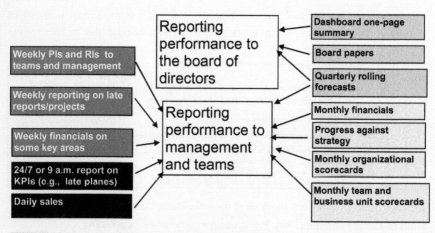

EXHIBIT 19.12 Performance Management Framework

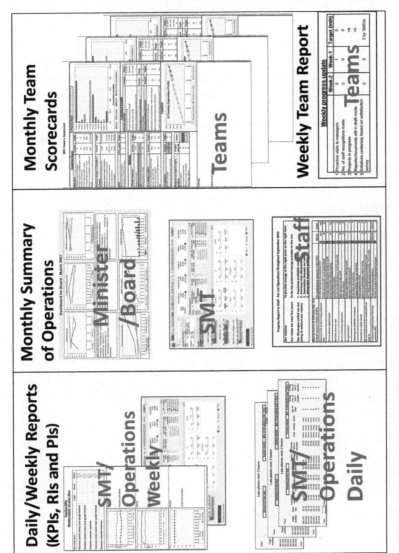

EXHIBIT 19.13 Performance Reporting Portfolio

of different levels in the organization and the reporting frequency that supports timely decision making.

Set out in Exhibit 19.13 is how the reporting of performance measures should work in a private, public, or not-for-profit organization.

Notes

1. David Parmenter, *Key Performance Indicators: Developing, Implementing, and Using Winning KPIs*, 2nd ed. (Hoboken, NJ: John Wiley & Sons, 2010).
2. Robert S. Kaplan and David P. Norton, *Translating Strategy into Action the Balanced Scorecard* (Boston: Harvard Business Press, 1996).
3. Jeremy Hope and Robin Fraser, *Beyond Budgeting: How Managers Can Break Free from the Annual Performance Trap* (Boston: Harvard Business Press, 2003).
4. Stephen Few, "Common Pitfalls in Dashboard Design," www.perceptualedge.com/articles/Whitepapers/Common_Pitfalls.pdf.
5. Stephen Few, *Information Dashboard Design: The Effective Communication of Data* (Sebastopol, CA: O'Reilly Media, 2006).

CHAPTER 20

Where to Invest in Your Accounting Systems for Maximum Benefit

Far too much money is reinvested in upgrading the general ledger (G/L). In a modern company, the G/L does only the basic task of holding the financial numbers for the year. Monthly reporting, latest forecast numbers, budget numbers, and even the drill-down facility available to budget holders often reside outside the G/L package, so why reinvest?

Avoiding the Hard Sell

The impression I have is that all the major G/L systems are designed by freshly minted MBAs who have never been a CFO in their lives. This is the only explanation I can think of for the unnecessary complexity that is embedded in most of the major G/L applications. The major G/L systems like SAP have now made implementing a G/L as complex as setting off to the moon. You need consultants, truckloads of them, to implement the systems.

If you are ever in a hotel lobby and you see a team arrive, smiling, beautifully dressed, with very expensive shoes and of course scratch-free leather briefcases as the members have always flown business class, go up to them and ask, "By chance are you SAP implementers?" You will be right 50 percent of the time.

It is important for the CFO to avoid the hard sell that the G/L providers make. They are experts at selling the systems through your emotional drivers. The Sarbanes-Oxley Act of 2002 has made millions for their bottom line. Instead, the CFO has to look carefully at the options that are available if you keep complexity out of the G/L.

Besides investing in an overly complex G/L, many CFOs are party to a huge investment in other systems that serve to lock in analysis at the micro level (e.g., activity-based costing applications). Jeremy Hope of *Beyond Budgeting* fame points out in his book *Reinventing the CFO*[1] that many such systems are dubious.

Better Systems to Invest in

Instead of changing your G/L, I believe the CFO and the finance team have better investment opportunities elsewhere, which will turn the accounting function into a paperless office. The order of priority should be:

- Implement a planning and forecasting tool and migrate all forecasting and budgeting processes onto it.
- Upgrade accounts payable systems (e.g., scanning equipment, electronic ordering and receipting).
- Acquire a reporting tool and migrate all reporting onto it.
- Add a drill-down front end to the G/L if it is not already part of your G/L (e.g., PowerPlay, Crystal Reporting).
- Install consolidation and intercompany software.
- Use your website to communicate transactions (customer statements and supplier remittances accessible 24/7 using password protection).
- Upgrade the G/L only after you have acquired the above systems and maximized the existing G/L.

Business upgrades to G/L and other core systems often simply replicate existing processes and do not take the opportunity to redesign those processes into new systems. There are many tools in modern systems that are never used!

CFO with blue chip international experience

Planning and Forecasting Tool

The case for investing in a planning and forecasting tool has already been made in Chapter 15. Simply get on with it now. Not to do so will be career limiting! As a corporate accountant, being an expert at Excel will show you are a technical dinosaur, one who has not embraced modern tools and does not understand the inherent risks in running core financial systems with a high-risk tool. It would be worth revisiting Chapter 15 once more.

Invest in Accounts Payable

Finance teams need to invest in accounts payable (AP) to reduce transaction volumes and make the AP operation paperless. For the finance team, the best return on your dollar investment is going to be in AP. As mentioned in Chapter 1, many AP processing procedures are more akin to the Charles Dickens era than to the 21st century. Why do we go from an electronic transaction in to the supplier's accounting system to a paper-based invoice? Surely we should be able to change this easily, with our major suppliers receiving electronic feeds already G/L coded.

Many U.S. multinationals have achieved this already. It requires an investment, skilled AP staff, and retraining of the budget holders. The rewards are immense. To appreciate the benefits, the AP team should regularly visit the website of the Accounts Payable Network (www .TheAPNetwork.com).

There have been major advancements in technology for AP teams. The return on investment in AP technology is greater than any other equivalent investment in other service departments within a business. Why then are some AP teams so underinvested? This is due to:

- Lack of understanding by the CFO of the technologies and their benefits
- The AP team not researching the technologies
- Poor selling of these technologies by application suppliers

Some of the ways to work toward a paperless AP function have been explored in Chapter 1. It would be worth revisiting that chapter once more.

Most accounting systems come with an integrated purchase order system. Some even enable orders to be sent automatically to preferred suppliers, whose price list has been reviewed via the system by the budget holder.

This is a major exercise and one that should be researched immediately. There will be an organization near your locality that has your accounting system where the purchase order system is working well. Visit that company and learn how to implement it.

Reporting Tool

The advancement of reporting tools has meant that the G/L is used merely as a collecting area for financial data for the month. A better practice today is to have a reporting tool collect this data from the G/L overnight, or in some cases weekly, so that the budget holders can drill into their revenues and costs during the month. Management accountants also will use this reporting tool when analyzing costs because it contains prior months' figures in a continuous stream, enabling them to do cross-year financial comparisons seamlessly.

Excel has no place as a reporting tool. Again, it is too prone to disaster. There is no problem where the system automatically downloads to Excel, with all the programming logic being resident in the system and basically bombproof. The problem arises when the system has been built in-house, often by someone who has now left the company, with the accuracy of formatting the G/L download relying on Excel formulas reading the imported file. This is simply a disaster waiting to happen.

A Drill-down Tool

The finance team needs to have an application whereby budget holders can access their transactions by account codes in a simple drill-down format. The information is first summarized, and they can then drill down to the transaction, if necessary.

It is important that budget holders take ownership of their part of the G/L. To this end we need to offer them a user-friendly interface to their part of the G/L. There are a number of tools that can make an old G/L feel like a 21st-century version.

Companies are reporting that they have had great success by downloading transactions (daily or weekly) from the G/L into their drill-down reporting tool application. In fact, the budget holders never look at the G/L. The drill-down tool also offers trend analysis that transcends the year-end, enabling budget holders to look at the last 18- or 24-month trend in expenditure.

Consolidation and Intercompany Software

Performing a consolidation in Excel should be a criminal offence. There are now excellent systems that organize this for you and enable the subsidiaries to have their own general ledger and account code structure. Their trail balance is simply mapped into the consolidated entity's account codes. In addition, sophisticated intercompany software is available that enables an automatic interface for intergroup transactions where one party, to the transaction, does the entry for both G/Ls!

Use Your Website to Communicate Transactions

By allowing secure access to electronic documentation 24/7 that you currently send out by email or post, you will save costs and aid your customers' and suppliers' processing efficiency. Customer statements and supplier remittances can be viewed by customers and suppliers, respectively, using password protection, 24 /7. Some organizations allow major customers and suppliers online read-only access to accounts receivable and AP, respectively.

Maximize the Use of the G/L

You are most likely using only 30 to 40 percent of your G/L's features or capability. Some better practices to maximize the value of your existing G/L are:

- Train, train, train your budget holders on how to use the G/L.
- Delegate the responsibility of maintaining their part of the G/L to budget holders.
- Invest in a G/L upgrade only if you already have a procurement system and a planning tool.
- Get your G/L consultant in next week for a day to see where you can better use your G/L's built-in features—you will be pleasantly surprised.

One CFO receives a visit three to four times a year from the G/L consultant, who reviews what the finance team is doing and then reminds them of other processing features within the G/L that will save them time. These were covered in the training but have been forgotten.

Note

1. Jeremy Hope, *Reinventing the CFO: How Financial Managers Can Transform Their Roles and Add Greater Value* (Boston: Harvard Business Press, 2006).

CHAPTER 21

Implementing a New Accounting System

If you have read Chapter 20 and still are convinced that you really have to upgrade your general ledger (G/L), then there are a number of better practices worth implementing:

- Do not underestimate the communication commitment—have a page on the intranet and talk about the successes in the project to date.
- Get the CEO to send out the memo telling people that they must attend the training session (see Appendix J).
- Celebrate every small success—the celebration alone is a great communication tool.
- Get a day or so of public relations (PR) support—ensuring that all presentations and key memos are bounced off the PR expert. You will be surprised how they can improve the sell component.
- Sell the changes to the budget holders—remember, you sell by the emotional drivers, not by logic.
- Ensure that the next chart of accounts is set up by someone who has the authority and persuasive communication skills to get management and budget holders to agree that there should be fewer than 100 account codes covering the profit and loss statement. See Chapter 13 for the rules for limiting account codes.
- Run a focus group workshop (see Exhibit 21.1) to ascertain the key issues, the problems that should be resolved, and so on.
- Have an accounting systems newsletter to cover the gems that are found from time to time in the system; start this in the last quarter of the project.
- Resist the temptation to customize the accounting system. Once you have made your choice, stick with it; otherwise at upgrade time

EXHIBIT 21.1 Agenda and Outline of G/L Focus Group Workshop

One-day focus group workshop on implementing a new accounting system—and getting it right first time

Objective:
- To ensure a key group of staff and management are fully aware of what is required to implement the new accounting system
- To fully understand the required level of involvement and the inherent hurdles this project will face

Location: xxxxx

Date and Time: xxxxx

Attendees: A focus group selected from experienced staff: covering the regions, branches, depots, and head office and covering the different roles from administrators to senior management team (SMT)

Requirements:
1. Workshop administrator to help coordinate attendees
2. At least three laptops, data show, screen, three electronic whiteboards, quiet workshop space away from the offices

9:00 A.M.	Introduction from CEO
9:10	The problems with the existing accounting system and better practice accounting systems by CFO/Financial Controller
	■ The problems
	■ Reasons why we are taking the system as "vanilla" (e.g., no modifications)
	■ Case studies
	■ Features of the new system
	■ Why so many G/L installations fail
	All SMT and major budget holders are invited to join the focus group. They leave after this session.
10:00	Commence workshop 1: Brainstorming the processing bottlenecks using Post-it reengineering
10:30	Morning break
10:50	Resume workshop 1, finish off reengineering
11:20	Presentation of how the selected G/L application has been implemented in better-practice companies (if selection made)
12:00 P.M.	Lunch
12:45	Commence workshop 2: Brainstorm a new chart of accounts looking to reduce the number to less than xxx
2:00 P.M.	Feedback from groups
2:20 P.M.	Afternoon break

EXHIBIT 21.1 *Continued*

2:40 P.M.	Short presentation on the decision based reporting by xxxxxxxxxxxxxxx
3:30 P.M.	Commence workshop 4 brainstorm new report formats
4:00 P.M.	In-house team complete workshop documentation on lap tops
4:30 P.M.	Presentation by the focus group to the SMT. The focus group state their opinion on the key issues to address and resources required.
5:00 P.M.	Finish of workshop

you will have a nightmare on your hands—even one modification is one too many.

- If you insist on customizing the G/L, make sure you put a copy of the code for all changes to the software in a time capsule in the company's bank (do not trust the filing systems of the information technology team or the consultants who made the changes).
- Make it clear to budget holders that the new G/L is heralding a new world where the finance team has delegated the responsibility of maintaining the G/L to budget holders (e.g., budget holders are expected to monitor their part of the G/L, there will be no spring cleaning at month-end for any mispostings, budget holders will enter accruals directly into the G/L, etc.).

CHAPTER 22

Better Use of the Intranet

Many organizations are failing to make the big leap forward in their use of the intranet because the senior management team (SMT) has failed to recognize its significance to the company's universe.

The intranet is now too important to leave it solely in the hands of the information technology team, as it is one of the most important tools to secure competitive advantage.

For example, a child described a *home page* as the center of a solar system, with information revolving around it. That kid will go far. That is exactly what it is for your organization, even if you may not have a very big solar system yet.

Your Intranet Should Be a Spider's Web

Nature teaches us many lessons. It is a shame we are so slow to learn. An organization, to excel, needs to build its intranet modeled on the garden spider's web. Let me explain.

The spider knows that the web must let the wind through yet catch all passing insects. Your intranet must trap all meaningful data yet let the "flotsam" pass through.

The spider, when building the web, connects to all available support structures. Your intranet needs to capture all aspects of your organization in order to be the one-stop shop for all your employees.

Spiders are constantly rebuilding their web throughout the night; your intranet likewise should be repaired, and linkages improved, on a daily basis.

The spider's web operates 24/7, just as your intranet should. Staff should be able to access their work so they can finish off a report at 1 A.M. from their home office.

Spiders' webs are sticky, and your intranet likewise needs to be designed to ensure employees are constantly in contact with it throughout the day. Eventually the intranet will become a fundamental part of their working life.

The Intranet as a Business Tool

The intranet is simply the best business tool a company has. If used correctly, the intranet will enhance performance, job satisfaction, communication, and knowledge transfer between teams and individuals. In other words, the intranet is far too important to leave solely in the hands of the technology team. In order to extract full competitive advantage, your intranet needs to be driven and supported by all teams, including finance, within the organization.

Show me an organization that has a vibrant and sticky intranet web with tentacles reaching everywhere, and I will show you an organization that is going places. An effective intranet becomes the hub of the company, the place where everyone goes to find the information, tools, and resources necessary to carry out their jobs. The intranet should be the fountain of all knowledge within the company and the gateway to all business applications.

Organizations are moving increasingly to this state. One publicly owned entity, for example, has a good mapping system covering all staff in the organization. Besides the standard photos, title, short CVs, and contact details (the basis of a good intranet section on staff), it includes a section on skills and knowledge. Imagine you are in the middle of a complex problem and you need an expert on statistics or discounted cash flow; all you need to do is search this area. The section on "skills and knowledge" is updated by the staff members themselves, with their managers having the opportunity to add their comments on the site.

Exhibit 22.1, which shows an intranet portal, gives a simplistic view of what an intranet can cover. It could be said that senior management has two options, either to embrace their *intranet* and fully support it or to fiddle while Rome burns. Organizations are placing useful data on the intranet so staffers do not have to access it from the *Internet* (e.g., they found out where staff searched on the world wide web and then put the links on the intranet). All the reports, presentations and images are available to staff to save time. All key business systems are accessed from the intranet, as well as the latest company news and press releases.

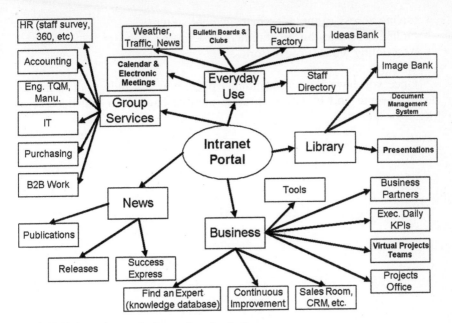

EXHIBIT 22.1 Content of a Better-Practice Intranet

Teams and business units will have their own pages setting out their services to staff and teams in the organization.

What the Finance Team Can Do

One thing you can do immediately as a member of the finance team is to set up your team's home page (see Chapter 9). The content on your finance team's section of the intranet should include:

- Financial reports, at a company level, division level, and department level
- Accounting policies and procedures manual
- Financial delegations
- Accounts receivable information
- Accounts payable information
- Forecasting application so budget holders can enter budget information and it is automatically routed to their manager for approval
- Expense claims so employees can submit claims online and these can be automatically routed to their manager for approval

- Online access to the asset management system
- Online access to the procurement system
- Accounting team success stories

Once you have built your intranet page, why not help your in-house clients prepare and update their team intranet page. You will become a friend for life.

PART III

Areas Where Costly Mistakes Can Be Made

The better practices in Parts One and Two, if implemented, will free up time and make a significant contribution to the organization.

The main goals worth achieving in this part of the book are:

Goal	Reason
1. Redesign all the performance bonus schemes in your organization so that they are based on the better practice foundation stones.	Performance-related pay is an area where the CFO can add much value by ensuring that the bonus schemes are carefully constructed.
2. Understand the ramifications of a takeover or merger (TOM).	TOMs can very easily kill an organization. The CFO needs to be well briefed on the many downsides of a TOM.
3. The CFO must be able to communicate the hidden cost of downsizing to management.	Downsizing is a task that CFOs are frequently asked to be involved in. The hidden costs of downsizing are best understood by the CFO.
4. Limit the number of reorganizations in your organization by conveying to the senior management team (SMT) the downsides of such an activity.	Reorganizations do not solve a problem; in most cases, they create a bigger one. The CFO must effectively communicate this to the SMT.

CHAPTER 23

Designing Performance Bonus Schemes

Performance bonuses give away billions of dollars each year based on methodologies where little thought has been applied. Who are the performance bonus experts? What qualifications do they possess to work in this important area, other than prior experience in creating the mayhem we currently have?

When one looks at the performance bonus experts' skill base, one wonders how they got listened to in the first place. Which bright spark advised the hedge funds to pay a $1 billion bonus to one fund manager who created a paper gain that never turned into cash? These schemes were flawed from the start; *super* profits were being paid out, no allowance was made for the cost of capital, and the bonus scheme was only *high-side focused*.

Foundation Stones

There are a number of foundation stones that need to be laid down and never undermined when building a performance bonus scheme (PBS) that makes sense and will move the organization in the right direction.

Base the PBS on a Relative Measure

You should base the PBS on a relative measure rather than a fixed annual performance contract. Most bonuses fail at this first hurdle. Jeremy Hope and Robin Fraser[1] have pointed out the trap of an annual fixed performance contract. If you set a target in the future, you will never know whether it was appropriate, given the particular conditions of that time. You often end up paying incentives to management when in fact you have lost market share. In other words, your rising sales did not keep up with the growth rate in the marketplace.

Relative performance target measures are where we compare performance with the marketplace. Thus the financial institutions that are making super profits out of this artificial lower-interest-rate environment would have a higher benchmark set retrospectively, when the actual impact is known. As Jeremy Hope says, "Not setting a target beforehand is not a problem as long as staff are given regular updates as to how they are progressing against the market." He argues that if you do not know how hard you have to work to get a maximum bonus, you will work as hard as you can.

Super Profits Should Be Retained

Super profits should be excluded from a performance bonus scheme and retained to cover possible losses in the future. In boom times, annual performance targets give away too much. These *super-profit years* come around infrequently and are needed to finance the dark times of a recession. Yet what do our remuneration experts advise? A package that includes a substantial slice of these super profits yet no sharing in any downside. This downside, of course, is borne solely by the shareholders.

There needs to be recognition that the boom times have little or no correlation to the impact the teams' performance. The organization was always going to achieve this, no matter who was working for the firm. As Exhibit 23.1 shows, if an organization is to survive, super profits need to be retained. If you look at Toyota's great years, the percentage paid to its executives was a fraction of that paid to the U.S. Detroit-based CEOs whose performance was not as successful.

This removal of super profits has a number of benefits:

- It avoids the need to have a deferral scheme for all unrealized gains.
- It is defensible and understandable to employees.
- The amount can be calculated by reference to the market conditions relevant in the year. Where the market has gotten substantially larger, with all the main players reporting a great year, we can attribute a certain amount of period-end performance to super profits.

In designing a bonus scheme, the super-profits component should be a deduction from the profits rather than creating a ceiling for the bonus scheme. If a bonus pool has maxed out, then staff members will rather play golf than work hard to win further business.

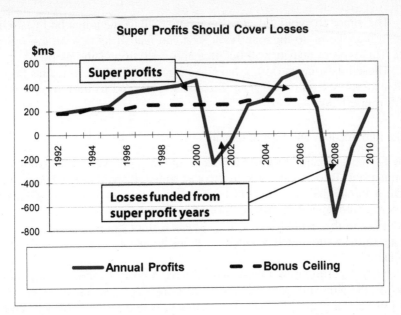

EXHIBIT 23.1 Retention of Super Profits

Free of Profit-Enhancing Adjustments

All profits included in a performance bonus scheme calculation should be free of all major profit-enhancing accounting adjustments. I predict that many banks will be making super profits in the years 2010 to 2015 as the massive write-downs are written back when loans are recovered to some extent. This will happen as sure as night follows day.

I remember a classic case in New Zealand where a CEO was rewarded solely on the basis of a successful sale of a publicly owned bank. The loan book was written down to such an extent that the purchasing bank merely had to realize these write-downs to report a profit, in the first year, that equated to nearly the full purchase price.This activity is no different from many other white-collar crimes that occur under the eyes of poorly performing directors.

One simple step you can take is to eliminate all short-term accounting adjustments from the bonus scheme profit pool of senior management and the CEO. These eliminations should include:

- Recovery of written-off debt
- Profit on sale of assets

The aim is to avoid the situation where management in a bad year will take a massive hit to the loan book so it can feather its nest on the recovery. This type of activity will be alive and well around the globe.

These adjustments do not have to be made for the loan team's bonus calculations. We still want team members motivated to turn around non-performing loans.

Take into Account Full Cost of Capital

The full cost of capital should be taken into account when calculating any bonus pool. Traders can trade in the vast sums involved only because they have a bank's balance sheet behind them. If this were not so, then the traders could operate at home and be among the many solo traders who also play in the market. These individuals cannot hope to make as much profit due to the much smaller positions their personal cash resources facilitate.

Each department in a bank should have a cost of capital, which takes into account the full risks involved. In today's unusual environment, the cost of capital should be based on a five-year average cost of debt and a risk weighting associated with the risks involved. With the losses that bank shareholders have had to absorb, the cost of capital in some higher-risk departments should be set as high as 25 percent.

With the artificially low base rate, in 2009–2010, a fool could run a bank and make a huge bottom line. All banks thus should be adjusting their cost of capital in their PBSs based on a five-year average.

At-Risk Portion of Salary

Any at-risk portion of salary should be separate from the performance bonus scheme. In the finance sector, it is traditional for employees to have a substantial share of their salary at risk. The bonus calculation has been a very primitive one.

The at-risk portion of the salary should be paid when the expected profits figure has been met (see Exhibit 23.2). Note that, as mentioned earlier, this target will be a relative measure, set retrospectively when actual information is known.

The surplus over the relative measure will then create a bonus pool for a further payment that will be calculated taking into account the adjustments already discussed.

Avoid Linkage to Share Price

Performance bonus schemes should avoid any linkage to share price movements. No bonus should be pegged to the stock market price, as the stock

EXHIBIT 23.2 At-Risk Component of Salary

	Remuneration		
	Mgr 1	Mgr 2	Mgr 3
Salary package	60,000	80,000	100,000
At-risk salary (bonus is paid separately)	12,000	16,000	20,000
Base salary, paid monthly	48,000	64,000	80,000
Relative measure, set retrospectively	not met	met	exceeded
Percentatge of at-risk portion paid	40%	100%	100%
At-risk portion paid	4,800	16,000	20,000
Share of bonus pool	0	5,000	10,000
Total period-end payout	4,800	21,000	30,000

market price does not reflect the contribution staff, management, and CEO have made.

Only a fool believes that the current share price reflects the long-term value of an organization. Just because a buyer, often ill informed, wants to pay a certain sum per share for a block of shares does not mean that this share price can be used to value the company.

Providing share options is also giving away too much of shareholders' wealth, often in a disguised way.

Linked to a Balanced Performance

Performance bonus schemes should be linked to a balanced performance. The balanced scorecard has offered another avenue to pay performance bonuses. However, PBSs using a balanced scorecard are often flawed on a number of counts:

- The balanced scorecard often is based on only four perspectives, ignoring the important "environment and community" and "staff satisfaction" perspectives.
- The measures chosen are open to debate and manipulation.
- There is seldom a linkage to progress in the organization's critical success factors (CSFs).
- Weighting of measures leads to crazy performance agreements, such as shown in Exhibit 23.3.

An alternative would be to link the PBS to the organization's CSFs. See an example of an airline PBS in Exhibit 23.4.

EXHIBIT 23.3 Performance-Related Pay Systems that Will Never Work

Category	Perspective Weighting	Measure	Measure Weighting
Financial	60%	Economic value added	25%
		Unit profit	20%
		Market growth	15%
Customer	20%	Customer satisfaction survey	10%
		Dealer satisfaction survey	10%
Internal	10%	Above-average rank on process industry ql	5%
		Decrease in dealer delivery cycle time	5%
Innovation and learning	10%	Suggestions/employee	5%
		Satisfaction survey	5%

Source: International Institute of Management

EXHIBIT 23.4 How the Performance-Related Bonus Could Be Linked to the Critical Success Factors (Airline)

	Operational Team	Public Relations Team	Maintenance Team	Accountants
Financial performance	30%	30%	30%	30%
Progress in CSFs				
Timely departure and arrival of planes	20%	0%	20%	0%
Timely maintenance of planes	10%	0%	30%	0%
Retention of key customers	10%	0%	0%	0%
Positive public perception of organization—being a preferred airline	10%	30%	0%	0%
"Stay, say, strive engagement with staff"	10%	20%	10%	20%
Encouraging innovation that matters	10%	20%	10%	20%
Accurate, timely information that helps decisions	0%	0%	0%	30%

In Exhibit 23.4, all teams have the same weighting for the financial results. Some readers will feel this is too low. However, when you research more on the balanced scorecard philosophy, you will understand that the greatest impact on the bottom line, over the medium and long term, will be in the organization's CSFs.

The operational teams at the airports have a major focus on timely arrival and departure of planes. You could argue that this CSF should have a higher weighting, such as 30 percent. However, these operational teams impact many other CSFs. They clearly impact the timely maintenance of planes by making them available on time and impact the satisfaction of first-class, business-class, and gold card holder passengers. The public's perception of the airline is reflected in the interaction between staff and the public, along with press releases and the timeliness of planes.

Ensuring that staff members are listened to, are engaged successfully, and are constantly striving to do things better (Toyota's *kaizen*) is reflected in the weighting of "stay say strive" and "encouraging innovation that matters." There is no weighting for "accurate, timely information that helps decisions" because other teams, such as information technology and accounting, are more responsible for this, and I want to avoid using precise percentages, such as 7 percent or 8 percent, which gives the impression that a performance pay scheme can be a scientifically based instrument.

The public relations (PR) team has a major focus on creating positive spin to the public and to the staff. All great leaders focus on this area. You need not look past Richard Branson in this respect. The weights for the PR team will focus them in the key areas where they can contribute. Innovation success stories and recognition celebrations will cause staff members to want to focus on this important area of constant improvement, which has been demonstrated so well in Toyota over the past couple of decades.

The maintenance and accounting teams' focus is narrower. The finance team has a higher weighting on "stay say strive" and "encouraging innovation that matters" to help focus its attention on these important areas. This will improve performance and benefit all the other teams the finance team impacts through its work.

Avoid Having Deferral Provisions

Performance bonus schemes should avoid having deferral provisions, which attempt to avoid paying out unrealized gains. All unrealized gains are just that. In many cases they are a *mirage*. While we need to reward those dealers who bought early into a climbing share, we need to recognize that the extent of the gain is largely due to a bounce back.

Already some banks have adopted a deferral mechanism on unrealized gains. While this is understandable, we need to consider likely the impacts:

- We do not want all stocks sold and bought back the next day as a window-dressing exercise that dealers/brokers could easily arrange with each other.
- The financial sector is driven by individuals who worship the monetary unit rather than any other more benevolent force. This is a fact of life. A deferral system will be very difficult for them to accept.
- Staff members will worry about their share of the pool when they leave; the last thing you want is a team leaving so its members can cash in their deferral pool while it is doing well.
- Underperforming staff members will want to hang around for future paydays out of their deferred bonus scheme.

It is my belief that while some sectors may be able to successfully establish a deferral PBS, in the financial sector, this is fraught with difficulties. It would be better to focus on the other foundation stones, especially the removal of super profits.

Tested to Minimize Gaming Risk

All performance bonus schemes should be tested to minimize the risk of being gamed by participants in the scheme. All schemes where money is at stake will be gamed. Staff members will find ways to maximize the payment by undertaking actions that often will not be in the general interest of the organization.

The testing of a new scheme should include:

- Reworking bonuses paid to about five individuals over the past five years to see what would have been paid under the new scheme and comparing against actual payments made.
- Consulting with some clever staff members and asking them, "What actions would you undertake if this scheme was up and running?"
- Discussing with your peers in other companies better practices that work—this will help move the industry standard at the same time as you avoid implementing a scheme that failed elsewhere.

Not Linked to Key Performance Indicators

Performance bonus schemes should *not* be linked to key performance indicators (KPIs). KPIs are a special performance tool, and it is imperative that they not be included in any performance-related pay discussions. KPIs

EXHIBIT 23.5 Trialing the Performance Bonus Scheme before You Go Live

	1991	1992	1993	1994	1995	1996	1997	1998	1999	2000
Annual profits (excluding all cost of capital charges)	180	180	200	220	240	350	370	390	410	450
Removal of accounting entries			(30)							
Super- profits clawback						(10)	(20)	(30)	(30)	(40)
Full cost of capital	(30)	(30)	(30)	(32)	(35)	(60)	(62)	(62)	(75)	(75)
Adjusted profit	150	150	140	188	205	280	288	298	305	335
Expected profit based on market share	140	140	140	160	180	260	260	265	280	290
Profits subject to bonus pool	10	10	0	28	25	20	28	33	25	45
Percentage of pool (33% in this example)	3	3	0	9	8	7	9	11	8	15

	2001	2002	2003	2004	2005	2006	2007	2008	2009	Last Year
Annual profits (excluding all cost of capital charges)	(240)	(60)	290	310	460	520	210	(700)	(125)	200
Removal of accounting entries			(20)		(40)	(40)				
Super profits clawback					(20)	(30)				
Full cost of capital	(25)	(28)	(40)	(42)	(65)	(70)	(30)	(30)	(35)	(30)
Adjusted profit	(265)	(88)	230	268	335	380	180	(730)	(160)	170
Expected profit based on market share			190	220	300	350	170	160		160
Profits subject to bonus pool	0	0	40	48	35	30	10	0	0	10
Percentage of pool (33% in this example)	0	0	13	16	12	10	3	0	0	3

EXHIBIT 23.6 Checklist to Ensure Foundations Are Laid Carefully

1. Be based on a relative measure rather than a fixed annual performance contract

All fixed in advance, annual targets for bonuses are removed	☐ Yes	☐ No
Relative measures are introduced to take account of:		
▪ Comparison against market share	☐ Yes	☐ No
▪ Comparison against other peers	☐ Yes	☐ No
▪ Changes in input costs (e.g., where base rate is zero banks)	☐ Yes	☐ No
Progress against the relative measures is reported three or four times a year	☐ Yes	☐ No

2. Super profits should be retained for the loss-making years to come

Super-profit scenarios analyzed	☐ Yes	☐ No
Historic trends analyzed to estimate when super profits are being made	☐ Yes	☐ No
Drivers of super profits identified (e.g., the interest margin banks had in 2009 meant that even a fool would have made super profits)	☐ Yes	☐ No
Super profits removed from net profit as a percentage of each $m made rather than having a ceiling	☐ Yes	☐ No
Model tested against last 10 or 20 years retained profit/losses to ensure formula is right	☐ Yes	☐ No

3. The profits in a bonus calculation should be free of all major profit-enhancing accounting adjustments

Eliminate all short-term accounting adjustments including:		
▪ Recovery of written-off debt	☐ Yes	☐ No
▪ Profit on sale of assets	☐ Yes	☐ No
▪ Recovery of goodwill	☐ Yes	☐ No

4. Take into account the full cost of capital

All departments that which have a specific profit-sharing scheme should have a cost of capital, that takes into account the full risks involved	☐ Yes	☐ No

5. Separate out at-risk portion of salary from bonus element

Test the new system on previous years	☐ Yes	☐ No
Human resources to discuss the change on a one-to-one basis with all managers affected	☐ Yes	☐ No
Prepare an example of the new scheme and publish in a secure area of the human resources team's intranet section	☐ Yes	☐ No

6. Avoiding linkage to share price movements

Remove all bonuses that are linked to share prices	☐ Yes	☐ No
Remove all share options from remuneration	☐ Yes	☐ No

EXHIBIT 23.6 *(Continued)*

7. Linked to a balanced performance

Remove all key performance indicators (KPIs) from bonus schemes	☐ Yes	☐ No
Evaluate progress against the success in the critical success factors	☐ Yes	☐ No

8. Avoid having a deferral scheme for all unrealized gains   ☐ Yes   ☐ No

9. All bonus schemes must be game tested

Rework bonuses paid to about five individuals over the last five years to see what would have been paid under the new scheme and compare against actual payments made	☐ Yes	☐ No
Consult with some clever staff members and ask, "What actions would you undertake if this scheme was running?"	☐ Yes	☐ No
Discuss with your peers in other companies better practices that work—this will help move the industry standard at the same time as you avoid implementing a scheme that failed elsewhere	☐ Yes	☐ No

10. Do not link KPIs with performance-related pay

Remove all KPIs from performance-related pay	☐ Yes	☐ No
Remove all KPIs from job descriptions	☐ Yes	☐ No
Remove all KPIs from annual performance agreements	☐ Yes	☐ No

11. Communicating with staff using public relations experts

Sold changes via the emotional drivers	☐ Yes	☐ No
Have prepared presentations that are targeted specifically at:		
▪ The board	☐ Yes	☐ No
▪ CEO	☐ Yes	☐ No
▪ Senior management team	☐ Yes	☐ No
▪ Staff (on performance-related pay schemes)	☐ Yes	☐ No

12. Road-test the bonus scheme on last complete business   ☐ Yes   ☐ No
cycle

are too important to be gamed by individuals and teams to maximize bonuses. While KPIs will show, 24/7, daily, or weekly, how teams are performing, it is essential to leave the KPIs uncorrupted by performance-related pay.

Certainly most teams will have some useful monthly summary measures, which I call *result indicators,* that will help them track performance and be the basis of any performance bonus scheme. See Chapter 19 for more information.

Schemes Need to Be Communicated

All PBSs should be communicated to staff using public relations experts. All changes to such a fundamental issue as performance-related pay need to be sold through the emotional drivers of the audience. With a PBS, this will require different presentations when selling the change to the board, CEO, senior management team (SMT), and management and staff. They all have different emotional drivers. We need to note that nothing is ever sold by logic (e.g., remember your last car purchase).

Thus, we need to radically alter the way we pitch the sale of the new performance-related pay rules to the CEO, the SMT, the board, and the affected staff. We have to focus on the emotional drivers that matter to all these parties. The emotional drivers will all be different.

Many change initiatives fail at this hurdle because we attempt to change the culture through selling logic, writing reports, and issuing commands via email. It does not work. The new performance-related pay scheme needs a PR machine behind it. No presentation, email, memo, or paper should go out unless it has been vetted by your PR expert. In addition, I would road-test the delivery of all presentations in front of the PR expert before going live.

All Schemes Should be Road-Tested

Performance bonus schemes should be road-tested on the last complete business cycle. When you think you have a good scheme, test it on the results of the last full business cycle, the period between the last two recessions. View the impact of the bonus on the net profit.

You need to appraise the PBS as you would a major investment in a fixed asset to whose payment you have committed a future stream of income. See Exhibit 23.5 for an example of this road test and Exhibit 23.6 for a checklist for performance bonus schemes.

Note

1. Jeremy Hope and Robin Fraser, *Beyond Budgeting: How Managers Can Break Free from the Annual Performance Trap* (Boston: Harvard Business Press, 2003).

CHAPTER 24

Avoiding a Rotten Takeover or Merger

It is often quoted, and even great leaders seem to forget, that "history has a habit of repeating itself." Company executives, directors, and the major institutional investors (whose support is often a prerequisite) need to learn the lessons and think more carefully before they commit to a takeover or merger (TOM).

How Takeover or Merger Goes Wrong

The main reasons why you should beware of a TOM as set out next.

The Synergy Calculations Are Totally Flawed

The Economist[1] ran a very interesting series on six major takeovers or mergers (TOMs). In the articles, the writers commented that over half of TOMs had destroyed shareholder value and a further third had made no discernible difference. In other words, according to a KPMG report discussed in one article, there is a one in six chance of increasing shareholder value.

TOM advisors and hungry executives are as accurate with potential cost savings estimates as they are with assessing the cost of their own home renovations (in other words, pretty hopeless).

Press clippings are easily gathered with CEOs stating that the anticipated savings have taken longer to eventuate. The reason: It can take up to four years to merge the information technology platforms together, and even when this is achieved, many of the future efficiency and effectiveness initiatives have been put on the back burner.

The synergy calculations never allow enough for the termination and recruitment costs involved in merging entities.

Loss of Focus on Customers

There is no better way to lose sight of the ball than a merger. Merging the operations will distract management and staff from the basic task of making money. While meeting after meeting occurs at the office and sales staff focus on their futures (either applying for positions elsewhere or joining in the ugly scramble for the new positions), the customers are up for grabs. Researchers, sales staff, and marketers are all busy back at their desks trying to perform damage-control exercises as they either jockey for the lifeboats or stay on board to try to keep the ship afloat. It would be an interesting Ph.D. thesis to assess the loss of customers due to merger activity.

Culture Clash

TOMs are like herding wild cats. Where have cultures merged successfully? In reality, one culture takes over another. This is okay when one culture is fundamentally flawed. However, in many mergers, both entities have cultures that work. Now you have a problem. Many competent staff members may choose to leave rather than work in a culture that does not suit their working style.

There Is No Heart in a Merged Organization

How long does it take for a company to develop a heart? This is more than just the culture; it includes the living and pumping lifeblood of the organization. I think it takes years, and some consistency among the management and staff. The merged organization thus cannot have a heart. The organization can be kept alive on life support, but just like a critical patient, it is effectively bedridden and will be in intensive care for some time.

Loss of Years of Intangibles (Passion, History, Research, Projects)

An organization is a collection of thousands of years of experience, knowledge, networking, research, projects, and methodologies. If a major blue chip company said that it was going to deestablish all its staff and management, shareholder analysts would think management had simply lost it. The stock values would fall. This is exactly what a merger does. Research and development is another victim. How do you keep on projects and maintain the level of momentum with unhappy research staff? At worst, you will be moving one team to a new location, making redundant those whom you believe are making the least contribution, and hemorrhaging talent. Research basically gets decimated. It would be interesting to look at the impact on research after the Wellcome Glaxo merger.

The Wrong Management Rises to the Top

I have a theory that the main beneficiaries of a merger are the piranhas, those managers who relish the fight to the top. For them, burying a dagger in someone's back needs to be a daily occurrence; it is the equivalent of our caffeine fix, and they are addicted to it. The result is quite interesting; the merged company very soon becomes dysfunctional as more and more of these caustic managers rise to the top. The senior management meetings make the feeding frenzy over a carcass on the plains of Africa look orderly. These managers do not live and breathe the organization; the ones who did have long since left as there is no heart in the new organization.

Financial Time Bombs Start Going Off

There are many financial time bombs that impact shareholder value.

Severance packages can create further waste as staff members, especially the talented staffers leave before generous severance terms disappear. Thus to retain such people, further salary incentives need to be made that create further pressure on the bottom line.

The TOM is often the time when the shareholders realize the dilution they have been a silent party to comes into full swing, the conversion of options. The surge of the share price as speculators play with the stock means that options can be exercised profitably by the executives who then leave the shareholders holding the rotten TOM.

Avoiding a Lemon

Some companies are still making fictitious money like Enron did. They are shams, and we need to avoid purchasing a lemon. The Enron documentary should be compulsory watching for all investors and employees with pensions invested in their companies. The lessons from Enron and other similar collapses provide a useful guide to predicting corporate collapses. I have designed a checklist that provides the warning signs of a lemon; see Exhibit 24.1. Score more than 5, and you had better *disinvest* before your funds are deinvested from you by others.

EXHIBIT 24.1 Warning Signs of a Lemon

	Is It Covered?	
Stock market loves the share for over a 2–3-year period	☐ Yes	☐ No
CEO has become a media-loved person	☐ Yes	☐ No
The company has adopted some bizarre human resources practices	☐ Yes	☐ No
There is an overhyped culture within the company	☐ Yes	☐ No
The key positions in the top are headhunted visionaries	☐ Yes	☐ No
The investment bankers are earning large transactions fees	☐ Yes	☐ No
There are no questioning articles in the press	☐ Yes	☐ No
Excessive company executive remuneration	☐ Yes	☐ No
Senior management team consists of many rags-to-riches stories	☐ Yes	☐ No
Outside superstars are recruited in with media fan-fare	☐ Yes	☐ No
A high proportion of the income comes from "invisibles"	☐ Yes	☐ No
The organization has created a new market/service that the market does not yet understand	☐ Yes	☐ No
Takeovers are becoming a regular occurrence in the company	☐ Yes	☐ No
There are signs that business ethics are questionable	☐ Yes	☐ No
Very innovative company	☐ Yes	☐ No
Taxi drivers are talking about the shares	☐ Yes	☐ No
The company has changed its executive jet twice in the last three years	☐ Yes	☐ No
Excessive media interest borne from media spin	☐ Yes	☐ No
Executives are charismatic in front of analysts and the press	☐ Yes	☐ No

Human Beings Find It Hard to Conceptualize the Intangibles

For many of us, conceptualizing the abstract is very difficult. A company is most definitely an abstract quantity. It is not a balance sheet; it is much more and much less. Executives in major corporations can write off the annual gross national product of a small country on a failed merger and still not lose sleep at night. The numbers are so large that they appear unbelievable, and the senior management team (SMT) seems to be able to pass them off as just poor management decisions. Yet they are a catastrophe for the investor whose savings are now reduced and the retiree who was relying on the dividends to cover yearly living expenses.

It is impossible for the average board and SMT to completely appreciate all the implications of a merger.

Mergers Are Seldom Done from a Position of Strength

Most mergers are defensive; management is on the back foot trying to make something happen. Defensive TOMs are not a great idea as the companies escaping from a threat often bring their problems into the marriage.

Alternatively, TOMs occur because management consider themselves invincible. They talk to the general public through the press, reveling in their moment in the limelight. Their brief track record of stellar growth is now extrapolated out of all proportion.

There Is Never Enough Time to Fully Evaluate the Target

A merger is like an auction. The buyer rarely has more than a cursory look at the goods before bidding. Management often does not want to find the dirty laundry as it would mean going back to square one again.

During the starry days of courtship, it is important not to limit due diligence in the haste to close the deal, as you tend to know less about each other than you think. The dirty laundry often takes years to discover and clean.

Takeover or Merger Scorecard

Exhibit 24.2 is a scorecard covering the aspects executives need to know before boldly going where others have mistakenly gone before (five out of six TOMs fail to achieve the synergism planned). If the merger must go ahead, then please look at the list in Exhibit 24.2 and get to it. I will not wish you good luck, as that would not be adequate enough.

Alternatives to a TOM

Why is it then that senior management and boards rush like lemmings for this self-annihilation? It is understandable why the investment community and shareholders make the mistake; they are simply naive. Try to find an analyst who has been a successful manager in business. The individual's skill is in adding numbers up and the ability to write seemingly sensible evaluations based on little or no knowledge of why mergers cannot work. Shareholders usually have little time for research or are just plain greedy, looking for supernormal returns and believing all the promotional material that merely lifts share prices over the short term.

EXHIBIT 24.2 Takeover or Merger Scorecard

1. Can your company turn away from a deal if it does not stack up?	☐ Yes	☐ No
2. Have you done an evaluation of the potential downside?	☐ Yes	☐ No
3. Are all the next team players experienced in accurately assessing the full costs of the TOM and accurately estimating synergistic savings?		
Advising brokers	☐ Yes	☐ No
TOM advisors	☐ Yes	☐ No
Board	☐ Yes	☐ No
Executive	☐ Yes	☐ No
4. Have all other alternatives to the TOM been fully explored?	☐ Yes	☐ No
5. Have safeguards been put in place to ensure that the benefits from this TOM accrue to shareholders, staff and local community as well as the executive share option holders?	☐ Yes	☐ No
6. Does your company have experience in doing a proper due diligence process?	☐ Yes	☐ No
7. Has your company enough time to do a proper due diligence process?	☐ Yes	☐ No
8. Has an impact assessment been undertaken on the organization if the TOM fails?	☐ Yes	☐ No
9. Has the company got enough cash reserves to weather any eventual storm arising from the TOM?	☐ Yes	☐ No
10. Have you performed a culture audit? (A TOM is like merging two families, and many problems are overlooked in the frenzied courtship.)	☐ Yes	☐ No
11. Have you locked in a portion of your advisors' fees to a successful realization of the proposed TOM benefits? (Remember, many of your advisors have never worked in an organization that has had a successful TOM.)	☐ Yes	☐ No
12. Have you performed an assessment of asset fit—quality, condition, and usage?	☐ Yes	☐ No
13. Is your target company a CAMEL—an organization that can withstand difficult times? It should be a company with adequate *c*apital, good *a*sset quality, good *m*anagement, record of sound *e*arnings growth, and good *l*iquidity.	☐ Yes	☐ No
14. Has an assessment been done on the locked-in terms and conditions? This is (especially relevant in certain countries e.g. Australia. acquiring an Australian company)?	☐ Yes	☐ No

EXHIBIT 24.2 (*Continued*)

15. Has an evaluation been performed of the current pressure on the environment in which the organization is trading? (At the time you are the weakest, postmerger, the industry is likely to have a major crisis.)	☐ Yes	☐ No
16. Has an assessment been performed on the technology systems integration? (Few understand the implications of a TOM and the time frames involved. The IT team may not have the skills to cope with the now-larger environment.)	☐ Yes	☐ No
17. Has the TOM been initiated through sound reasoning? (Many mergers based on a defensive or cost-cutting strategy fail.)	☐ Yes	☐ No
18. Have you carefully selected the target? Or if you have been approached, have you really ascertained why the company want to sell?	☐ Yes	☐ No
19. Have you checked the adequacy of provisioning for potential bad debts and underperforming loans?	☐ Yes	☐ No
20. Is the business tied to contractual conditions that enable customers to pull out of profitable contracts (a lesson that the Australian bank NAB learned)?	☐ Yes	☐ No
21. Have you established an integration plan that would include the setting up of a council to oversee the key integration projects?	☐ Yes	☐ No
22. Is the current relationship between the companies favorable? (In other words, they have not been fierce rivals in the past.)	☐ Yes	☐ No
23. Do you have the resources to select the new management structure ASAP?	☐ Yes	☐ No
24. Have you got a contingency plan for the potential loss of key staff? (Uncertainty and very generous severance clauses may force executives you want to keep to activate the severance clause for fear of missing out on the generous terms.)	☐ Yes	☐ No
25. Are you prepared to go through the potential pain of lower revenue as management and staff are diverted by the merger?	☐ Yes	☐ No
26. Are you prepared to be made surplus to requirements when the dust has settled and the bloodletting is finished?	☐ Yes	☐ No
27. Have you set up a clear strategy for *after* the merger, including who is getting what job, thus avoiding the cancer of uncertainty?	☐ Yes	☐ No

(*Continued*)

EXHIBIT 24.2 (*Continued*)

---

28. Have you set up an in-house think tank whose task is to   ☐ Yes   ☐ No
speed up integration and to extract knowledge from the
different parts of the joint company and use it in the new
organization?

29. Have you ensured that the joint CEOs are able to work   ☐ Yes   ☐ No
together until the designated word CEO leaves?
(Remember, appearances count.)

There are options other than a TOM. You can:

- Remain a boutique operator with strategic alliances. This may be better than risking the fate of many failed TOMs.
- Pay back shareholders the surplus reserves and let them reinvest elsewhere.
- Improve performance by focusing on underperforming assets (that is often the reason why the other company is interested in you in the first place).
- Look to grow the old-fashioned way by expanding from within.
- Invest as a silent partner (Warren Buffett style) in small but fast-growing companies with complementary services and extract value by internationalizing their innovations.

I met an investment banker on a recent flight who told me about the takeover and merger game that is being played by large investment bankers around the world. It never made any sense to me, because everybody knows only one in six mergers breaks even and many have lost billions off the balance sheet.

The game is called "transactional fees" and involves the study, by the investment bankers, in minute detail of the motivational factors of the key players. They end up knowing more about the private lives of the CFO, CEO, board members, and fund managers than they would like their partner to know. Investment bankers go to the CEO and CFO with a proposed merger and acquisition deal, and they often fail. The CFOs and CEOs know that these deals seldom work.

The investment bankers then go to the influential board members, and the CFO and CEO have to fight it out in the boardroom, which they typically will win. The investment bankers, who have now spent hundreds of thousands of dollars in research, are not finished. They go to the fund managers, who are the major shareholders, and say, "The board has lost the plot; they do not recognize the value in this deal!" The fund managers put pressure on the board, whose members in turn say to the CEO and CFO, "If we do not do this deal, the fund managers will change the board structure—but before that, we will see that you go first." The CEO says, "What the hell, we will do it." Here is the interesting part. The CEO is offered a big sum to go quietly, and this, with the investment bankers' fees are now amortized, through poorly thought out accounting principles, slowly kills the combined company for years to come.

Note

1. "How Mergers Go Wrong," *The Economist*, July 22–August 26, 2000.

CHAPTER 25

Hidden Costs of Downsizing

As a CFO, you should never underestimate the long-term impact of downsizing staff. Whever possible, I believe the CFO should argue that it is better to fund the shortfall out of retained earnings. The cost of firing and rehiring, when added to the public relations disaster it creates, often is much higher than holding on to the staff.

By my calculations (see Exhibit 25.1), an organization with 500 full-time employees that is contemplating dismissing between 50 and 70 staff members would be no worse off if the staff members were kept on and redeployed, where possible, for up to 2.2 to 2.5 years. In reality, through clever use of new initiatives implemented by these staffers some revenue would be generated, further supporting their payroll costs and thus stretching out the downsizing time frame.

When faced with a situation where the business is contracting, there are a number of options you need to explore:

- Can you redeploy the staff and buy some time so staff members have time to seek further employment while employed? This is a managed staff reduction process and will save a huge amount of money on redundancies while at the same time giving your staff an opportunity to find employment. This, of course, does not work in a major recession.
- Working with the human resources team, formally establish a voluntary redundancy program. This has some downsides, as you can't directly target staff members with lesser skill sets.
- Undertake a reorganization, and have everybody reapply for their jobs. This is the coward's way and has huge hidden costs, including the best staff leaving as they walk out the door with a golden parachute and straight into employment elsewhere. This leaves you with the also-rans and the piranhas (those nasty individuals busily burying hatchets in all those around). All organizations that have had reorganizations tend to end up with dysfunctional management teams.

EXHIBIT 25.1 Hidden Costs of Dismissing Staff

Based on 500 Full-Time Equivalent Organization

	General Managers' Time	Managers' Time Organizing	Staff to Stay On	Staff Laid Off
Staff involved	4–6	90–100	340–350	50–70
		No. of weeks worked		
Un-productive time due to uncertainty	6–8	2–3	4–5	4–5
Time spent re-applying for own job	n/a	1–2	1–2	1–2
Interview time	2–3	2–3	0.5	0.5
Redundancy payments	n/a	n/a	n/a	10–16
No.—weeks worked per person	8–11	5–8	5.5–7.5	15.5–23.5
Total weeks for category	32–66	450–800	1870–2625	775–1645
Total salary cost	$4.8m–7.8m			
Redundancy support	1.7m–2.8m			
Cost of rehiring				
Cost of training				
Unproductive time (new staff)				
TOTAL cost	$6.5m–10.6m			
Peroid it would have supported laid-off staff	Between 2.2 and 2.5 years of salary of the laid-off workers			

The experts in this area are the human resources team; never make decisions or move to the next stage without full consultation with them. I hope you are never involved in a massive downsizing, but if you are, prepare for it very carefully. Ensure that you have been as innovative with your solutions as possible. If done well, it could create an achievement that lasts for a career.

CHAPTER 26

A Reorganization Too Many

A major reorganization is as complex as putting in a new runway at Heathrow Airport while keeping the airport operational. The steps, the consultation, the dynamics, and so forth are as difficult. Then how is it that we are unable to fully understand the ramifications and costs of a reorganization, and why do organizations appear to have an addiction to reorganizations?

This chapter, while it may not give a cure for the addiction, may help management be more aware of the symptoms so that advice can be sought.

Ramifications and Associated Costs

The CFO has historically been far too silent when a reorganization is muted. If anyone is to talk sense to the board and senior management team, it has to be the CFO. The CFO needs to ascertain the costs of such an exercise. To assist, I set out next what happens. The cost estimates, included here are based on a national organization with 5,000 full-time employees.

- There is a period of chaos, where staff members are disillusioned and many key staff in the third- and fourth-tier management ranks look to leave (normally in the first six months). You will need to incorporate some costs here based on discussions with your mentors.
- The bedding-in process starts to kick in somewhere between the seventh and twelfth months. The completion of all the redundancies takes longer than expected and, yes, more than a few will come back as contractors at a higher cost. These costs must not be ignored.

- Costs go through the roof, especially consultants' fees. You will need help with the reorganization.
- Designing a new logo (if rebranding) costs can be anywhere between $30,000 and $70,000.
- New letterhead new signage and stationery (if rebranding) is between $200,000 and $300,000.
- Culture change advice will cost $50,000 to $100,000.
- Alignment of procedures costs $20,000 to $50,000.
- Recruiting for new positions assistance costs from $100,000 and $200,000 (yes, we need to allow everybody to apply).
- The cost of commissioning any IT system that is required for the new structure will be between $750,000 to $2,000,000.
- Unwinding of the property leases that may become surplus can take up to 24 to 36 months.

About 24 months after the reorganization was announced, productivity is back to normal; thus for the duration you effectively have been going backward. In the 24- to 36-month period advantages may kick in provided that the reorganization has been successful. It is useful to remember that only one out of seven takeovers or mergers actually works. While reorganizations may have a greater success rate than this, it may well be less than 50 percent.

An Addiction to Reorganizations

CEOs seem to think restructuring operations is good for efficiency, improving service, and, of course, their future aspirations. In some sectors it is an addiction. Government agencies are forever splitting up and then amalgamating. The only purpose I see is to distribute some of the public purse to the private sector advisors, consultants, and contractors (some of whom were previous employees).

As Francis Urquhart[1] would say, "Some of you may think that restructuring a department frees the newly formed teams to deliver, others may think that the confusion, miscommunication that often goes with a reorganization undermines people's confidence in what they do and in their team, giving rise to a period of stagnation. You may think that, but I cannot possibly comment."

Typical Reasons for a Reorganization

Let us analyze the typical reasons for a reorganization.

Reorganizing to Improve Efficiency

Merging two units/teams together or splitting teams up and re-forming into new teams certainly does create a climate change. The question is whether it leads to efficiency. In order to become more efficient, there needs to be a behavioral and procedural change. Staff members need to change work habits so that logical efficiencies can be introduced.

One energy sector company has made much progress with continuous improvement programs. Senior managers are heavily involved in the change management, and now this is part of the culture. The company has workshops to identify areas where change needs to occur, and people at the meetings agree to take on the process of change. They have had a number of successful projects.

One finance company has had a number of successes with business reengineering. It has made significant inroads by using preferred suppliers and eliminating paperwork or passing over the paperwork to suppliers. Continuous improvement is now part of company culture. There is an ongoing requirement for staff members to keep up in their field, bonuses are paid if you pass a tertiary exam, and so forth.

The interesting point about these two stories is that they arose from business reengineering as opposed to business reorganization. Any efficiencies reorganizations achieve are simply those that are associated with reengineering the processes. Thus, one can surmise it would have been better to have performed a reengineering exercise in the first place.

One mistake that the uninitiated often make is assuming that large savings are available when merging corporate service functions, such as merging two accounting functions together. In many cases the costs of changing systems far outweigh the savings from eliminating any duplication of labor costs.

Reorganizing to Improve Service

As stated earlier, a reorganization or merger is like putting in a new runway at Heathrow Airport. Surely, you might think, simply laying down foundations, concrete, and a bit of infrastructure is not that hard. You try telling that to the management at Heathrow Airport.

Likewise, a reorganization is a lot more complex than your planning will have indicated. Day-to-day routines are disrupted with meetings to discuss the new organization, staff members applying for new positions, staff members searching the papers and recruitment agencies for alternative jobs—need I go on? Service does not improve, not in the first two years anyway.

For service to improve, you need a behavioral change. Staff members need to buy into becoming more customer oriented, measuring their performance in a balanced way. You have only to see the quotes on the wall in any Tony's Tyre Service (a tire company in New Zealand) customer waiting room to understand that staff members live and breathe service.

Every job is a self-portrait of those who did it. Autograph your work with quality.
Quality only happens when you care enough to do your best.

A positive behavioral change does not often occur with a reorganization; in fact, quite the reverse occurs in the first two years. So if you are looking for better service, maybe a service program is what is needed rather than a reorganization.

Reorganizing Will Show There Is a New CEO

Many CEOs like to stamp their authority by throwing out systems they do not understand and reorganizing the business to fit a model they are more familiar with. They like to show there is a new broom in the organization. This is typical of a CEO with an ego problem. Many reorganizations occur within the first 6 to 12 months of a new CEO arriving, and often these CEOs are making decisions without full knowledge of the business. The cost to the enterprise is huge. In fact, as part of the recruitment process, one should evaluate the reorganizations the CEO has done.

Exhibit 26.1 is a checklist that should be evaluated before a reorganization occurs.

There Are Alternatives to a Major Reorganization

Appoint a CEO Who Is a Successful Change Agent

I believe an inspirational CEO will create more value than any reorganization ever will. In fact it would be worthwhile looking to see if inspirational leaders ever fall back on reorganization to solve a problem. I can recall the early days of George Hickton, a great New Zealand CEO, taking over the reins of a newly formed government department. Very soon, with a combination of new blood and inspirational leadership, the government department was revolutionized. I believe it was one of the most impressive organizations I have had the pleasure of working for. I can recall the time when George Hickton was presenting at the Institute of Chartered Accountants conference where the front row was taken up by his direct reports who were both interested and passionate about what the CEO was talking about. This was a rare sight, and I expected David Attenborough,

EXHIBIT 26.1 Reorganization Scorecard Checklist

Reorganization Scorecard

1. Have you done an evaluation of the potential downside?	☐ Yes	☐ No
2. Have the senior managers got a convincing story to tell that will capture the minds and hearts of staff—without this staff become disillusioned very quickly and start turning away from the organization?	☐ Yes	☐ No
3. Are all the following participant experienced in accurately assessing the full costs of the reorganization?		
■ The Board/Ministers' office/Council	☐ Yes	☐ No
■ Senior management	☐ Yes	☐ No
■ Advisors you have used	☐ Yes	☐ No
4. Have all other alternatives to the reorganization been fully explored?	☐ Yes	☐ No
5. Have you got a reorganization web page on the intranet site explaining the current status?	☐ Yes	☐ No
6. For all those staff members who have been identified as surplus to requirements, has a reality check been done to ascertain how many of them may be your company's oracles/?(people who have much company history, knowledge, and wisdom)?	☐ Yes	☐ No
7. Have reasonable estimates been made for consultancy fees?		
■ New organization logo, if necessary	☐ Yes	☐ No
■ New letterhead and signage and stationery, if necessary	☐ Yes	☐ No
■ Culture change advice	☐ Yes	☐ No
■ Alignment of procedures	☐ Yes	☐ No
■ Recruiting costs for new positions	☐ Yes	☐ No
8. Have reasonable estimates been made for temporary staff, redundancy pay, and contractors?	☐ Yes	☐ No
9. Have reasonable estimates been made for legal costs—which can be significant if the change process isn't done well?	☐ Yes	☐ No
10. Have reasonable estimates been made for alignment of procedures?	☐ Yes	☐ No
11. Are you prepared to have key projects grind to a halt as staff members lose interest, leave, or are diverted on reorganization exercises?	☐ Yes	☐ No

(Continued)

EXHIBIT 26.1 *(Continued)*

Reorganization Scorecard

12. Have you allowed for lower productivity in the next 18 months as the dust settles? (Think of the lost time due to most managers reapplying for their own positions, endless reorganization meetings, etc.)	☐ Yes	☐ No
13. Have you got a contingency plan for the potential loss of key staff?	☐ Yes	☐ No
14. Have you scheduled in-house team-building exercises, as the reorganization will have created some disharmony among managers as they jockey for position?	☐ Yes	☐ No
15. Have all property-related costs been fully accounted for? (Subletting surplus office accommodation takes much longer than the leasing agent would lead you to believe.)	☐ Yes	☐ No
16. Have you discussed reorganization with two or more of your peers from other organizations?	☐ Yes	☐ No
17. Have you created a checklist on all changed IT requirements?	☐ Yes	☐ No
18. Have you organized any enticements for staff members to help make them stay on? (They are going to be suffering in this reorganization.)	☐ Yes	☐ No
19. Have your organized training?	☐ Yes	☐ No
20. Have you updated the website for the new structure?	☐ Yes	☐ No
21. Have you created press releases for publications and letters to stakeholders, contractors, suppliers, and customers?	☐ Yes	☐ No
22. Have you developed a training program to help managers during the recruitment process?	☐ Yes	☐ No
23. Have you estimated the time and cost of unfair dismissal cases?	☐ Yes	☐ No
24. Are you prepared to create havoc in some of your staff members' lives? (A reorganization is going to create a lot of destruction of staff family life as the temperature reaches a boiling point.)	☐ Yes	☐ No
25. Have you planned to have events that will put some fun back in the workplace? (Reorganizations are pleasure killers.)	☐ Yes	☐ No

safari shorts and all, to come through the curtains at any moment saying, "You are witnessing an event which is rarely caught on camera."

Move Buildings

A few years ago a major oil company had a top-heavy head office. The new CEO realized that the best way to change was to sell the large and spacious head office and acquire a smaller head office building, about one third of the size of the original building. He called the business heads in and said, "Fit in that building, and the staff which members who cannot make it will be made redundant." It transpired, after the move, that there were layers of management whose sole purpose was to attend meetings. Surprisingly enough, when these managers and meetings ceased to exist, the oil company found that operations were unaffected.

Rotate Offices

Arthur Andersen & Co.'s Manchester office, in the UK, United Kingdom had another solution. Each year the senior management team (i.e., the partners) were instructed to move offices. This had the desired effect of energizing and giving the partners a chance to get on top of the paper war. The partners agreed that the hassle was a positive experience, albeit you needed to ask them a couple of weeks after the move!

Improve the Leadership from Within

A reorganization may be an attempt to get around the problem that is created by inadequate or ineffective leadership from the senior management team and the management tier that reports just below that. One way of improving the issue is to undertake a leadership survey, which is a more in-depth look at leadership than a 360-degree feedback can achieve.

You then support these leaders with mentors and follow with an upskilling leadership program. You need to seek mentors who have the X factor. Many would welcome the chance to pass on their knowledge and experience. I guess that if half the people who masterminded a reorganization had talked it through with their mentor, if they had one, many reorganizations would have stayed on the drawing board.

Before You Look at a Reorganization

Before you look at a reorganization, reflect on these points:

- Talk to your peers who have done a reorganization to reassess the likelihood of success and the cost involved.
- The next 18 months may be a period of lower productivity—is the organization prepared for this?
- Focus on your key employees first, to ensure that the reorganization will not disenfranchise them.
- Evaluate the alternatives; there may be a better option.
- Two reorganizations in a three- to four-year period indicates an addiction.

Note

1. *House of Cards*, BBC Production.

CHAPTER 27

Listing on the Stock Exchange

Having firsthand experience of how to list a company on a stock exchange will undoubtedly add many zeros to the bank balance of those lucky CFOs who have had this opportunity. Listing a company on a stock exchange should be done from a position of strength. Being at the mercy of the advising investment bank and chief underwriters is not only costly but an exercise that will not always end up with a happy outcome. CFOs need to learn from their peers who have already walked over the red-hot coals.

Gather Useful Experiences

If ever a CFO needed experience before undertaking a task, this is it: taking a company onto a stock exchange. The handling of this activity requires a confidence that is acquired from prior experience.

Ideally a large private company would seek a CFO who had already handled one or two floats successfully. If, however, you are in the position of doing this for the first time, consider these suggestions:

- Network with CFOs who have been successful in this area. It is easy to get their guidance once you have massaged their ego. Successful people often find time to share their success with others.
- Get yourself a mentor or two who have been there and done it. Someone who has retired is ideal as you may be able to call on his or her assistance in the myriad of important meetings you will have. Sometimes there may be a fee, but it will be a fraction of the exorbitant fees that investment bankers charge.

Selecting the Advisors

Sometimes you will not have a choice here, as the clever investment bankers will have orchestrated the process already. You simply have been taken along for the ride. Your job is to stay on the surfboard rather suffer the consequences of being caught up in the big wave.

If you are in the position of selecting your advisors, some helpful advice includes:

- Research the advisors with the best record by talking with successful CFOs and your mentor(s).
- Understand the strengths of each firm and who are the star players.
- When firms offer their services, you have the opportunity to lock in the key players, as firms will often parade them about. When the job is secured, however, the minions take over. Include in the contract a clause that states that "XXX and YYY will be full time on the project."
- Structure the deal very carefully. You are the client and therefore are entitled to add clauses to suit your needs. Understand the negotiation work of Harry Mills. I can recommend his book *Negotiate: The Seven Step Master Plan.*[1]
- Ensure there are provisions to prevent the investment bank from offloading large portions of shares just after the float, should the issue be undersubscribed. Such an offload could set the share price back for some time.
- Invest time and money researching the background of each member of your investment bank advisory team. They will know who your partner is and the names of your children, so do the same research.

Have a Well-Oiled Public Relations Machine

You will need to have lifted the profile of the board, company, CEO, and CFO in order to maximize the positive market reaction. You need to present a picture that your team can walk on water. In other words, you need to become slightly famous. This is not a time for modesty. You need to present a picture of knowledge and authority if you want to win the confidence of new investors.

It is too late to be embarking on a public relations campaign to lift the profile of the CEO and CFO during the float. As a CFO, you should have been on this journey for a few years already. A good place to start is to read Steven Van Yoder's *Get Slightly Famous*[2].

The Prospectus

Quite frankly, prospectuses are appalling. Often each one looks like the last one. There is good reason for this, as the advisers has copied the template from their last one. If you were to write a book the way the prospectus is written, you would not sell 10 copies.

Remember, it is your prospectus, not the investment bank's. You determine what and how you are to communicate. Public relations experts can help to sell your message well. Most certainly, breaking the investment bank's rules on formatting should be a given. The formatting is a result of years of freshly minted MBAs cutting and pasting from previous prospectuses. Never has there been a thought as to what makes a prospectus a good and easy read.

My late father, a lawyer, would dutifully read these prospectuses and somehow make some sense of them. Few investors would have the time or inclination to do this. The typical prospectus is thus unreadable and unread. Many investors rely principally on the press or advice from their advisors, who themselves are relying on press comments. Hence the importance of a good relationship with the press and a high profile of the CEO, CFO, and other members of the senior management team in the business pages. If a float is on the horizon, you should be planning to deliver special press briefings about the company as soon as possible.

Due Diligence Coordinator

The investment bank will need to satisfy itself about the value of the company, and then the prospectus will need to be audited. It is also possible that a major company may wish to buy a sizable share of the company at the time of the float. Thus you could have up to three separate teams visiting the company to go over the books.

The first step to improving communication between finance staff and the due diligence teams is to have a full-time, in-house due diligence coordinator. This person should be a staff member, not necessarily in finance, who knows most people in the company and knows where everything is; in other words, he or she is "an oracle."

You may find that the ideal person is someone who has recently retired. The important point is that he or she should have no other duties during the due diligence process other than helping the due diligence teams. Give the individual a nice room and say, "When not helping the due diligence teams, you can simply put your feet up." Do not be tempted to give the person additional duties. The coordinator's tasks include:

- Allocating appropriate facilities for the due diligence room(s) (desks, phones, security).
- Providing an induction session for the due diligence staff.
- Gathering any documentation that the due diligence teams need and setting up a well-organized file for them.
- Chasing after any information requests the due diligence teams have made that are still outstanding.
- Setting up designated contact points in every function (e.g., whom to speak to in the marketing department).
- Organizing meetings with the designated person in the section the due diligence teams need to visit.
- Arranging meetings at key times between the CFO and the due diligence teams.

Preparing the Forecast

There will be tremendous pressure for the organization to come up with a good forecast for the next three years of operations. It is sobering to note that you, as CFO, have to put your name to it. The investment bankers and the auditors will run for cover, pointing out that they relied on your representations in certain areas. With litigation on the rise, there will be many CFOs in court fighting against indictments for misleading investors.

I have already covered in detail the rules of good forecasting (see Chapters 14 and 15). For example:

- Never forecast in Excel; if you do, you deserve to be judged in court as incompetent (see Chapter 17).
- Forecast using the key drivers of the business, such as key product demand, key customers, and so on.
- Forecast at category level rather than at account code level.
- Keep the forecast high level, as detail simply provides the misleading view that you can see into the future.
- Spend more time standing back from the forecast to ensure it makes sense.
- Have a bulletproof quality assurance check of the model to ensure it is functioning correctly.

Getting the Timing Right

I spoke to a wise CFO who has floated a company and he said that often organizations are not really ready for a float, in many cases it is not the right place to be and is often done for the wrong reasons. In order to be ready an organization needs:

- An earnings record that showing some stability
- Visibility of the future so prospectus forecasts can be achieved
- Investor relationship expertise (must have this in place before flaot)
- Ability to meet forecast (you have to know what you can and cannot disclose)
- Experience with dealing with "Wall street"
- An internal audit committee and compliance expertise
- A well oiled PR machine (being quoted means that customers, suppliers and staff worry about the share price)

The wise CFO went on to say to me that the time involved is horrendous. The prospectus, the road shows, disclosure of material contracts etc take a lot of time. To make matters worse the advisers are happy to camp overnight so sleep is a rare commodity. His passing quote is to be ignored at your peril *Double your worst estimate and you will be about right.*

Sources of Useful Information

A basic Internet search will yield much useful information on getting listed on a stock exchange. Noteworthy websites include:

- Summary of the rules (www.stockexchangesecrets.com)
- An overview of listings on the main market of the London Stock Exchange (www.withersworldwide.com)
- Financial steps in an initial public offering (IPO) for a small or medium-size enterprise (www.qfinance.com)
- The cost of going public: why IPOs are typically underpriced (www .qfinance.com)

Notes

1. Harry Mills, *Negotiate: The Seven Step Master Plan* (Wellington, NZ: The Mills Group, 1997).
2. Steven Van Yoder, Get "Slightly" Famous! Become a Celebrity in Your Field and Attract More Business with Less Effort (Pt. Richmond, CA: Bay Tree Publishing, 2007).

CHAPTER 28

Managing the Treasury

The CFO's role in managing the treasury department is wide and varied. On one hand, the treasury function has been set up like an internal bank and, on the other hand, we have organizations with little treasury activity and where their banks are the main provider of funds. Many costly mistakes can be made by the CFO as treasurer, such as not managing the relationship with your main banks, investing in instruments you do not fully understand, speculating on the foreign exchange market, borrowing short and investing long, and not managing your debt maturity profile.

An Open and Honest Relationship with Your Banks Will Pay Off

In many organizations, the CFO is responsible for managing borrowing requirements, maintaining an open and honest communication (resisting the internal pressure to be economical with the truth), obtaining a credit rating from one or more rating agencies and liaising with the regional loan officers of the banks. A wise CFO told me that a CFO has to make sure the organization delivers in line with expectations and treats their lenders like shareholders. The wise CFO pointed out that he even has a road-show for lenders on every result announcement.

One finance team I know invites representatives from their main bank to the organization's annual awards. Naturally the bank is encouraged to sponsor a prize and come, as do all the other guests, in fancy dress. The night is a taxi-home event and is enjoyed by all and talked about for months afterward. Naturally enough, the organization always has a smooth run when seeking a loan. One might suggest that good timing would be to seek additional bank loan facilities in the period before the function.

Do Not Get into Deals You Do Not Understand

Many of the traded instruments whose purpose is meant to mitigate risk are in fact creating greater risk. They are designed by freshly minted mathematical experts who understand the numbers but not the reality of business. They have never run a company in their life. The problem starts when your treasury staff, less mathematically talented and in fear of looking dumb, look confidently at you and say they understand the transaction. Instruments are rife with risk. You may be undertaking a transaction with a counterparty whose credit risk is greater than yours. You may be required to deposit margin monies in trust bank accounts that are not very secure.

There are often simple ways to mitigate the risk, and these should be investigated first. If the instrument is perfect for you, undertake it only if you as the CFO and a couple of directors fully understand the ramifications of the instrument and how it behaves with changes in interest or exchange rates.

You Can Never Guess the Future, So Be Half Right and Half Wrong

Many CFOs, along with their treasury staff, get sucked in by the ever-changing foreign exchange market. You know when this has happened when you see a Reuters screen on the CFO's desk. A simpler approach is to avoid making foreign exchange calls altogether. Have a simple policy of covering 50 percent of the 6- or 12-month liability and moving this toward the 75/25 percent range if you feel the currency is moving in one direction. Taking full cover or not covering at all is taking risk that your organization does not need.

Foreign Exchange Trading Can Be a Zero-Sum Game

It is a small step from undertaking forward currency transactions to a full trading desk. CFOs argue that we are more talented than the market and thus can make money. This happened at British Petroleum in the mid-1980s. The treasury staff very quickly became the highest-paid staff in the organization, with large bonuses, based on their gambling success.

All of this activity is not aligned with the critical success factors of the business and has the great chance of undermining the financial stability of the organization. Dealers who are on a bad run start to avoid taking the losses and start running them, betting larger and larger sums in the vain hope that their view will turn out to be right "big time" if we just run the exposure for another day. Before you know it, you have a Barings Bank situation on your hands.

At the end of the day, gambling on the foreign exchange market is a zero-sum game. The losers remove themselves from the table, and then your chances of being on the right side of the deal decrease as the better players outwit you. Besides, no matter how clever your dealers are, there is often enough logic around to persuade yourself that the currency could go up or down.

Obtaining Credit Lines When You Do Not Need Them

They say that a bull or pit bull terrier can smell fear and then all hell breaks loose. Bank managers are the same. If you ever go cap in hand to a bank when you are desperate, it is too late. Bankers smell the fear and then wisely withdraw their support, further worsening the situation.

Clever CFOs always seek credit lines for that rainy day, when the balance sheet is looking strong and they have that take-it-or-leave-it attitude. The costs of the unused facilities are minor in the scheme of things. We are talking about the life or death of the company.

Staggering the Maturity of Loans

Far too often large debt repayments fall due at the time when banks are in their "short hands, long pocket" mood. You can never forecast when these credit crunch times are going to hit so you had best stagger the maturity of the loan book over a reasonable period, as shown in Exhibit 28.1.

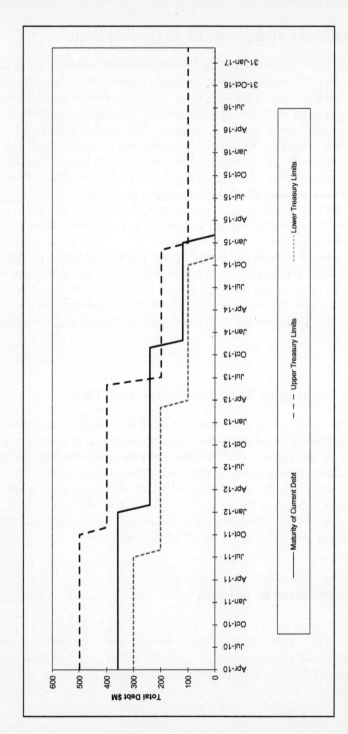

EXHIBIT 28.1 Staggering the Loan Book

I will never forget working in an investment bank that prided itself in being able to take on foreign exchange forward contracts that nobody else would do. The bank manage to get its risk profile the wrong way around. It was taking larger positions the father out time was, thus exposing itself to huge risks. It was only a matter of a few years before it all came undone.

Sources of Useful Information

A basic Internet search will yield much useful information on managing treasury. Noteworthy sites include:

- Nicholas Leeson: "Going For Broke" (www.time.com)
- Treasury Best Practice Community—for professional treasury practitioners (www.TreasuryBestPractice.com)
- Guide to treasury best practice and terminology (www.TreasuryBest Practice.com)
- News website for corporate treasurers (www.gtnews.com)
- Key challenges for treasury (www.gtnews.com)

Checklist of Areas to Focus on in the Next Six Months

Here are the better practices that you can take to get started very quickly in changing the way you handle the processes within your finance team.

Key Tasks to Complete	Tick here if covered	
Accounts Payable (AP)		
Is AP closed on the last working day or earlier?	☐ Yes	☐ No
Are accruals closed off before AP closure?	☐ Yes	☐ No
Have you introduced the purchase card?	☐ Yes	☐ No
Have you integrated systems with the major suppliers so they can send electronic invoices with your general ledger codes on them?	☐ Yes	☐ No
Do you have a web-based expense claim system that can be completed by staff no matter where they are in the world?	☐ Yes	☐ No
Have you introduced scanning technology for all paper-based invoices from your minor suppliers? (All major suppliers will become electronic feeds over time.) The electronic image can then be sent to the budget holder for approval if there is no purchase invoice.	☐ Yes	☐ No
Have all check payments been eliminated, with the last one mounted on the CEO's office wall?	☐ Yes	☐ No

(*Continued*)

Key Tasks to Complete	Tick here if covered	
Are remittances loaded in a secure area of your website so that suppliers can download them by using their password?	☐ Yes	☐ No
Have you got an automated procurement system with electronic ordering and receipting where an invoice can be paid without further approval after being matched to the order and receipting?	☐ Yes	☐ No
Have you got budget holders electronically approving exception invoices (where there is no order, no electronic receipting of services or invoice differs from order) within 24 hours?	☐ Yes	☐ No
Have you introduced consignment stock where the supplier is responsible for constant replenishment (e.g., core stock items [which requires online access to relevant stock records] and stationery)?	☐ Yes	☐ No
Have you sourced national contracts for stationery, travel, and so forth?	☐ Yes	☐ No
Have you asked for consolidated invoices from suppliers, especially power, telecommunications, and stationery?	☐ Yes	☐ No
Have you changed invoicing cycles on all monthly accounts, such as utilities, credit cards, and so on (e.g., invoice cycle including transactions from May 27 to June 26 and being received by June 28)?	☐ Yes	☐ No
Have you instructed major suppliers to request an order from your budget holders?	☐ Yes	☐ No
Do you return all supplier invoices without a purchase order, asking suppliers to attach the purchase order?	☐ Yes	☐ No
Are all large-volume, small-dollar transactions going through the purchase cards (e.g., say, all under $2,000)?	☐ Yes	☐ No
Do you perform frequent electronic funds transfers payment runs?	☐ Yes	☐ No
Do you use self-generated invoices (buyer-created invoices)?	☐ Yes	☐ No
Have you sent a welcome letter to all new budget holders and given them training?	☐ Yes	☐ No
Have you introduced a shame-and-name list to focus budget holders on compliance?	☐ Yes	☐ No

Key Tasks to Complete	Tick here if covered	
Do you reward good budget holder behavior?	☐ Yes	☐ No
Have you performed business reengineering in AP?	☐ Yes	☐ No
Have you ceased all supplier reconciliations?	☐ Yes	☐ No
Have you considered using the suppliers' taxation numbers for their account codes?	☐ Yes	☐ No
Do you have an intranet site for the AP manual, AP team photos, and AP success stories?	☐ Yes	☐ No
Do you perform simulation exercises when recruiting accounts payable staff?	☐ Yes	☐ No
Do you maintain account management within AP (e.g., Pat looks after suppliers A through G)?	☐ Yes	☐ No

Timely Month-End Reporting (see Appendix B)
Decision-Based Reporting

Does your reporting show a linkage among commentary, statements, notes, and graphs?	☐ Yes	☐ No
Is your monthly reporting comparing actuals versus most recent forecast for that month?	☐ Yes	☐ No
Have you introduced a report on the progress with implementing the strategic initiatives?	☐ Yes	☐ No
Have you included a report on the risks/costs pressures the organization faces?	☐ Yes	☐ No
Have you adopted the A3 page (U.S. standard fanfold) summary report for the CEO?	☐ Yes	☐ No
Have you adopted the A3 page (U.S. standard fanfold) investment proposal?	☐ Yes	☐ No
Do you limit variance reporting to major category headings?	☐ Yes	☐ No
Do all finance staff see the finished financial report?	☐ Yes	☐ No
Have you set up icons in your reporting application to highlight variances over a certain amount (whether they are within tolerance, positive, or negative)?	☐ Yes	☐ No
Do you stick to a page per topic (e.g., one-page profit and loss statement, one-page balance sheet, one-page cash flow, one-page capital expenditure, etc., with the accompanying notes on that page)?	☐ Yes	☐ No
Do you have a report that summarizes the status of projects?	☐ Yes	☐ No

(Continued)

Key Tasks to Complete	Tick here if covered	
Have you read Stephen Few's white papers (www.perceptualedge.com)?	☐ Yes	☐ No
Are your reports "big picture" only (e.g., short and concise)?	☐ Yes	☐ No
Can budget holders do their monthly report in less than half an hour?	☐ Yes	☐ No
Do you report on your key performance indicators daily/weekly?	☐ Yes	☐ No
Have you limited the daily, weekly, and monthly routines that are in Excel?	☐ Yes	☐ No

Limiting the Time Invested in Board Reporting

Have you worked out the cost of preparing the board papers each time?	☐ Yes	☐ No
Are all board requests now scoped (e.g., "We want you to xxx, and do not invest more than $5,000 of time on it)?	☐ Yes	☐ No
Has the board been approached to accept papers from the originator (e.g., CFO signs back page saying "I concur but not written by me")?	☐ Yes	☐ No
Has the board been approached to appraise the benefit of putting all board papers on an electronic "board paper" tool?	☐ Yes	☐ No
Has the board been approached to have more timely meetings closer to month-end?	☐ Yes	☐ No
Has a review of board papers been performed with the chairman to eradicate unnecessary papers?	☐ Yes	☐ No
Has the board dashboard been prepared covering the main key result indicators?	☐ Yes	☐ No
Have you commenced a marketing drive to restructure board operations, setting four to six meetings a year instead of the monthly meeting?	☐ Yes	☐ No

Streamlining an Annual Planning Process (see Apendix I)

Managing the Accounting Team

Do you hold half-yearly team away days (e.g., covering training, accounting and interpersonal skills, revisiting corporate objectives, and setting goals)?	☐ Yes	☐ No

Key Tasks to Complete	Tick here if covered	
Do direct reports have a one-to-one meeting with you at the same time each month (e.g., Pat 2 p.m. first Tuesday)?	☐ Yes	☐ No
Have you adopted the better practice recruiting techniques?	☐ Yes	☐ No
Are you recognizing staff performance enough?	☐ Yes	☐ No
Do you have an accounting function balanced scorecard?	☐ Yes	☐ No
Does your team meet out of office at social events?	☐ Yes	☐ No
Do you spend less than 20 percent of the work week in meetings?	☐ Yes	☐ No
Do you hold in-house tailored courses for the finance team (a good benchmark is three days per year)?	☐ Yes	☐ No
Is tertiary education (e.g., MBA programs) included in your training program?	☐ Yes	☐ No
Do all your direct reports have a mentor?	☐ Yes	☐ No
Do you have a mentor?	☐ Yes	☐ No
Have you commenced the 13-week serving leadership program set out in Chapter 6?	☐ Yes	☐ No

Speeding Up the Annual Audit Process (see Appendix D)

Accounts Receivable

Do you provide immediate notice of overdue debt to the sales team?	☐ Yes	☐ No
Have you established clear credit practices and communicated these practices to staff and customers?	☐ Yes	☐ No
Are you professional when accepting new accounts, and especially larger ones (e.g., perform the same credit checks that a bank would when lending the same amount)?	☐ Yes	☐ No
Do you monitor sales invoicing promptness and accuracy?	☐ Yes	☐ No
Do you charge penalties on overdue accounts?	☐ Yes	☐ No
Do you use the banks as cash handlers?	☐ Yes	☐ No
Do you collect over 50 percent of debt by direct debit?	☐ Yes	☐ No

(Continued)

Key Tasks to Complete	Tick here if covered	
Do you offer an ongoing rebate (or a monthly prize drawing) to customers for allowing payment to be processed by direct debit?	☐ Yes	☐ No
Is senior management involved in collecting?	☐ Yes	☐ No
Do you accept credit cards for smaller high-risk customers?	☐ Yes	☐ No
Have you introduced the 15-month trend debtors' graph?	☐ Yes	☐ No
Have you linked price increases with prompt payment rebates?	☐ Yes	☐ No
Do you cut off accounts receivable at noon on the last working day, with the afternoon sales being dated as the first day of the new month?	☐ Yes	☐ No
Do you invoice all "monthly invoices" to customers with an earlier cutoff (e.g., May 26 to June 25)?	☐ Yes	☐ No
Do you invoice all transactions to the 25th of the month, with a second invoice for the remaining period of the month?	☐ Yes	☐ No
Do you send electronic invoices to your major customers, including their relevant general ledger codes?	☐ Yes	☐ No
Have you streamlined the processes between subcontractors and customers to ensure a prompt and accurate billing process?	☐ Yes	☐ No

Marketing the Accounting Team

Do you have an accounting function intranet page?	☐ Yes	☐ No
Is the accounting function intranet page updated at least every two weeks?	☐ Yes	☐ No
Do management accountants, AP, property, office services, CFO, and so forth walk about the office to see internal stakeholders?	☐ Yes	☐ No
Do you attend corporate function launches, etc.?	☐ Yes	☐ No
Do you contribute to your organization's newsletter/ intranet?	☐ Yes	☐ No
Are you adding value to the senior management team (surprising them, giving them success stories)?	☐ Yes	☐ No
Do you hold "cup for a cause" events (e.g., finance team holding a coffee break at their workspace, with guests giving a donation to a specified charity)?	☐ Yes	☐ No

Key Tasks to Complete	Tick here if covered	

Client Management

Have you done an in-house customer satisfaction surveys on the finance team?	☐ Yes	☐ No
Do you constantly give budget holders new insights into their business unit operations every time you meet them?	☐ Yes	☐ No
Have you included trend information (rolling 12- or 24-month graphs) and KPIs in the reporting on business units?	☐ Yes	☐ No
Have you provided training sessions for staff (e.g., accruals, G/L)?	☐ Yes	☐ No
Do you introduce a new cost-saving initiative each month?	☐ Yes	☐ No
Do you help business unit managers with their new reforecasts?	☐ Yes	☐ No
Do you help business unit managers with their projects?	☐ Yes	☐ No

More Emphasis on Weekly Reporting

Are KPIs reported 24/7, daily, weekly?	☐ Yes	☐ No
Are yesterday's sales reported by 9 a.m. the following day?	☐ Yes	☐ No
Are key customers' sales reported on a weekly basis?	☐ Yes	☐ No
Do you report some weekly information of key direct costs?	☐ Yes	☐ No
Are you reporting weekly on late projects?	☐ Yes	☐ No
Are you reporting weekly on late reports?	☐ Yes	☐ No

Working Smarter

Do you hold a daily team debriefing at the end of the day?	☐ Yes	☐ No
Do you limit the number of meetings you have in the mornings (your prime service delivery time)?	☐ Yes	☐ No
Are you using "action meeting" methods?	☐ Yes	☐ No
Have you stopped opening your emails first thing in the morning?	☐ Yes	☐ No
Does your team talk about innovation each day?	☐ Yes	☐ No
Do you have a team mission statement (e.g. "To be awesome at what we do!")?	☐ Yes	☐ No

(Continued)

Key Tasks to Complete	Tick here if covered	
Are your team training sessions systematic and organized?	☐ Yes	☐ No
Do you resolve conflict between team members effectively and efficiently?	☐ Yes	☐ No
Have you invested enough in the induction process for new staff joining the finance team?	☐ Yes	☐ No
Have you created a service ethic in the accounting team culture?	☐ Yes	☐ No
Do you have fun activities in the workplace?	☐ Yes	☐ No

Limit the Profit and Loss to 50 Account Codes

Have you reduced the chart of accounts to a minimal amount?	☐ Yes	☐ No
Have you applied the 1 percent rule for expense account codes (3 to 5 percent for revenue account codes)?	☐ Yes	☐ No

Month-End Reporting Checklist

There are a wide range of steps that can be taken for tackling month-end processing. Set out next is a checklist for you to see if you are utilizing all of them.

Checklist of Implementation Steps

All management made aware of the problem.	☐ Yes	☐ No
Buy-in obtained.	☐ Yes	☐ No
Multifunctional project team set up (reporting, marketing, operations, IT, production planning).	☐ Yes	☐ No
Quick month-end reporting team (QMERT) empowered to make decisions.	☐ Yes	☐ No
Focus on continuous improvement and teamwork.	☐ Yes	☐ No
Mandate from senior management team that all service operations are to adhere to new deadlines issued by the QMERT.	☐ Yes	☐ No
Identified non-value-added tasks, such as posting of automated accruals, automated journals, and allocations, and move them earlier.	☐ Yes	☐ No
Rigorously apply the Pareto principle (80/20), focusing on the big numbers, and establish materiality levels (e.g., >$XX for any debit entry in an accrual list, >$XX for any accrual total from a department, etc).	☐ Yes	☐ No
Manual journal entry line items to be reduced by over 50 percent (80 percent has been achieved).	☐ Yes	☐ No

(Continued)

Checklist of Implementation Steps

Banned spring cleaning from month-end routines (it is done in the quiet periods midmonth	☐ Yes	☐ No
Set up an overs-and-unders schedule to catch material adjustments (this allows the natural set-off to occur, reducing the processed adjustments)	☐ Yes	☐ No
Limited all adjustments to the accounts to those that are material to the "true and fair" view of the month-end report	☐ Yes	☐ No
Eliminate all interdepartmental corrections at month-end.	☐ Yes	☐ No
Eliminate management review of budget holders' numbers as budget holders now have responsibility to resolve issues.	☐ Yes	☐ No
Management report condensed into two pages, one page of performance measures and one on the financial performance of the business unit.	☐ Yes	☐ No
Use estimates to avoid slowing down the process.	☐ Yes	☐ No
Senior management team members have agreed to changes to reports communicated far in advance.	☐ Yes	☐ No
Budget holders have tracked activity throughout the month, eliminating the usual surprises found during the close process.	☐ Yes	☐ No
Allocations are now processed without seeing departmental spending.	☐ Yes	☐ No
Preparations for month-end close moved before period-end instead of after.	☐ Yes	☐ No
The team is issuing constantly communicating on achievements.	☐ Yes	☐ No
Moved all month-end cutoffs to the last working day (Day −1) or the day preceding day (day −2) (e.g., AP cutoff, accruals cutoff).	☐ Yes	☐ No
Interview key users to determine information requirements.	☐ Yes	☐ No
Develop concise decision-based reports.	☐ Yes	☐ No
All key systems upgraded to be online in real time.	☐ Yes	☐ No
Removed duplicate data entry.	☐ Yes	☐ No
Removed manual reconciliations.	☐ Yes	☐ No
Budget holders trained, encouraged, and told to analyze their figures during the month and take corrective action for mispostings, and so on.	☐ Yes	☐ No
Management accountants assigned to specific budget holders.	☐ Yes	☐ No

Checklist of Implementation Steps

Bring management meetings to the third working day after month-end, effectively locking in the benefit.	☐ Yes	☐ No
Adopt a continual focus on process improvement (e.g., every month some new change is implemented to improve processing).	☐ Yes	☐ No
Set up league tables or shame-and-name listings, allowing natural competition between sectors to reduce errors. (Nobody likes being on the bottom.)	☐ Yes	☐ No
Start counting errors.	☐ Yes	☐ No
Run a Post-it reengineering workshop to streamline month-end processes.	☐ Yes	☐ No
Allowing subsidiaries to keep their own accounting systems (where a migration would not be cost-effective).	☐ Yes	☐ No
Closing on the same day each month (e.g., nearest Friday, nearest Saturday, to the calendar month-end, 4-, 4-, 5-week reporting periods per quarter).	☐ Yes	☐ No
Closing off capital projects one week before month-end.	☐ Yes	☐ No
In last week, process only essential operating entries.	☐ Yes	☐ No
Accepting a level of accuracy between 5 and 10 percent.	☐ Yes	☐ No
Issuing a flash report to the CEO by close of play on day +1.	☐ Yes	☐ No
Pushing processing back from month-end by avoiding having payment runs, intercompany adjustments, and so forth, at month-end.	☐ Yes	☐ No
Refocus of "variance to budget" reporting to year-to-date variances, which are more stable, or, better still, to latest forecast for the month.	☐ Yes	☐ No
Limit budget holder's reports to one page (about ten lines of numbers, a couple of graphs, and a third of a page for commentary).	☐ Yes	☐ No
Letting the financial report written by the management accountant go unaltered to the CEO and the board.	☐ Yes	☐ No
Final number and commentary ready by at least close of business day 3.	☐ Yes	☐ No

Month-End Bottlenecks and Techniques to Get around Them

These bottlenecks and techniques are sourced from a benchmarking study of accounting functions that has over 300 accounting teams from all sectors comparing their practices and achievements against one another.

Bottleneck	Proposed Course of Action
1. High processing at month-end	Push processing back from month-end by avoiding having payment runs at month-end. Better practice is to have weekly or daily direct credit payment runs but none happening within the last and first two days of month-end. The last thing you need is to receive a large number of invoices.
2. Intercompany adjustments	Ban all intercompany adjustments at month-end except for internal profit adjustments.
3. Closing off accounts payable	Immediately close off accounts payable on the last working day or, better still, noon on the last working day, with transactions in the afternoon carried forward to the first day of the new month. I have come across no company that can justify closing off accounts payable after the last day of the month.

(Continued)

Bottleneck	Proposed Course of Action
4. Closing off the accruals	Close off accruals on day −2; see below.
5. Closing off accounts receivable, especially handling the last day's sales invoices	Immediately close off accounts receivable on the last working day or, better still, noon on the last working day, with transactions in the afternoon carried forward to the first day of the new month.
6. Inventory cutoff, including the handling of work in progress	Make the cutoff on last working day.
7. Last week's time sheets	For non-revenue-generating time sheets: ■ Get staff to complete by day −3. ■ Include best guess for remaining two days. ■ Project forward on last week. For revenue-generating time sheets: ■ Time sheets from staff required by 9 a.m. last working day. ■ Include best guess for the afternoon. ■ If staff members do not know what they are doing by the start of the day, maybe they should be working for your competitors.
8. Old accounting system	Much can be achieved with an old system. An old system is not an excuse for not reaching day 3 reporting. If you still believe it is, you need a paradigm shift in your thinking.
9. Supplier interfaces	Look to sort out the timely and accurate receipt of electronic data from all major suppliers. Consider self-invoicing, where you generate the supplier invoice based on delivered details and the contract price. The invoice contains all details, such as tax reference number and a unique invoice number using, say, the first three letters of your company, two letters of theirs, and four numbers (e.g., dsbbd3457).

Bottleneck	Proposed Course of Action
10. Awaiting budget holders' reports	Limit budget holders' reports to one page. (See Chapter 3 for an example report). Give budget holders half a day to provide their brief commentary. At the close of business on the last working day (day −1) all cutoffs are complete and numbers sent to budget holders. Budget holders have until noon day +1 to complete their commentary on major variances. The variance must be over $XX and >10 percent of budget before a comment is required.
11. Report-writing stage	Let go of report writing and produce more useful information during the month; see below for details.
12. The monthly forecast	Replace the month-end forecast with a quarterly rolling forecast built in a robust planning tool (see Chapter 15). Reforecasting monthly is meaningless as it does not involve budget holders, creates a year-end number that yo-yos each month, and delays the month-end accounts (as it is the last exercise in the reporting cycle).

Speeding Up the Annual Audit Process Checklist

Key Tasks

Planning Meeting with Auditors

1. Preparation of agenda, which should include:
   a. Status of prior-year significant audit findings (to assess whether they should be an issue this year).   ☐ Yes   ☐ No
   b. Unresolved internal control and accounting issues.   ☐ Yes   ☐ No
   c. Draft milestones discussed and agreement reached.   ☐ Yes   ☐ No
   d. Fine-tuning the content of this checklist.   ☐ Yes   ☐ No
   e. Proposed deadlines.   ☐ Yes   ☐ No
   f. Discussions of new standards and policy.   ☐ Yes   ☐ No
   g. Procedures to alert one another to any potential issues or known obstacles that could affect the audit opinion.   ☐ Yes   ☐ No
   h. Role of internal audit team, their planned work, documentation, and degree of reliance that can be placed on their work.   ☐ Yes   ☐ No
2. Schedule out your desired dates for:
   a. Commencement and completion of interim audit field work.   ☐ Yes   ☐ No
   b. Scheduled progress meetings.   ☐ Yes   ☐ No
   c. Pre-year-end meeting to address accounting issues, with action plans and deadlines (where possible).   ☐ Yes   ☐ No
   d. Sign-off of the words in financial statements.   ☐ Yes   ☐ No
   e. Commencement and completion of final audit field-work.   ☐ Yes   ☐ No
   f. Final audit *issues found meeting*.   ☐ Yes   ☐ No
   g. Audit committee meeting.   ☐ Yes   ☐ No
   h. Release of auditor-signed financial statements.   ☐ Yes   ☐ No

(Continued)

Key Tasks

3. Ensure one or two representatives from headquarters and □ Yes   □ No
   from operations attend this meeting with the auditors.

Between Planning Meeting with Auditors and Their First Visit

1. Formal agreement to deadlines in writing by CFO and   □ Yes   □ No
   auditors.
2. Finalize the auditors' "information needs" list for interim
   and final visits.
   a. Agreement on the content of the information needs   □ Yes   □ No
      list—this list should contain all key items required by
      the auditors prior to the commencement of the final
      audit fieldwork.
   b. Determine the layout and content of working papers for □ Yes   □ No
      each financial statement component, along with the
      scheduled completion date.
   c. All schedules that would take longer than two hours to □ Yes   □ No
      prepare should be discussed with the auditors to ensure
      the investment is worth it.
   d. Responsibility for the preparation of each schedule in □ Yes   □ No
      the information needs list should be assigned
      immediately to specific employees by your office, and
      this information communicated to the auditors.
3. Role of internal audit team: Working papers of the internal □ Yes   □ No
   audit team should be completed and documented to a
   standard allowing the external auditors to place some
   reliance on them and thus reduce the scope of their
   work.
4. Update documentation of internal controls.
   a. Document the systems of internal controls.   □ Yes   □ No
   b. Auditor informed of significant changes in specific   □ Yes   □ No
      internal controls.
   c. All work carried out by internal audit team should be   □ Yes   □ No
      documented.
5. Communication with staff in your organization.
   a. Designate an audit coordinator,   □ Yes   □ No
   b. Designate a contact point in every function,   □ Yes   □ No
   c. Staff and the audit staff should be made aware of who   □ Yes   □ No
      the audit coordinator is.
   d. Have staff members mark their calendars when the   □ Yes   □ No
      auditors will be performing the interim and final fieldwork.

Key Tasks

e. Distribute the information needs list to the appropriate staff.   ☐ Yes   ☐ No

f. Meet with staff a few weeks prior to the arrival of the auditors to assess their progress.   ☐ Yes   ☐ No

g. Discuss conflict management with staff during audit. (The auditors' needs and the normal duties of your staff will create conflict.)   ☐ Yes   ☐ No

Audit Team Interim Visit

1. Organize an off-site get-together between finance team and audit team during the interim visit.   ☐ Yes   ☐ No

2. Arrange and make ready for the auditors' arrival an appropriately sized room or desk space, phone, storage space, secure filing, adequate power connections, parking spots, and so on.   ☐ Yes   ☐ No

3. Introduce the auditors to the audit coordinator and discuss the types of questions and concerns that can be brought to the coordinator's attention.   ☐ Yes   ☐ No

4. Provide to the auditors a contact list listing the key people for each section, their phone numbers and office locations.   ☐ Yes   ☐ No

5. Assign an individual to locate documents for the auditors. (Your staff should be able to gather information quicker and with less disruption than the auditors could.)   ☐ Yes   ☐ No

6. Reconfirm and hold the progress meeting between CFO and audit manager/partner.   ☐ Yes   ☐ No

Pre-Year-End Meeting to Address Accounting Issues

1. Raise all the likely accounting issues. (Discuss draft with management to agree on issues up front.)   ☐ Yes   ☐ No

2. Obtain a sign-off from the auditors as what their audit opinion on these accounting issues is likely to be.   ☐ Yes   ☐ No

3. Discuss and agree quantification of any differences of opinion.   ☐ Yes   ☐ No

4. Agree with the auditors that the month 12 result will be the year-end-result. Any material adjustments greater than $XX that have an impact on the profit and loss and balance sheet will be recorded in an overs-and-unders schedule. (This allows the natural set-off to occur, reducing the need to process adjustments.)   ☐ Yes   ☐ No

(Continued)

Key Tasks		

Assembling a Well-Structured Financial Statement File for the Auditors

1. Supports all numbers in the financial statements.	☐ Yes	☐ No
2. Supports all numbers presented in the notes to the financial statements.	☐ Yes	☐ No
3. Includes all schedules and reports used to compile the financial statement numbers.	☐ Yes	☐ No
4. Schedules and reports should tie directly to the accounting records.	☐ Yes	☐ No
5. Explanations of any significant variances from this year' s to last year's results.	☐ Yes	☐ No
6. Copies of all monthly finance reports.	☐ Yes	☐ No

Audit Team Final Visit

1. Arrange and make ready for the auditors' arrival an appropriately sized room or desk space, phone, storage space, secure filing, adequate power connections, parking spots, and so on.	☐ Yes	☐ No
2. Introduce the auditors to the audit coordinator and discuss the types of questions and concerns that can be brought to the coordinator's attention.	☐ Yes	☐ No
3. Provide to the auditors a contact list noting the key people for each section, their phone numbers, and office locations.	☐ Yes	☐ No
4. Assign an individual to locate required supporting documentation for the auditors. (This may be the audit coordinator.)	☐ Yes	☐ No
5. Hand over financial statement file.	☐ Yes	☐ No
6. Reconfirm and hold the progress meetings between CFO and audit manager/partner.	☐ Yes	☐ No
7. Hand over the overs-and-unders schedule to the audit team—all adjustments found during final audit greater than $XX that have an impact on the profit and loss and balance sheet will be added to this schedule.	☐ Yes	☐ No

Handling the Audit Adjustments and Representations

1. Provide management representation letters in prescribed format.	☐ Yes	☐ No
2. Organize provision of legal counsel representation letters.	☐ Yes	☐ No
3. Post all agreed final audit adjustments to the financial statements.	☐ Yes	☐ No

---

Key Tasks

Post-Year-End Audit Activities

1. Hold a meeting between the audit senior and the audit   ☐ Yes   ☐ No
   coordinator to discuss achievements, problems
   encountered, and possible solutions for next year.
2. Organize post-year-end party to celebrate the end of a big   ☐ Yes   ☐ No
   task.
3. Invite all those involved including the internal auditors.   ☐ Yes   ☐ No

---

Checklist of Strategic Focus Areas

This checklist sets out the better practices that should be implemented once you have freed up time from implementing the initiatives set out in Appendices A to D. Many of these initiatives will leave a lasting legacy in your organization.

Key Tasks to Complete		
Throw Away the Annual Planning and Associated Monthly Budget Cycle		
Do you understand how to report without a monthly budget?	☐ Yes	☐ No
Have you read Jeremy Hope and Robin Fraser's book, *Beyond Budgeting?*	☐ Yes	☐ No
Quarterly Rolling Planning/Forecasting (see Appendix G)		
Cost Apportionment		
Do you keep head office costs where they belong (e.g., avoid apportioning them to the business units)?	☐ Yes	☐ No
Is product costing kept for one-off exercises?	☐ Yes	☐ No
Ban Excel from Daily and Week Finance Team Routines		
Are you replacing daily, weekly, and monthly Excel routines with more robust solutions?	☐ Yes	☐ No
Is the team starting to reskill in 21st-century applications (reporting, drill down, forecasting tools)?	☐ Yes	☐ No

(Continued)

Key Tasks to Complete		

Identify the Organization's Critical Success Factors

Does the senior management team (SMT) and board understand the difference between the *success factors* and the *critical success* factors (CSFs) of your organization?	☐ Yes	☐ No
Have you run an exercise to find your organization's success factors?	☐ Yes	☐ No
Have you run an exercise to find which success factors are the critical ones (the CSFs)?	☐ Yes	☐ No
Does the SMT understand how CSFs and strategy fit together?	☐ Yes	☐ No

Developing Winning Key Performance Indicators and Reporting Them in a Balanced Scorecard

Have you sold the need for a key performance indicator (KPI) project through the emotional drivers?		
Do you understand the difference between the four types of performance measures (KRIs, RIs, PIs, and KPIs)?	☐ Yes	☐ No
Have team members listened to the free webcasts on KPIs by David Parmenter accessed via www.davidparmenter.com?	☐ Yes	☐ No
Have you read David Parmenter's book *Key Performance Indicators: Developing, Implementing, and Using Winning KPIs*, 2nd ed., details available from www.davidparmenter.com?	☐ Yes	☐ No
Do you understand the 10/80/10 rule?	☐ Yes	☐ No
Can you recall the characteristics of KPIs?	☐ Yes	☐ No
Do you and the senior management team understand the 12-step process of implementing KPIs?	☐ Yes	☐ No
Do you and the senior management team understand the role the organization's CSFs play in developing performance measures that work?	☐ Yes	☐ No
Do you have a dashboard for the board of directors?	☐ Yes	☐ No
Do you have a balanced scorecard for management?	☐ Yes	☐ No
Do you have a balanced scorecard for teams?	☐ Yes	☐ No
Do you have an icon-based report telling staff monthly how the organization is progressing with its CSFs?	☐ Yes	☐ No
Do you have a staff icon-based monthly report covering the whole organization's performance on one page?	☐ Yes	☐ No

Maximize Your Accounting Systems

Have you invested in a planning and forecasting tool and migrated all forecasting and budgeting processes onto it?	☐ Yes	☐ No

Key Tasks to Complete		
Have you invested in your accounts payable systems (e.g., scanning equipment, electronic ordering and receipting)?	☐ Yes	☐ No
Have you invested in a reporting tool and migrated all reporting onto it?	☐ Yes	☐ No
Have you invested in a drill-down application (e.g. Crystal reporting, PowerPlay, Qlikview, etc.) that is fed by the general ledger (G/L) so budget holders can access their transactions easily?	☐ Yes	☐ No
Have you invested in your intranet and website so that customer statements and supplier remittances can be viewed by customers and suppliers, respectively, using password protection, 24/7?	☐ Yes	☐ No
Are you constantly training your budget holders on how to use the G/L?	☐ Yes	☐ No
Have you delegated the responsibility of maintaining their part of the G/L to budget holders?	☐ Yes	☐ No
Have you brought back the G/L consultants for, say, half a day to see where you can better use your G/L's built-in features?	☐ Yes	☐ No
Implement a New Accounting System	☐ Yes	☐ No
Did you get the CEO to send out the "you must attend the training session letter"? (See Appendix J.)		
Have you organized a one-day focus group workshop on implementing a new accounting system?	☐ Yes	☐ No
Have you celebrated every small implementation success (the celebration alone is a great communication tool)?	☐ Yes	☐ No
Have you organized a day or so of public relations support to help sell why budget holders should get behind the new system?	☐ Yes	☐ No
Have you sold the new G/L by the budget holders' emotional drivers? (Remember, you do not sell by logic.)	☐ Yes	☐ No
Have you applied the 1 percent rule for expenditure account codes and the 3 to 5 percent rule for revenue account codes?	☐ Yes	☐ No
Have you run a focus group workshop to maximize the new features?	☐ Yes	☐ No
Have you set up an accounting systems newsletter to cover the gems (the G/L system shortcuts that save processing time)?	☐ Yes	☐ No

(Continued)

Key Tasks to Complete

Have you resisted the temptation to customize the G/L? (Even one modification is one too many.)	☐ Yes	☐ No
If you have customized the G/L, have you made sure you put a copy of the code on all changes to the software in a time capsule, in the company's bank?	☐ Yes	☐ No

Make Better Use of the Intranet   ☐ Yes   ☐ No

Does your intranet include financial reports, at the company, division, and department levels (outside the G/L)?		
Do you have your accounting policies and procedures manual on the intranet?	☐ Yes	☐ No
Are your financial delegations on the intranet?	☐ Yes	☐ No
Is accounts receivable information on the intranet so sales staff can monitor customers who have outstanding debt?	☐ Yes	☐ No
Does your intranet include the accounts payable statistics (e.g., managers who have most invoices outstanding)?	☐ Yes	☐ No
Have you posted payments to major suppliers on your website so they can access them 24/7 using an access code and password?	☐ Yes	☐ No
Can reforecasting and budgeting be updated via the intranet?	☐ Yes	☐ No
Do you submit expense reports online and auto-route expense claims for approval?	☐ Yes	☐ No

How a Quarterly Rolling Forecast Can Be Laid Out in a Planning Tool

Here is an example of rolling forecasting with a planning tool, forecasting out six quarters. The first six months are shown with monthly numbers. The tool will have forecast dated for the previous 6 quarters for trend analysis. Forecast six months out as well as a view of the previous six months. Planners can compare different versions of their forecasts. Managing version comparisons in spreadsheets is extremely difficult.

IBM Cognos TM1 Web

Rows: Measures [Measures]
Columns: Periods [Periods]
[Base]

	Month +1	Month +2	Month +3	Qtr +1	Month +4	Month +5	Month +6	Qtr +2	Qtr +3	Qtr +4
Revenue (schedule)	13000	13600	14200	40800	12700	12100	12700	37500	41500	42500
Cost of sales	-5700	-6000	-6200	-17900	-5600	-5300	-5600	-16500	-18300	-18700
⊞ GROSS PROFIT	7300	7600	8000	22900	7100	6800	7100	21000	23200	23800
Sales and Wages (schedule)	3400	3300	3200	9900	3100	3500	3400	10000	11000	12000
Personnel Expenses	450	430	450	1330	820	880	840	2540	1290	1310
Premises, Plant and Equipment	590	580	600	1770	570	600	550	1720	1730	1530
Communications	350	360	380	1090	350	350	350	1050	1100	900
Marketing	350	420	440	1210	420	460	430	1310	1340	1440
Training	240	200	210	650	200	220	190	610	630	720
Corporate Overheads	550	540	550	1640	530	550	530	1610	1640	1520
Miscellaneous	250	260	270	780	280	270	270	820	830	790
Travel and Accommodation (schedule)	400	450	430	1280	470	460	460	1390	1400	1370
⊞ TOTAL EXPENSES	6580	6540	6530	19650	6330	6850	6600	19780	20960	21580
Interest Received (paid)	-40	-30	-20	-90	-50	-30	-40	-120	-130	-120
Taxation p	-200	-310	-440	920	-220	20	-140	-330	-630	-630
⊞ NET PROFIT AFTER TAX E	480	720	1010	2140	500	-60	320	770	1480	1470
Headcount	510	500	500	500	490	530	510	510	515	520
Sales Per Employee ($) per month	$25,000	$27,000	$28,000	$27,000	$26,000	$23,000	$25,000	$25,000	$27,000	$27,000
Gross Profit % on product y	45%	45%	45%	45%	45%	45%	45%	45%	50%	50%
Gross Profit % on product x	55%	55%	55%	55%	55%	55%	55%	55%	50%	50%

Source: IBM Cognos TM1 www.ibm.com

Example of how the model uses formulas.

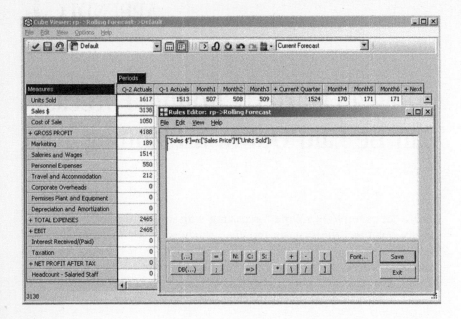

In this sales forecast view, tailored within the planning system, planners can focus on major products and product groupings (versus all products), the key customers per each set, and rounded numbers.

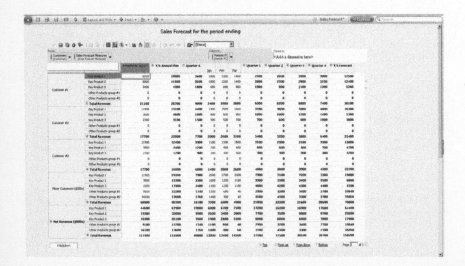

In this example, managers are able to focus on business decisions about their staff levels. New hires (who, when and where). Existing staff who are planning to leave can be assigned an end date. The tool will then automatically calculate the total payroll for the department, including taxes based on the underlying assumptions. Managers can complete this type of payroll forecasting very quickly.

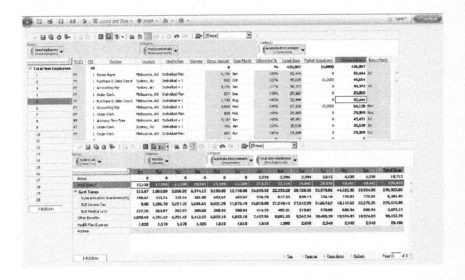

Implementing a Quarterly Rolling Forecast Checklist

This checklist is an evolving tool and is designed to help ensure that while you are juggling the balls, you do not drop the ones that matter.

Secure Senior Management Team Commitment

1. Sold the change through senior management team's (SMT) and the board's emotional drivers (historic evidence, including costs, better practices, benefits to them) via a presentation, ☐ Yes ☐ No

2. Get the board and SMT to agree to separate targets from forecasts. ☐ Yes ☐ No

3. Get commitment for the foundation stones of a quarterly rolling planning process.
   a. Separation of targets from forecasts (telling management the truth rather than what the managers want to hear). ☐ Yes ☐ No
   b. A bottom-up process performed quarterly. ☐ Yes ☐ No
   c. Forecast past year-end (e.g., six quarters ahead). ☐ Yes ☐ No
   d. The monthly targets are set, a quarter ahead, from the quarterly rolling forecast (QRF). ☐ Yes ☐ No
   e. A quarter-by-quarter funding mechanism. ☐ Yes ☐ No
   f. The annual plan becomes a by-product of the QRF. ☐ Yes ☐ No
   g. Forecasting at a detailed level does not lead to a better prediction of the future. (We do not need to forecast at account code level.) ☐ Yes ☐ No
   h. The QRF should be based around the main events/key drivers. ☐ Yes ☐ No

(Continued)

315

i. A fast light touch (an elapsed week).	☐ Yes	☐ No
j. Based on a planning application (e.g., Winforecast, adaptive planning, Corvu, Prophix, Cognos Planning, TM1)—not Excel.	☐ Yes	☐ No
4. Work closely with the executive assistants regarding calendar bookings so senior management team is present during the first forecast.	☐ Yes	☐ No
5. Ensure that management understands what is going to be delivered and what their involvement is (expectation management).	☐ Yes	☐ No
6. Ensure that the CEO is very visible during the road show.	☐ Yes	☐ No

Select QRF Project Team

7. Ensure that the QRF project team has no more than four members.	☐ Yes	☐ No
8. Use people with forecasting, systems structure, and design expertise.	☐ Yes	☐ No
9. Look for personality fit between prospective project team members.	☐ Yes	☐ No
10. Have an end user or budget holder (BH) on the project team.	☐ Yes	☐ No
11. Have the team listen to the free webcast on quarterly rolling forecasting by David Parmenter accessed via www.davidparmenter.com.	☐ Yes	☐ No

Establish Your Quarterly Rolling Pattern (e.g., March, June, September, etc.)

12. Avoid peak or holiday months when planning the weeks the quarterly forecasting is to be performed.	☐ Yes	☐ No
13. Link to monthly/quarterly/six-month external reporting requirements.	☐ Yes	☐ No
14. Determine when the forecast cycle is to be performed (e.g., commence second Monday of March, June, September, December).	☐ Yes	☐ No
15. Set pattern that fits with any legal reporting deadlines.	☐ Yes	☐ No
16. Communicate dates to BHs.	☐ Yes	☐ No

Revisit Last Year's Forecasting Process and Ascertain Lessons Learned

17. Interview two to three members of the senior management team for a debriefing.	☐ Yes	☐ No
18. Interview four to six BHs for a debriefing on the last year's forecasting process.	☐ Yes	☐ No

19. Workshop with a focus group to ascertain hurdles and barriers to QRF.   ☐ Yes   ☐ No

20. Report back findings to senior management team and obtain sign-off for next phase.   ☐ Yes   ☐ No

21. Gather historic information that can be used to help with the new forecasting system (e.g., trends, averages, etc.).   ☐ Yes   ☐ No

Evaluate System Requirements (Including Focus Group Meeting)

22. Hold a focus group one-day workshop, made up of a mix of key individuals around the different businesses and administrators who have a good understanding of operational issues.   ☐ Yes   ☐ No

23. Focus group workshop to ascertain the likely scenarios.   ☐ Yes   ☐ No

24. Have one application demonstrated at the focus group workshop.   ☐ Yes   ☐ No

25. Report on recommended application and how it is to be built.   ☐ Yes   ☐ No

26. Draft road map for development.   ☐ Yes   ☐ No

27. Select at least four to five in-house staff members to become experts on the forecasting system. (Do not forget the CFO.) and ensure they are in the focus group   ☐ Yes   ☐ No

28. Assess the organization's skill set regarding implementation. (Extra training may be required to fill gaps.)   ☐ Yes   ☐ No

Commence Acquisition of Planning Application

29. Appraise systems and short-list to three before requests for proposal.   ☐ Yes   ☐ No

30. Team to visit different sites of preferred solution.   ☐ Yes   ☐ No

31. If major project, prepare a request for information, as new systems are coming online all the time. (This adds time to the project.)   ☐ Yes   ☐ No

32. Establish selection criteria and short-list down to three to five for the proposal.   ☐ Yes   ☐ No

33. Reduce to the best two applications.   ☐ Yes   ☐ No

Organize Test of the Best Two Applications

34. Request short-listed suppliers to demonstrate their application on some key features. Agree to two to three days of consultancy fees and evaluate results. (The winner is expected to offset these days from the quoted price.)   ☐ Yes   ☐ No

(Continued)

35. Sign off on deal.	☐ Yes	☐ No
36. Ensure key consultants are locked in to the job.	☐ Yes	☐ No

Train In-House Designated Experts on the New Application

37. Provide in-depth training to the four to five in-house staff members who are to become experts on the forecasting system. (Do not forget the CFO.)	☐ Yes	☐ No
38. Organize off-site visits so the experts can see other applications and learn from their experience.	☐ Yes	☐ No

Build New Model

39. Agree with consultants that in-house team is to build the model with advice from consultants.	☐ Yes	☐ No
40. Ensure that more than one staff member is involved in design (so you have cover if someone leaves).	☐ Yes	☐ No
41. Complete documentation of logic.	☐ Yes	☐ No
42. Apply Pareto's 80/20 rule and go into detail for major expenditure and revenue items (e.g., personnel costs should have much more detail, should forecast revenue by major customer).	☐ Yes	☐ No
43. Key assumptions easily identifiable in the budget model.	☐ Yes	☐ No
44. Brainstorm with the senior management team (SMT) what their likely scenarios are.	☐ Yes	☐ No
45. The model is based on the key drivers, ascertained through research and discussions with the SMT, including:		
▪ Introduction of the new product(s).	☐ Yes	☐ No
▪ Close-down of an operation.	☐ Yes	☐ No
▪ Delay of a major initiative.	☐ Yes	☐ No
▪ Extrapolations on expenditure profiles that can be best computed by trending data.	☐ Yes	☐ No
▪ Major shift in assumptions.	☐ Yes	☐ No
46. Consultants give training workshops and one-to-one support, but do not perform the modeling.	☐ Yes	☐ No
47. Follow the KIS (keep-it-simple) principle.	☐ Yes	☐ No
48. Make provision to accommodate BHs' calculations in model.	☐ Yes	☐ No
49. Where relevant, link forecasting tool to performance indicators. Have you automated as many cost categories as possible (e.g., consumables, telecommunication costs, office accommodation costs)?	☐ Yes	☐ No

50. Ensure budget holders are directly involved in the forecasting process (e.g., no delegation). ☐ Yes ☐ No

51. Lock in a short forecasting process. ☐ Yes ☐ No

52. Deliver more interesting information from forecast process (e.g., trend graphs, performance measures). ☐ Yes ☐ No

53. During forecasting period (one or two weeks), update frequently how the budget holder numbers are progressing. ☐ Yes ☐ No

54. Constantly market your success stories. ☐ Yes ☐ No

Pilot Planning Application in Two Areas

55. Set up new forecasting regime in two or three units, a quarter ahead, to iron out the bugs and to promote the efficiencies. ☐ Yes ☐ No

56. Fine-tune system based on results and feedback. ☐ Yes ☐ No

Conduct Road Show of New Rolling Forecast Application

57. Prepare presentation (road test in front of PR expert). ☐ Yes ☐ No

58. Test delivery, especially the workshop exercises. ☐ Yes ☐ No

59. Deliver road show. ☐ Yes ☐ No

60. Improve road show, on the road, based on feedback. ☐ Yes ☐ No

61. Explain that BHs are encouraged to give realistic forecasts rather than what they think management wants to hear. ☐ Yes ☐ No

Roll Out Training of Planning Application (Using In-House Experts)

62. Find those staff who thrive with new technology and train them first. ☐ Yes ☐ No

63. Learn from previous forecast mistakes and train staff to avoid them. ☐ Yes ☐ No

64. Train all significant BHs by one-on-one training. ☐ Yes ☐ No

65. Set up from the outset a quarterly follow-up training course. ☐ Yes ☐ No

66. Assess the training needs of the project champion (e.g., some training gaps may need to be filled). ☐ Yes ☐ No

Complete Quality Assurance Processes on First Rolling Forecast

67. Establish in-depth quality assurance procedures. ☐ Yes ☐ No

68. Set up index for QRF file and a standard for working papers. ☐ Yes ☐ No

(Continued)

69. Provide reasonability checks.   ☐ Yes   ☐ No
70. Audit the forecast application prior to use.   ☐ Yes   ☐ No
71. In the calendar of the forecasting committee (CEO, two   ☐ Yes   ☐ No
    general managers, and CFO), book in the key dates when
    they need to be in committee to interview budget
    holders—book a year ahead.

Performing a Quarterly Rolling Forecast Checklist

This checklist is designed to ensure you cover all the bases each time you run a forecast.

Perform Pre-Work for Quarterly Run

1. Automate any additional expense categories you can (e.g., where trend analysis is as good as or better than a budget holder's (BH's) estimate). ☐ Yes ☐ No

2. Update standard costings for travel, accommodation, transfers, and daily allowances to all common destinations. ☐ Yes ☐ No

3. Introduce continuous improvements based on prior-quarter survey feedback. (Perform a survey on a sample of budget holders (BHs).) ☐ Yes ☐ No

4. Complete payroll details and prepopulate all BHs' schedules. ☐ Yes ☐ No

5. Issue quarterly rolling forecast timetable on the intranet. ☐ Yes ☐ No

6. Obtain up-to-date demand forecasts from key customers where possible. ☐ Yes ☐ No

7. Set key assumptions and materiality levels before the forecast round. ☐ Yes ☐ No

8. Prepare presentation for BHs emphasizing "fast light touch" forecast. ☐ Yes ☐ No

9. Send CEO invitation to attend quarterly rolling presentation, all budget holders, stating permission is to be sought from CEO if not attending workshop. ☐ Yes ☐ No

(Continued)

10. Deliver presentation explaining to all BHs how it is   ☐ Yes   ☐ No
    going to be done, assumptions, lessons from last run,
    and so on. (This replaces the issuing of instructions.)

11. Organize additional support to help with one-to-one   ☐ Yes   ☐ No
    support (using local accounting firms—their staff would
    have to attend the workshop).

12. Provide briefing to new support staff from local   ☐ Yes   ☐ No
    accounting firms (if used).

13. Establish schedule of who is to provide whom with   ☐ Yes   ☐ No
    one-to-one support during the forecast process.

14. Have a trend graph for every cost and revenue category   ☐ Yes   ☐ No
    so BHs can sense if their forecasts look reasonable.

15. Limit BHs' forecast requirements to no more than 10 cost   ☐ Yes   ☐ No
    category lines.

16. Process any changes highlighted from last forecast and   ☐ Yes   ☐ No
    audit the formulas in the forecasting application.

17. Remind forecasting committee (CEO, two general   ☐ Yes   ☐ No
    managers, and CFO) of their responsibilities during the
    lock-up.

Support BHs during Forecast Preparation

18. Provide more one-to-one support.   ☐ Yes   ☐ No

19. Provide a daily progress report to CEO of BHs who are   ☐ Yes   ☐ No
    running late—the shame-and-name report.

20. Provide incentives for prompt forecast returns (e.g., give   ☐ Yes   ☐ No
    movie vouchers).

21. Ensure BHs have provided insightful commentary,   ☐ Yes   ☐ No
    including any unusual deviations on the trend graphs.

22. Ensure BHs understand the flexibility of a quarterly   ☐ Yes   ☐ No
    funding regime.

Complete Quality Assurance Procedures

23. Ensure all returns are in.   ☐ Yes   ☐ No

24. Check all key ratios calculated by the the forecast model   ☐ Yes   ☐ No
    for reasonableness.

25. Review all revenue and expenditure graphs to ensure   ☐ Yes   ☐ No
    the trends look reasonable.

26. Ensure all key papers have been saved on the master   ☐ Yes   ☐ No
    file.

27. Rework forecasts where they have known and agreed   ☐ Yes   ☐ No
    errors—with BHs' permission.

28. Check correct treatment of costs on major projects.   ☐ Yes   ☐ No

29. Interviews of BHs by forecasting committee where the forecast is significantly different.	☐ Yes	☐ No
30. Look for missed major expenditure items.	☐ Yes	☐ No

Forecasting Committee

31. Advise BHs of times for them to turn up and present their case to the forecasting committee (e.g., requesting additional funding, wanting to maintain unsubstantiated funding).	☐ Yes	☐ No
32. Forecasting committee confirmed their attendance.	☐ Yes	☐ No
33. Forecasting committee interviewed all relevant BHs.	☐ Yes	☐ No
34. Adjust forecasts based on feedback from forecasting committee.	☐ Yes	☐ No
35. Forecasting committee confirmed forecast.	☐ Yes	☐ No

Presentation of Forecast to Budget Holders

36. Delivery of second presentation—the final forecast numbers—to BHs. (This helps make the quarterly forecast contestable.)	☐ Yes	☐ No
37. Make presentation available on the intranet.	☐ Yes	☐ No

Review Process—Lessons Learned

38. Set up intranet-based feedback survey on quarterly rolling forecast process. Ask what three things went well and what three things could be improved next time. (Once or twice a year would suffice.)	☐ Yes	☐ No
39. Plan next forecast run.	☐ Yes	☐ No
40. Ascertain BHs who require special assistance next time.	☐ Yes	☐ No
41. Check for any timing differences when the last month-end numbers are finalized (e.g., is there a major event that will now happen in the first month that was not forecast to occur, or vice versa?).	☐ Yes	☐ No
42. Update reporting application with new targets for the upcoming three months.	☐ Yes	☐ No

Streamlining an Annual Planning Process Checklist

Many accountants find themselves having to maintain an annual planning process even though they would rather be doing quarterly rolling planning. This checklist is designed to help make the antiquated process quicker and at the same time plant the seed for quarterly rolling planning. This checklist assumes you have a robust planning tool. Those working in Excel will need to add a prayer section to the checklist.

Key Tasks

Run a Workshop to Analyze Pitfalls and Sell the Concept of Quarterly Funding

1. Notify those who should attend.   ☐ Yes   ☐ No
2. CEO to send email stating permission is to be sought   ☐ Yes   ☐ No
   from CEO if not attending the annual planning
   workshop.
3. Lock in an agreement on the foundation stones:
   - Bolt down your strategy and strategic initiatives first   ☐ Yes   ☐ No
     (e.g., have the senior management team gone on an
     executive retreat before the annual planning starts?).
   - There is no need to have a budget for every account   ☐ Yes   ☐ No
     code in the general ledger; instead use the use the 10
     percent rule.
   - Annual plan is not to be broken down into 12   ☐ Yes   ☐ No
     monthly targets; monthly breakdown will come from
     the quarterly rolling planning process.

(Continued)

Key Tasks

- The annual plan does not give an annual entitlement to spend; that is given each quarter during the quarterly rolling planning update. ☐ Yes ☐ No
- Budget committee ready for the one-week lock-up in the second week of the annual planning process. ☐ Yes ☐ No
- There is to be a 10-working-day time scale, and there is a ban on travel or vacations during these two weeks. ☐ Yes ☐ No
- Each budget holder (BH) has one chance to discuss his or her annual plan with the budget committee, and the decision from the meeting is final. ☐ Yes ☐ No
- Each BH is required to forecast only up to 10 category headings. (Each category is a group of account codes.) ☐ Yes ☐ No
- Each BH is required to forecast only a category heading that represents over 10 percent of total revenue or total costs, whichever is relevant. ☐ Yes ☐ No

4. Have you sold the change to a 10-day annual planning process through emotional drivers? ☐ Yes ☐ No

Perform Pre-Work

5. Automate as many expense categories where trend analysis is as good as, or better than, a BH's estimate (e.g., consumables, telecommunication costs, accommodation). ☐ Yes ☐ No
6. Establish standard costings for travel and accommodation so BHs can quickly work out their travel costs (using standard costs). ☐ Yes ☐ No
7. Download all payroll details so BHs can quickly and accurately calculate their salaries and wages. ☐ Yes ☐ No
8. Issue annual planning timetable on the intranet. ☐ Yes ☐ No
9. Obtain up-to-date demand forecasts from key customers where possible. ☐ Yes ☐ No
10. Set key assumptions and materiality levels. ☐ Yes ☐ No
11. Prepare presentation for BHs (slides and handouts). ☐ Yes ☐ No
12. CEO to send invitation to attend annual planning workshop. ☐ Yes ☐ No
13. CEO to send email stating permission is to be sought from CEO if not attending presentation. ☐ Yes ☐ No

Key Tasks

14. Deliver presentation to all BHs of how it is going to be done—this replaces the issuing of budget instructions. ☐ Yes ☐ No

15. Organize additional support to help with one-to-one support in remote locations (using local accounting firms—their staff would have to attend the presentation). ☐ Yes ☐ No

16. Commenced the migration from Excel over to a planning and forecasting application. (Do not forget the cheaper forecasting tools, which could be a temporary fix.) ☐ Yes ☐ No

17. Establish schedule of who is to provide whom with one-to-one support during the forecast. ☐ Yes ☐ No

18. Have a trend graph for every revenue and expenditure category. ☐ Yes ☐ No

19. Establish a budget committee (CEO, two general managers, and CFO), and explain their responsibilities. ☐ Yes ☐ No

Support Budget Holders during Budget Preparation

20. Provide one-to-one support to BHs. ☐ Yes ☐ No
21. Provide a daily progress report to CEO of BHs who are running late—the shame-and-name report. ☐ Yes ☐ No
22. Provide incentives for prompt budget returns (e.g., movie vouchers). ☐ Yes ☐ No
23. Ensure BHs have provided insightful commentary. ☐ Yes ☐ No
24. Provide BHs with comparison graphs so they can see how reasonable their forecasts look against the past trends. ☐ Yes ☐ No

Complete Quality Assurance Procedures

25. Ensure all annual plan returns are in. ☐ Yes ☐ No
26. Check all key ratios for reasonableness of forecasts. ☐ Yes ☐ No
27. Review all revenue and expenditure graphs to ensure the trends look reasonable. ☐ Yes ☐ No
28. Ensure all key papers have been saved in the annual planning directory. ☐ Yes ☐ No
29. Rework budgets where forecasts contain errors—with BHs' permission. ☐ Yes ☐ No
30. Check correct treatment of costs on major projects (particularly consulting fees). ☐ Yes ☐ No
31. Look for missed major expenditure items. ☐ Yes ☐ No

(Continued)

Key Tasks

Budget Committee

32. Advise BHs of times for them to turn up and present their annual plan to the budget committee. ☐ Yes   ☐ No

33. Budget committee confirm their attendance during the budget committee lock-up. ☐ Yes   ☐ No

34. Budget committee have completed interviews with all BHs. ☐ Yes   ☐ No

35. Adjust annual plans based on feedback from the budget committee. ☐ Yes   ☐ No

36. Budget committee confirmed final numbers in the consolidated annual plan. ☐ Yes   ☐ No

Presentation of Annual Plan to Budget Holders

37. Presentation of the final annual plan numbers to BHs (not compulsory to attend presentation). ☐ Yes   ☐ No

Review Process—Lessons learned

38. Set up intranet-based feedback survey on annual plan process. ☐ Yes   ☐ No

39. Plan the quarterly rolling planning forecast runs. (These updates will set the monthly targets and replace the need for next year's annual planning cycle.) ☐ Yes   ☐ No

40. Check for any timing differences when the year-end numbers are finalized. (BHs have forecast prior to year-end so they did not know the final status of major projects/deals. Some deals may need to be carried forward into the next year's numbers or vice versa.) ☐ Yes   ☐ No

---

Useful Letters and Memos

Email from accounts payable sent to new budget holders:

Date _____

Dear _____

Welcome from the accounts payable team

The accounts payable team is committed to adopting and implementing best practices. To this end we need to work in an effective partnership with all budget holders.

Practices in our organization may differ significantly from those you are used to.

We would like to meet with you for 20 minutes or so to go through our procedures, which will help you in your role as a budget holder. We have a short 20-minute PowerPoint presentation, which we will present on a laptop at your desk. Please advise us of a suitable time within the next few weeks.

In the meantime, you might like to visit our intranet page on XX.

We look forward to offering you a seamless service.

Kind regards,

AP Team Leader

Memo from CEO sent to all budget holders re attending general ledger (G/L) training:

Date _____

Dear _____

Attending G/L training

You will be aware that we have decided to implement a new accounting package. According to research, these implementations are prone to failure.

The general ledger licenses and associated costs will be over $XX,000. Thus it is imperative that we make this project a success and get it right the first time!

We are also using this implementation to alter radically the way we process accounting transactions. This means that we are implementing processes that will mean you are spending fewer nights and weekends working on administrative matters.

You will need to attend in person. Please select one course and email back today. I will be taking a personal interest in this and will be monitoring course attendance and no-shows.

Should you feel that you are unable to attend, please first contact me so we can discuss the reasons.

Kind regards,

CEO

Memo from CEO inviting all budget holders to attend fast month-end training:

Date _____

Dear _____

Attending fast month-end workshop

You will be aware that we have decided to radically change the way we prepare our monthly accounts. Our aim is to free both you and the accounting team from many routines that do not add value.

It is my firm belief that, after this workshop, we will be able to spend more time working in our critical success factors and spend fewer evenings and weekends working on administrative matters.

You will need to attend in person. Please select one course and email back today. I will be taking a personal interest in this and will be monitoring course attendance and no-shows.

Should you feel that you are unable to attend, please first contact me so we can discuss the reasons.

Kind regards,

CEO

Memo from CEO inviting selected individuals to attend a fast month-end Post-it reengineering workshop:

Date _____

Dear _____

Attending fast month-end workshop—target by 3 working days or less

Sounds impossible, doesn't it, when you consider that we spend XX days on each month-end producing numbers well after the horse has bolted. We have been investing many long evenings and weekends away from our home carrying out a task that is not adding value.

The finance team is proposing a radical change based on best practices. The board and I are convinced it will work. It is estimated to save us over $XX,000 in time and much more when adding in the full opportunity cost.

It is my firm belief that, after this workshop, we will be able to spend more time working in our critical success factors and spending fewer evenings and weekends working on administrative matters.

I am inviting you as I value your contribution. You will need to attend in person. Please clear your diary so you can attend. I will be attending the first session and I look forward to seeing you there.

Should you feel that you are unable to attend, please first contact me so we can discuss the reasons.

Kind regards,

CEO

Memo from CEO sent to all budget holders re compulsory attending of a fast annual planning workshop:

Date _____

Dear _____

A two-week annual planning process—workshops on XX and XX

Sounds impossible, doesn't it, when you consider the four months of pain last year, involving endless discussion, argument, and many long evenings and weekends away from our home.

The finance team is proposing a radical change based on the world's best practices. The board and I are convinced it will work. It is estimated to save us over $XX,000 in time and much more when adding in the full opportunity cost.

An important part of the process is XXX XXX XXX.

You will need to attend in person. Please select one workshop and email back today. I will be taking a personal interest in this and will be monitoring course attendance and no-shows.

Should you feel that you are unable or do not need to attend, please first contact me so we can discuss the reasons.

Kind regards,

CEO

Memo from CEO sent to all subsidiary companies re new month-end processes:

Date _____

Dear _____

A "nonevent month-end"—no more m/e intercompany disputes

You are no doubt aware that at month-end, we have numerous intercompany disagreements. This delays month-end reporting and means excessive time is spent delivering news well after the horse has bolted.

Modern organizations in the 21st century do not have this problem, and I want our organization to replicate their better practices.

To this end we will be investing in an intercompany application that means one party, the seller, will update both general ledgers simultaneously. I will advise when this occurs.

As from today, the new intercompany rules are as follows:

- The party making the sale will close their ledger off on day −2; all sales on the last day will be treated as next months transactions and processed then.
- The balance on the accounts payable ledger is to emailed to the intercompany debto, who has to process an adjustment to agree.
- All disputes are to occur after month-end.

I will be taking a personal interest in this area and will be monitoring all major intercompany adjustments.

Should you not understand these rules, please first contact the CFO.

Kind regards,

CEO

Letter from accounts payable team leader to suppliers:

Date _____

Dear _____

We have thrown away the checkbook—and are at a loss as to how to pay you

We are a modern company and have now thrown away the checkbook, which is a technology from Charles Dickens's time. In fact, the last check is mounted in a frame in the CEO's office. Other than trying to recycle that mounted check—of which there is little chance, as the CEO is proud of its symbolic meaning—we have no means of paying you.

You should be aware that we have sent you a number of direct credit forms for completion.

One solution is that you complete this direct credit form today and fax it to us at XXX; another solution is that you direct debit us; alternatively we could start a barter system. (I am joking!)

(Continued)

We value the relationship we have with your company and are looking at ways we can link our IT systems with yours so that we process a transaction between us only once. Our IT experts will be in contact with your IT experts sometime in the future.

Let's move into the 21st century together!

Kind regards,

AP Team Leader

Memo from CEO to invite selected staff to attend a focus group workshop (needed for quarterly rolling planing and KPIs projects:

Date _____

Invitation to attend a one-day focus group to look at XXX

It is important that we have a focus group workshop to kick-start this assignment as:

- There are many pitfalls in such a project, and many projects have failed to deliver in other companies.
- A wide ownership is required, and a focus group can have a huge impact on the selling process.
- The foundation stones need to be understood and put in place early on in the project.
- A focus group will give valuable input on how the implementation should best be done to maximize its impact.

We are seeking a focus group selected from experienced staff members covering the regions, branches, and head office and the different roles, from administrators to the senior management team. I believe you would offer much to this exercise and request that you set aside the time to assist.

I welcome your support on this important project. The project team of XX, XX, XX, and XX will need and appreciate your support.

Please confirm availability to attend this focus group workshop, after having discussed it with your manager. I look forward to meeting you at the workshop.

Kind regards,

CEO

Memo for a member of the team for going the extra mile:

Date _____

Dear _____

Re Completing project XX

I would like to comment on the exceptional skills you demonstrated in completing the XX project on time and within budget. You managed all this while maintaining the routine day-to-day tasks!

Please accept this voucher as a small token of the organization's appreciation.

I have discussed the recognition with the CEO who also would like to show her appreciation, in person. I have arranged a morning coffee, at the CEO's office, next Tuesday at 10.30 a.m.

Kind regards,

XXX

Letter to a supplier who has gone the extra mile:

Date _____

Dear _____

Re Breathtaking improvement

I would like to comment on the exceptional skill your staff and your contractors have demonstrated in the recent installation of XX. The finished product has exceeded my expectations and has been well worth the wait.

Should you need a reference, please feel free to give potential customers my number.

Kind regards,

XXX

Letter to the auditors to organize a quick sign-off of year-end accounts

Dear _____

Re Year-end audited accounts

Over the past few years our year-end has been very costly in lost opportunities. Management and staff have spent far too much time in this exercise.

We wish to adopt world's best practice and complete our accounts within 5 working days, achieve a sign-off within 15 working days post year-end. As auditors, your firm will be aware of the better practices we wish to adopt.

We would like to hold a meeting within the two weeks to ascertain your commitment and agreement on the better practices that need to be adopted.

The outcome should be beneficial to both parties, as we will be much better prepared for your visits, will appoint an audit coordinator role, and so forth.

The agenda of this meeting will cover:

a. Status of prior-year significant audit findings
b. Unresolved internal control and accounting issues
c. The quick year-end better practices
d. Content of audit checklist
e. Proposed deadlines
f. Discussions of new accounting standards and policies
g. Procedures to alert each other to any potential issues
h. Role of internal audit team
i. Content of an "information needs" list

We request that the audit partner, audit manager, and audit senior to attend this meeting. We will have a representative from the audit committee, the CFO, and financial controller attending.

Kind regards,

XXX

Letter to the auditors who signed off quickly:

Date _____

Dear _____

Re Year-end sign-off

I would like to comment on the exceptional skill your staff have demonstrated during the audit. Your cooperation in a swift audit has been most beneficial and has freed up time to focus on making this year a good year.

I would also like to thank you for your "balanced" management letter, which celebrated the areas where we have improved as well as commented on areas for improvement. We can report that we have already made good progress in the suggested areas.

Should you need a reference, please feel free to give potential clients my number.

Kind regards,

XXX

Letter to a mentor:

Date _____

Dear _____

Re Seeking guidance

For a long time now I have treasured the times I have spent with you. Your wise council counsel has been most beneficial.

I would very much like to meet you periodically to seek your guidance on matters such as career progression, training I should take to fill in experience and skill gaps, industry issues, and advice on problems.

I thought we could hold these meetings over lunch, at my expense, at your convenience.

Kind regards,

XXX

Date_____

Dear_____

Re Year-end sign-off

I would like to comment on the exceptional skill your staff have demonstrated during the audit. Your cooperation in a swift audit has been most beneficial and has freed up time to focus on making this year a good year.

I would also like to thank you for your balanced management letter, which celebrated the areas where we have improved and commented on areas for improvement. We can report that we have already made good progress in the suggested areas.

Should you need a reference, please feel free to give potential clients my number.

Kind regards,

XXX

A Satisfaction Survey for an Accounting Function

Initially once a year and then twice a year, run a statistically based sample survey on your in-house customers. Send them the survey set out in this appendix. The key features are:

- Ask two open-ended questions that will generate most of the benefit for the survey: "What are the three things we do well?" and "What are the three things we can improve on?" Never ask about the problems, as half of them will not be fixable.
- Categorize all responses to these questions in a database and sort out by positive comments and suggestions for improvement.
- Use a 5-point scale
- Separate out accounting system dramas from the services your team provides by asking a series of system-related questions.
- Send them by email or use a web-based survey package as sourced from www.SurveyMonkey.com.
- Never ask questions you will not act on
- Make the questionnaire simple and able to be completed in 10 minutes.

Finance Team User Satisfaction Questionnaire

The purpose of the user satisfaction survey is to aid the finance team to deliver a quality service. In this questionnaire we are seeking to investigate your satisfaction with your relationship with the **Finance team since XX/**

XX/XX. Your response (in the shaded areas) will help us make sure we deliver a quality service.

The comment fields are a very helpful part of a feedback to the finance team. Please invest time in making your comments as specific as possible and give examples where appropriate. Your ratings and your comments are totally confidential. XXX (the company conducting the survey) will prepare the statistical data and display comments so as to conceal the identities of respondents. Please return no later than XX/XX/XX by email to XXX.

How satisfied are you with the finance systems in the following areas? Please use the next rating scale for the survey.

Rating

5 = Very satisfied, 4 = Satisfied, 3 = Neither satisfied nor dissatisfied, 2 = Dissatisfied, **1 = Very dissatisfied**, X = Not applicable, cannot rate

Finance System	Cannot rate	Ease of use	Ease of accessing data you need	Adequacy of reporting	Usefulness of system procedures manual	Adequacy of help desk support
Purchasing order system						
Accounts payable system						
Expenses claim system						
Purchase card system						
Accounts receivable system						
General ledger/ Reporting system						
Payroll system						
Forecasting system						

How satisfied are you with the following finance activities?

Finance Activities	Cannot rate	Timeliness	Accuracy (inc. QA)	Proactive/ responsiveness	Expertise of staff	Output (fit for purpose)
Processing of sales invoices						
Processing of purchase invoices						
Fixed assets processing/ reporting						
Payment of expenses						
Coordination of annual report						
Coordination of external auditors						
Coordination & support of budget process						
Coordination of forecasting year-end position						
Coordination of quarterly rolling forecasting process						
Advice to business units (on variance analysis, planning, financial implications of policy, etc.)						
Monthly financial information available to budget holders						
Monthly finance report to senior management						
Forecasting support						
One-to-one training						
Other (specify): _____						
Other (specify): _____						

Please rate your satisfaction with the finance team's communication (only those teams you have contact with):

How satisfied are you with the:	Accounts payable	Accounts receivable	Management accounting	Payroll	Systems accountants
Team's accessibility and promptness in replying to your queries?					
Proactive role of the team in anticipating issues?					
Team's understanding of issues from your perspective?					
Team's service ethic? (friendliness, approachability, positive attitude, supportiveness, commitment to continuous improvement)					
Degree of respect the team demonstrates toward you? (e.g., arriving on time for meetings, delivering to deadlines, honoring promises, responding to emails)?					
Willingness to take ownership of issues (inc. responding constructively to criticism)?					
Teamwork and ability to redirect key issues to appropriate person within team?					
Decision making within the workgroup (prompt, stand the test of time, rarely rescinded)?					
Team's follow through/ability to close issues?					

Please rate your satisfaction with the finance function's working style (only rate those teams, within Finance, you have contact with).

How satisfied are you with the:	Accounts payable	Accounts receivable	Management accounting	Payroll	Systems accountants
Frequency of face-to-face communication (e.g., not hiding behind emails)?					
Way we communicate operational/routine issues?					
Way we communicate complex issues?					
Overall effectiveness of our communication?					
Meetings that we host (keeping the meeting on track and on time)?					
Contribution we make to meetings you host (being prepared, our level of participation, follow-up action we undertake)?					
Presentations we deliver?					
Content of the business group's intranet site?					
Reports we prepare for you?					

Please provide a comment, in this section, to explain 1 or 5 ratings.

What do you consider to be the three main strengths of this service? (If you have used the "5" rating, please give examples).

_____

_____

_____

What do you consider are three main areas for this service to develop? (If you have used the "1" rating, please give examples. Please also give suggestions of specific changes you would like, if appropriate.)

_____

_____

_____

Please insert your name. It will be used for administrative purposes only.

If the findings of this survey were to be presented, would you be interested in attending the presentation?   _Yes/No_ (**_Circle your response_**).

Thank you for participating.

345

Index